# THE DESCRIBER'S
# DICTIONARY

*Dimboxes, Epopts, and other Quidams:*
*Words to Describe Life's Indescribable People*

*Bernstein's Reverse Dictionary, 2nd Ed. (Ed.)*

*The Ultimate Spelling Quiz Book*

*The Random House Dictionary for Writers and Readers*

# THE DESCRIBER'S DICTIONARY

*A Treasury of Terms
and Literary Quotations for
Readers and Writers*

## DAVID GRAMBS

*W. W. Norton & Company
New York        London*

The text of this book is composed in 12/14-5 Bembo with
the display set in Bembo.
Composition and manufacturing by The Haddon Craftsmen, Inc.
Book design by Margaret M. Wagner

Library of Congress Cataloging-in-Publication Data
Grambs, David.
The describer's dictionary / by David Grambs.
p.   cm.
1. English language—Synonyms and antonyms.   2. Description
(Rhetoric)   I. Title.
PE1591.G67   1993
423'.1—dc20                                        92-957

ISBN 0-393-03399-6

W. W. Norton & Company, Inc.
500 Fifth Avenue, New York, N.Y. 10110
W. W. Norton & Company Ltd.
10 Coptic Street, London WC1A 1PU

*For Di*

# CONTENTS

## PEOPLE

# PREFACE

Consider the case of a traveler or student who wants to describe, in a letter, what the scenic landscape and local dwellings are like in a remote and beautiful area of Ecuador where she is staying. She can't think of the word for a basin-like depression between two mountain peaks, or the word for the shape of a particular Indian symbol. She is not having an easy time finding the right words—if they are to be found—in her trusty thesaurus.

Or take the case of a student naturalist finishing his first article for a magazine. He needs the term meaning "living along a river" as well as the technical adjective for "peacock-like." He can't come up with them in his dictionary or *Roget's*.

Or suppose a newspaper reporter wants to open an important investigative story she is doing with an "evocative," detailed description of an imposing nineteenth-century courthouse building in the town central to her story. Her knowledge of architectural terms stops at the word *column*. She wants the correct terminology, but she wants the writing to be her own. Where can she quickly find the descriptive vocabulary to make that courthouse a vivid presence or setting to her readers?

Or consider the aspiring science-fiction writer who is honing a pithy description of a character based on a strange old man he once met. He wants the right word—a different word—for "wrinkled." Also, he can't think of that other la-di-da three-syllable word from French meaning "plumpness."

The intent of *The Describer's Dictionary* is to make a variety of descriptive words expediently available, or referable, in a way that neither a thesaurus nor a dictionary does. (It does not deign or claim to detail fine points of meaning, notably between synonyms, for which a standard dictionary is better suited.) Optimally, the book should be most helpful as a kind of descriptive-term memo pad or checklist for anybody needing quick access to just the right vocabulary for conveying in words some sort of picture.

Description is (with argumentation, exposition, and narration) one of the four traditional forms of discourse. It is the art of realistic depiction, or what the literary like to call verisimilitude. This is a craft that begins with a basic descriptive vocabulary. In the main, the idea here is to supply not terms for objects and creatures but terms for describing those objects and creatures. Don't look between these covers for any abstractions, isms, ologies, or similarly intellectual or philosophical vocabulary.

"Physical" and "adjectival" best describe the approach of *The Describer's Dictionary*.

Physical because it is a gathering of words exclusively for describing the physical world—much of it, at least—in which we live.

Adjectival because, unlike most specialized reference books, this one has more adjectives (or adjectival forms) than nouns in its pages. To describe things, or animals, or people, it helps to know your basic substantives, as plain identifying or designating nouns are fundamental in any description. But modifiers, or attributives, are the main stuff of description, and I've favored the adjectival form here.

The format should make it easier to find purely physical terms than you can in a standard *Roget's,* where chockablock run-on lists (and a usually confusing index) make distinctions between related words less than clear; or than you can in an alphabetical dictionary, where defining is the primary purpose. This format falls, not surprisingly, somewhere between that of a thesaurus and that of a dictionary. Simple "lead-in" definitional phrases precede most groupings of terms, but in many instances familiar words are merely thematically clustered for easy reference; their meanings should be clear enough, and the reader's intelligence is not underestimated. Adjectival forms, again, predominate. Obviously, most of these modifiers have their corresponding noun, adverb, or even verb counterparts, and I've made the bold assumption that readers will not have too much trouble ascertaining the latter, if occasionally with a quick check of a standard dictionary.

Regarding the way the book is organized, common sense rather than a particular schema has been my guide—or seat-of-the-pants intuition rather than any rigorous scientific codifying principle (as in a thematically subsumed thesaurus). Certainly other arrangements would have been possible. I only hope that the presentation—and spacing that divides groupings of related terminology—works well enough that you will always be able to zero in fairly quickly on a particular subject area or word sought.

The book's terminology serves the craft of physical description, and more specifically visual description (with the exception of a small section on tactile adjectives pertaining to surfaces and another on common descriptives for people's voices). It covers phenomena ranging from universal shapes and geometric patterns to general attributes of animals and human beings. *The Describer's Dictionary* also includes useful vocabulary for describing a building or house or (the art of what is technically called chorography) a particular tract of landscape.

Terminologies can easily overlap. The different sections of the book are by no means entirely exclusive of one another, and many of the illustrative quotations confirm this, containing several words that will be found under different headings in the text. For example, modifiers for shapes or forms may be useful in describing buildings or animals. A number of the terms under "Patterns and Edges" could as easily appear in the "Surfaces and Textures" section, and the words found under "Light and Colors," of course, have virtually universal application.

If a picture is worth a thousand words, perhaps an actual literary descriptive passage may be worth more than a hundred definitions. Illustrative quotations from prose literature are an important complement within these pages. If a book is to provide readers with categorized terminology for visual description, why shouldn't it also afford examples of vivid pictorial writing by some of the finest writers in the English language?

From both fiction and nonfiction, you'll find a variety of such passages throughout the book. Almost all are from native writers of English, as opposed to translations from world classics. They are not here as mere dressing. There is, I think, a kind of felicitous synergism created when words-to-refer-to are accompanied by brief passages readable in their own right, glowing snatches of prose by reputable and even great writers. The quotations help to bring the text's terminology to life (particularly for those who believe all reference books are inescapably deadly dry), and I hope that they make the book, more than a reliable word reference, an ever browsable little treasury of worthy prose-description gems. Whether you're a professional writer or merely somebody who could use this book for the occasional descriptive touch in a school paper or personal letter, some of these patches of published description should offer a little tug of inspiration or—if that is too arch-literary a word—encouragement.

At the same time, the often evocative quotations are a constant reminder that apposite terminology is often only a starting point of good descriptive writing. It is how well the terms are used that counts for so much. From novelists to scientists to nature writers, many of the excerpts herein demonstrate abundantly how important a gift for combining or maximizing the forcefulness of salient words can be. Good writing often involves ineffably subtle touches and obliquities of style. An eye for the striking detail, a sense of phrasing, and the ability to conjure up a good simile or metaphor can make the difference between a commonplace description and an eminently quotable passage. Some of the passages remind us also that some of literature's best portrayals of characters are rendered in a transparently simple, unsensory diction that is not per se "descriptive."

Let me be quick to add that not all terms (or spellings) found in the quoted passages, borrowed from outside, as it were, will be found in the book's word-listing text. The quotes are intended to illustrate uses of relevant terminology, but being from many writers and sometimes different periods are scarcely any kind of perfect fit with the selective lexicon that I've settled upon. Many writers create their own descriptives (or hyphenated descriptives), and often these will not be found in dictionaries—including this one. This—these quotations—is a good reminder to us that in prose writing, too, the whole is usually greater than the sum of its parts.

This book alone will not make you a first-rate descriptive writer or metaphor maker—you shouldn't need to be told that. But it attempts to lay out the words you may want to choose from a bit more plainly than a thesaurus will; and, with its interspersed borrowed passages, it should help you in focusing on the delineational task at hand.

*The Describer's Dictionary* is of necessity selective in the areas that it covers. The describable contents of our terrestrial world and universe are incalculable and their possible descriptive attributes numberless. To attempt to catalogue all conceivable (and conceptual) terms that could be brought to bear on all the perceivable inanimate and animate phenomena of our planet, including all human artifacts, is a little too quixotic an order for a single, modest book.

*The Describer's Dictionary* does not include nautical terminology, medical descriptives, or the thousands and thousands of terms relating to furniture and clothing throughout human history. It does not presume to replace technical glossaries for countless fields of expertise, identify trees or automobiles or gems, or teach you names of animal body parts used by zoologists. But it does—and this is the guiding principle behind the book—present hundreds of solidly fundamental modifiers and designations, of shape, color, pattern, surface, and general aspect, that should make it easier for you to describe clearly just about any thing or any being palpable and visible. That is, although this work does not include such a term as *samovar,* it does include most of the words that you'd need for giving a reader or person not present a good description of one.

Some of the book's terms are more technical than others, and some are quite rare. These Latinisms (as most of them are) notwithstanding, *The Describer's Dictionary* is meant as a reference for the general reader—the average person, not the specialist. It simply happens that many of the more precise or holophrastic (denoting the most in the fewest words or letters) useful words in descriptive English are somewhat technical or unfamiliar. Architectural terms are one example, and Latinate adjectives for shapes or forms are another.

Technical terms have their place even outside of technical publications. Used judiciously, they can be informative to the general reader (introducing a new word) and enrich prose that otherwise uses familiar terminology.

I hope *The Describer's Dictionary* will be a handy touchstone for anybody having occasion to try to paint pictures with the English language.

# ABOUT THE BOOK'S TERMINOLOGY

Many words in the various sections of the book should be familiar (if not always remembered or personally used). Other adjectives and nouns are more technical and probably quite unfamiliar.

It's important to emphasize, first, that all the words and phrases are arrayed in these pages as *reminders,* or for possible use in description. Second, because a definitional phrase or common word is followed by a more arcane adjective is not to imply that the latter is preferable or more "correct." In fact, it is more often the case that expert writers in particular fields, such as naturalists and art historians, use simple rather than technical language in their verbal depictions (as is shown in so many of the book's accompanying illustrative passages).

Thus, the simple "wrinkled" can be just as apt as "rugose," perhaps often more apt; and the existence of "hippocrepiform" notwithstanding, most writers, including academic specialists, will be far more likely to say simply "horseshoe-shaped." It is always a question of context or audience—or wanting to use the occasional, optional synonym for variety of expression.

*The Describer's Dictionary,* then, though it should bring to your attention many technical words that can be succinctly useful, is not to be misconstrued as a brief for favoring the bigger or ten-dollar word. Common or rare, the words are all part of our great English language. To paraphrase the famous remark of the mountain climber Mallory as to why one climbs a mountain, the words in the following pages are presented simply because they are there.

# ACKNOWLEDGMENTS

For their considerate help with either the text or the illustrative quotations, I'd like to thank David Berne, David Black, Rich Collins, Bea Jacoby, Ellen Levine, Carl Rossi, and Mark W. Thompson. At W. W. Norton, I'm indebted to Starling Lawrence, Richard Halstead, Lucy Anderson, and Barbara Grenquist.

For her creative design suggestions, I'm especially grateful to Linda Corrente.

# THE DESCRIBER'S
# DICTIONARY

# THINGS

# Shapes

His white mantle was shaped with severe regularity, according to the rule of St. Bernard himself, being composed of what was then called burrel cloth, exactly fitted to the size of the wearer, and bearing on the left shoulder the octangular cross peculiar to the order, formed of red cloth.

SIR WALTER SCOTT, *Ivanhoe*

The shapes of the letters are remarkably strong, written with expertise and confidence in symmetrical lines. Vertical strokes, both straight and rounded, are penned thickly with bold triangular pennant heads. Horizontal strokes are thin and are frequently used to join letters, sometimes with a slight triangular terminal.

PETER BROWN, *The Book of Kells*

Some of the most austerely stylised figures of all are made by the Dogon, a tribe living in Mali, in the Western Sudan. Their sculptors reduce bodies to cylinders, arms to rods, eyes to diamonds, breasts to cones. Yet their images often have a brooding monumental presence that makes many a naturalistic statue pale into vapidity.

DAVID ATTENBOROUGH, *The Tribal Eye*

*having a shape or form*
shaped, formed, configured, conformed, fashioned

*having no shape, shapeless*
unshaped, formless, amorphous, inchoate, unformed, unfashioned

*having a usually simple plane shape (lines or curves)*
geometric

*having the same shape or boundaries*
coextensive

*having a similar form*
conforming, similiform, equiform

*having a different form*
diversiform, variform

*having many forms*
multiform, multifarious, polymorphic, polymorphous, multiplex, omniform, omnifarious

*having a shape with equal sides and angles*
regular

*not having a shape with generally equal sides and angles*
irregular

*having an unconventional or uneven shape*
irregular, contorted, misshapen, malformed, deformed, twisted, grotesque

*29*

Mysticism always gripped the Welsh creative imagination, as we can see from the few Celtic artefacts still extant in the country. There is nothing straightforward to the manner of these objects, nothing right-angled or self-explanatory. They are neither realist in style nor entirely abstractionist—pictures which have evolved into patterns, triangles blurred into rhomboids, ritual combinations of curls and circles which may have some magic meaning, but have been stylized into an art form. When living creatures appear, they are caricature humans, schematic animals, and time and again there emerges the strange triskele, the wavy pattern of connected spirals which seems to have had some arcane fascination for the Celtic mind.

JAN MORRIS, *The Matter of Wales*

Aulus recommended a mass-attack in diamond formation. The head of the diamond would consist of a single regiment in two waves, each wave eight men deep. Then would follow two regiments marching abreast, in the same formation as the leading one; then three regiments marching abreast. This would be the broadest part of the diamond and here the elephants would be disposed as a covering for each flank. Then would come two regiments, again, and then one. The cavalry and the rest of the infantry would be kept in reserve. Aulus explained that this diamond afforded a protection against charges from the flank; no attack could be made on the flank of the leading regiment without engaging the javelin-fire of the overlapping second line, nor on the second line without engaging the fire of the overlapping third.

ROBERT GRAVES, *Claudius the God*

*having an axially (or in relation to a central line) balanced shape*
  symmetrical
*having an axially unbalanced shape*
  asymmetrical, dissymmetrical

*more prominent or sizable on one side*
  one-sided, lop-sided
*having the sides reversed (as in a mirror)*
  heterochiral
*having proper or harmonious dimensions relationally*
  proportional, proportionate, commensurate, eurythmic
*not having proper dimensions relationally*
  disproportional, disproportionate, uncommensurate

*longer in one dimension*
  elongated, oblong, oblongitudinal, lengthened, extended,
  stretched, prolongated, elliptical, distended, protracted
*shorter in one dimension*
  shortened, truncated, foreshortened

*becoming wider*
  widening, expanding, broadening, dilating, splayed
*becoming narrower*
  narrowing, tapering, tapered
*having or coming to a point*
  pointed, pronged, spiked, acuate, acuminate, mucronate

*having the form of a line or lines*
  linear, lineal, lineiform
*straight and uncurved in line*
  rectilinear, rectilineal, linear, lineal
*not straight*
  crooked, bent, askew, awry, oblique

We have just seen some of the geometrical properties of the Great Pyramid considered as a solid; it is of course not a tetrahedron, but has four lateral triangular faces sloping to a square base.

MATILIA GHYKA, *The Geometry of Art and Life*

(. . . on a carved stone in the Naples Museum is engraved the "Sublime" Isosceles Triangle of the Pentagram, subdivided into the smaller similar triangle and its "gnomon," et cetera); and he tried to explain the plans of Gothic churches and cathedrals (Beauvais, Cologne, Rheims, Notre-Dame, et cetera) by grafting directly onto the rectangular naves pentagons or pentagrams, the centres of which coincide with "focal" points like the centre of figure of the apse, or the altar. His star-diagrams are beautiful approximations (in some cases quite rigorous). . . .

MATILIA GHYKA, *The Geometry of Art and Life*

A *Vexierbild* (puzzle-picture) by Schon, a Nuremberg engraver and pupil of Dürer, has been described by Rottinger: of large dimensions (0.44 metre × 0.75 metre) it is formed of four trapezoidal rows in which striped hatchings are continued by landscapes peopled with living figures. Towns and hills, men and animals are reabsorbed and engulfed in a tangle of lines, at first sight inexplicable. But by placing the eyes at the side and very close to the engraving one can see four superimposed heads inside rectilinear frames. Perspective causes the apparent images to disappear and at the same time the hidden outlines to appear.

JURGIS BALTRUSAITIS, *Anamorphic Art*

*represented in outline only*
 outlined, outlinear, contoured, delineatory, in profile,
 silhouetted

*having a sharp bend or angle*
 angular, geniculate, orthometric (see *hook-shaped*)

*standing at a right or 90° (L- or gamma-shaped) angle*
 upright, perpendicular, normal, orthogonal, rectangular,
 orthometric

*having a less than right angle*
 acute-angled

*having three acute angles*
 triquetrous

*having a greater than perpendicular angle*
 obtuse-angled

*having an acute or obtuse (or non-right) angle*
 oblique-angled, obliquangular

*angle greater than 180°*
 reflex angle

*being an angle formed by two planes*
 dihedral

*on a plane or unbroken surface*
 flat, level, planar, tabular, flattened, even, applanate,
 homaloidal

*on a slant*
 slanting, aslant, inclined, oblique, on a bias, diagonal, askew

*bent abruptly*
 geniculate, inflexed, intorted

*bent abruptly backward*
 retroflex, cacuminal

*showing short and sharp veelike turns*
 zigzag, staggered, chevroned, cringle-crangle

If the long sides, given by joining the Station positions, were to be related to the Moon in the same way, the Station positions would need to form not a rectangle, but a parallelogram with corners that were not right angles. Shifting Stonehenge only 50 miles to the north or south would change the required angles by as much as 2°.

FRED HOYLE, *On Stonehenge*

He loved how this house welcomed into itself in every season lemony flecked rhomboids of sun whose slow sliding revolved it with the day, like the cabin of a ship on a curving course. JOHN UPDIKE, *Couples*

Pointed bastions have been added to the corners of the almost square Roman city. From these it was possible to send an enfilade along the sides of the ramparts. But the bastions, themselves, presented quite a large flank which also could be fired upon. Therefore they must be sharply pointed which technically is a poor form for earthern [*sic*] structures. It was quickly discovered that the rectangular contour was the least practical for a fortification of ramparts with bastions. A pentagon was better than a rectangle and a hexagon was still better. But best of all would be a town periphery in the form of a polygon.

STEEN RASMUSSEN, *Towns and Buildings*

Immediately on passing through Porta del Popolo the visitor enters a square, Piazza del Popolo. Today it is an oval but at that time it was a long, narrow trapezoid converging toward the gateway and with long garden walls on either side. Fac-

*having a shape formed by lines rather than by curves (hence having angles*
>  angular

*having a curve or curves (roundness or rondure)*
>  curvilinear, curved, curvate, bowed, curviform, arcing, arciform

*slightly curved*
>  curvulate

*curved upward*
>  upcurved, upturned, arched, arcuate, vaulted, concamerated

*curved downward*
>  downcurved, downturned, decurved, decurvate

*curved forward*
>  procurved

*curved backward*
>  recurved, recurvate

*curved inward*
>  incurved, incurvate, involute, hooked, aduncous

*curved outward*
>  excurved, excurvate

*curving back toward itself*
>  hooked, crooked

*curved around farther than a semicircle*
>  gibbous

*curved up and around and closed or almost closed*
>  looped

*describing a curve that is bold or lengthy*
>  sweeping

*describing a series of reverse curves*
>  whiplash

*curving or arcing (two curved lines) to a point*
>  cusped

ing the city, one saw the three thoroughfares thrusting deep into the town. The two triangular building sites form an effective front with two symmetrical domed churches strongly emphasizing the solid mass of the houses advancing toward the open space of the piazza.

STEEN RASMUSSEN, *Towns and Buildings*

The thing was not unlike an uncut diamond of the darker sort, though far too large, being almost as big as the top of my thumb. I took it, and saw it had the form of a regular octahedron, with the carved faces peculiar to the most precious of minerals.

H. G. WELLS, "The Diamond Maker"

The body of the machine was small, almost cylindrical, and pointed. Forward and aft on the pointed ends were two small petroleum engines for the screw, and the navigators sat deep in a canoe-like recess, the foremost one steering, and being protected by a low screen with two plate-glass windows, from the blinding rush of air. On either side a monstrous flat framework with a curved front border could be adjusted so as either to lie horizontally or to be tilted upward or down.    H. G. WELLS, "The Argonauts of the Air"

I recognised the tortuous, tattered band of the Milky Way, with Vega very bright between sun and earth; and Sirius and Orion shone splendid against the unfathomable blackness in the opposite quarter of the heavens. The Pole Star was overhead, and the Great Bear hung over the circle of the earth. And away beneath and beyond the shining corona of the sun

*curving to a central point with a "dip" (contraflexure) inward on either side of the apex*
> ogival

*making a perfect closed curve (two dimensions)*
> circular, round, ring-like, annular, cycloid, cycloidal, rotund

*flat and circular*
> discoid

*hollowed inward*
> concave, bowl-like, basin-like, crater-like, dished, sunken, depressed

*rounded and bulging outward*
> convex, protuberant, gibbous, cupped, cupriform

*concave on one side and convex on the other*
> concavo-convex, convexo-concave

*more curved on the concave than on the convex side*
> concavo-convex

*more curved on the convex than on the concave side*
> convexo-concave

*concave on two or both sides*
> biconcave

*convex on two or both sides*
> biconvex, amphicyrtic

*circular in three dimensions or ball-like*
> round, spherical, spheral, globular, globose, orblike, globate, rotund, spheriform, bombous, conglobate

*nearly round*
> obrotund

*like a half-circle*
> semicircular, hemicyclic

*like a half-moon (or lune)*
> semilunar, demilune

*round but wider in the middle or flattened at the top*
> oblate

were strange groupings of stars I had never seen in my life—
notably, a dagger-shaped group that I knew for the Southern
Cross.            H. G. WELLS, "Under the Knife"


. . . it was the planet Saturn rushing towards me. Larger and
larger it grew, swallowing up the heavens behind it, and
hiding every moment a fresh multitude of stars. I perceived
its flattened, whirling body, its disc-like belt, and seven of its
little satellites. It grew and grew, till it towered enormous,
and then I plunged amid a streaming multitude of clashing
stones and dancing dust-particles and gas-eddies, and saw for
a moment the mighty triple belt like three concentric arches
of moonlight above me, its shadow black on the boiling
tumult below.        H. G. WELLS, "Under the Knife"


The stalagmites of Armand are a rather unusual variety—
they appear to be made of rounded, irregular, hollow cones,
which are concave upwards.

TONY WALTHAM, Caves


If you draw a small irregular shape on the oblong edge of the
pack, every tiny part of that picture will change when you
shear the oblong to form a rhomboid. Only the area remains
the same; and only the sides, which are straight and parallel,
remain straight and parallel. But oceans and continents are
not parallelograms!      DAVID GREENHOOD, Mapping


By the time the Iceberg drifts past Cape York the pack-ice is
looser and studded with bergs of every size and description.

*round but longer vertically (as along a polar axis)*
> prolate

*more or less round*
> spheroidal, ellipsoidal

*egg-shaped*
> ooid, oval, ovoid, ovaliform, oviform, elliptical, ellipsoidal

*ovoid with the wider end up*
> abovoid

*showing coils or twists*
> convoluted, convolved, whorled

*winding (as if around a pole) in shape*
> spiral, helical, gyral, heliciform, sirulate, cochleate,
> corkscrew, tortile, curlicue

*spiral but narrowing toward the bottom*
> turbinate

*having numerous turns or bends*
> bending, winding, twisting, tortuous, sinuous, serpentine,
> meandering, anfractuous, waving, wavy, undulant,
> undulating

*like a complex or confusing network*
> maze-like, mazy, labyrinthine, plexiform

*having or in the form of connecting links*
> chain-like, festooned, catenary, catenate, concatenate,
> concatenated

*enclosing (with either straight or curved lines) a space and constituting a figure*
> closed

*not (either straight or curved lines) enclosing a space or constituting a figure*
> open

The biggest are still the ones from the fiords behind Jakob-shavn but there are also many smaller bergs that have crumbled off the ice cliffs in Melville Bay. There are humped and crested bergs, like the backs of dinosaurs; round and ridged ones, like giant scallop shells; tall, turretted squares like castles; tilted blocks which rise to sheer cliffs, like the bows of ocean-liners. There are tent-shaped, conch-shaped, gable-shaped, and fluted bergs. This glittering mass is pushed by the current, stronger now, westward through the thinning pack.          RICHARD BROWN, *Voyage of the Iceberg*

On the computer-enhanced images they could see a patchwork of sinuous valleys like those found on Mars. There were also areas of grooved terrain, similar to that found by *Voyager* on the surface of one of Jupiter's satellites, Ganymede. Elsewhere, the surface of Miranda resembled the cratered highlands of our own Moon, and there were also giant scarps higher than the Grand Canyon. In the centre of the satellite was a large rocky area shaped rather like a chevron, and two multi-ringed features rather like archery targets bracketed it.          ARTHUR SMITH, *Planetary Exploration*

Mounted on the decagon on struts is the high-gain antenna, the all-important dish through which all communications to and from Earth pass. The 3.66 m diameter dish is an aluminium honeycomb structure surfaced on both sides with laminated graphite-epoxy.

ARTHUR SMITH, *Planetary Exploration*

It was an almost perfect cone of snow, simple in outline as if a child had drawn it, and impossible to classify as to size,

*making a closed plane figure of straight lines*
polygonal

*many-sided*
multilateral, polygonal

*having many angles*
multiangular, polyangular

*being a two-dimensional figure*
plane

*being a three-dimensional figure*
solid

*being a solid figure with many sides*
polyhedral, polyhedric

*being polyhedral with all vertices in two parallel planes*
prismatoidal

*many-sided with parallelogram sides and the bases or ends parallel and congruent*
prismatic

*prismatic with parallelograms as bases or ends*
parallelepipedal

*being a parallelepiped with rhombuses for faces*
rhombohedral

*having two sides*
bilateral

*having two faces or fronts*
bifacial

*three-sided*
triangular, deltoid, trilateral, wedge-shaped, cuneate,
trigonal, cuneiform, trigonous, deltoid

*triangular with unequal sides*
scalene

*triangular with two equal sides*
isosceles

height, or nearness. It was so radiant, so serenely poised, that he wondered for a moment if it were real at all. Then, while he gazed, a tiny puff clouded the edge of the pyramid, giving life to the vision before the faint rumble of the avalanche confirmed it.         JAMES HILTON, *Lost Horizon*


The Russian defences consisted of a semi-elliptical-shaped fort containing 62 casemates on each of two floors from which heavy guns mounted in the centre could sweep the bay almost at water level. Behind the ellipse, and part of the fort, stood a large horseshoe-shaped work on two floors with casemates armed with heavy guns to flank the landward approaches. In the hills behind lay three round towers, also casemated, their guns commanding the countryside. All the masonry was granite, constructed in polygonal form similar to the method used by the Austrians at Verona.

QUENTIN HUGHES, *Military Architecture*


Anyone climbing the steps stood straight into the sky, and the wind in their clothes and the sky with its scarves of cloud and the trumpet shapes of the trees, made the figures like gay and flimsy dancers cut from paper.

RUMER GODDEN, *Black Narcissus*


The volcano rises as an isolated and well-formed cone about 3000 m above the floor of the Banda Sea. The perfection of the cone is marred by two very large and one small slump scars on the upper slopes and by fan-shaped slump deposits at corresponding positions at the base of the slope, underwater. Two of the slump scars are subaerial at the top; they have

*triangular with equal sides*
  equilateral
*triangular inversely*
  obcuneate, obdeltoid

*being a three-dimensional pointed figure with a base and triangles (usually four or three) for sides*
  pyramidal
*inversely pyramidal*
  obpyramidal
*being a triangular (with three upright sides) pyramid*
  tetrahedral

*having four sides and four angles*
  quadrilateral, quadrangular, quadrangled, tetragonal
*four-sided with all right angles and equal sides*
  square, foursquare, quadrate
*four-sided with all right angles (right-angled parallelogram)*
  rectangular
*four-sided with opposite sides parallel and equal*
  parallelogrammatic
*four-sided with two sides parallel*
  trapezoidal, antiparallelogrammatic
*four-sided (parallelogram) with equal but non-right-angled sides (or not a square)*
  rhombic, rhombical
*four-sided (parallelogram) with unequal non-right-angled sides*
  rhomboid
*somewhat like a rhomboid figure (rhombus or rhomb)*
  rhomboidal
*four-sided with no parallel sides*
  trapeziform, trapezial

steep, radial side walls and form deep embayments in the small, otherwise circular islands.

H. W. MENARD, *Islands*

Volcanic islands generally are circular or elliptical cones or domes, and it is easy to visualize the influence of their shape upon erosion by imagining simple circular cones that lie in seas without waves and on which rain falls uniformly. The consequent rivers that develop on a cone are radial because the slopes of the cone are radial. The side slopes of the river valleys tend to be relatively constant but the longitudinal slopes are steeper in the headwaters than at the shoreline. Thus the valleys of the radial streams are funnel shaped; they are narrow and shallow at the shoreline and spread into great, deep amphitheaters in the interior.

H. W. MENARD, *Islands*

This square-shaped labyrinth is made entirely of straight lines, which are much easier to scratch than concentric curves.

ADRIAN FISHER AND GEORG GERSTER, *Labyrinth*

The great breakthrough, however, was in the development of the medieval Christian labyrinth design. This had eleven rings instead of seven, a characteristic cruciform design, and most significantly, the paths ranged freely through the quadrants, rather than methodically proceeding quarter by quarter in the Roman way. A manuscript in the Vatican dated AD860-2 contains a prototype of this innovatory medieval Christian design, and the tenth-century Montpellier manu-

*being a four-sided figure with two equal acute and two equal obtuse
angles (or a long rhomboid figure with the diagonal perpendicular to the
horizontal)*
    diamond, lozenge-shaped

*solid with six square faces*
    cubic

*somewhat cubic in shape*
    cuboid, cuboidal

*having an evenly extended or elongated round shape*
    cylindrical, columnar, columnal, pillar-like, shaft-like

*narrowly cylindrical*
    tubular, tubulate

*more or less cylindrical but tapering at one or both ends*
    terete

*being a rounded figure (with a circular base) that tapers upward to a point*
    conical, conic, funnel-shaped

*somewhat conical*
    conoid, conoidal

*conical with the pointed end below*
    obconic

*like two opposite-pointing cones having the same base*
    biconical

*being a five-sided plane figure (polygon)*
    pentagonal

*being a six-sided plane figure*
    hexagonal

*being a seven-sided plane figure*
    heptagonal

*being an eight-sided plane figure*
    octagonal

*being a nine-sided plane figure*
    nonagonal

script portrays the design more formally. It was executed in two main forms, circular and octagonal.

ADRIAN FISHER AND GEORG GERSTER, *Labyrinth*


Why the images standing beneath the quarries had been set up in such a disorderly fashion, why they were left blind and without red cylinders on top, and why statues with keel-shaped backs were not to be found outside the quarry area remained a mystery to her.

THOR HEYERDAHL, *Easter Island: The Mystery Solved*


Orion is outlined by four bright stars at the corners of an imaginary trapezoid. Within the space defined by these four points, and seeming to draw them together into a pattern, is a row of three stars tilted at an angle—Orion's belt. Arcing downward from the belt is another group of fainter stars—his sword.

GALE LAWRENCE, *A Field Guide to the Familiar*


First of all, when you consider the shape of a chickadee's body, you will notice that it's round. Whereas a blue jay is elongated, and a nuthatch tapered and slightly flattened, a chickadee is like a little ball. This roundness helps the small bird balance itself in the topsy-turvy positions it assumes while it's searching for insect eggs on the twigs and outer branches of trees.

GALE LAWRENCE, *A Field Guide to the Familiar*


Earth flows move slower than debris flows and mudflows. They usually have a spoon-shaped sliding surface with a

*being a ten-sided plane figure*
  decagonal

*being a twelve-sided plane figure*
  dodecagonal

*being a (three-dimensional) polyhedron with four faces*
  tetrahedral

*being a polyhedron with five faces*
  pentahedral

*being a polyhedron with six faces*
  hexahedral

*being a polyhedron with eight faces*
  octahedral

*being a polyhedron with twelve faces*
  dodecahedral

*being a polyhedron with twenty faces*
  icosahedral

*being a polyhedron with twenty-four faces*
  icositetrahedral

*picture-like as a representational form*
  glyphic, pictographic, hieroglyphic

## PARTICULAR SHAPES OR LIKENESSES

*acorn-shaped*
  glandiform, glanduliform

*almond-shaped*
  amygdaloid, amygdaliform

*alphabet-like*
  alphabetiform

*amoeba-shaped*
  amoebiform, amoeboid

crescent-shaped cliff at the upper end and a tongue-shaped bulge at the lower end. . . .

PETER BIRKELAND AND EDWIN LARSON,
*Putnam's Geology*

Ultimately, the valley slopes take on a sigmoidal form with the upper convex slope formed by creep and a lower con-cave slope formed by wash processes.

PETER BIRKELAND AND EDWIN LARSON,
*Putnam's Geology*

If we look through a window at a mass of buildings, or any external objects, and observe that part of the glass to which each object, line, or point, appears opposite, we find that their apparent situation is very different from their real. We find that horizontal lines sometimes appear oblique, or even perpendicular, that circles, in certain situations, look like ellipses, and squares like trapezoids or parallelograms.

JACOB BIGELOW, *The Useful Arts*

Two of the most famous, long landmarks of Manhattan are the Flatiron Building, erected in 1902, and the Times Build-ing (recently remodeled as the Allied Chemical Building), in 1904. Both have odd, trapezoidal floor plans, dictated by the pie-shaped real-estate slices Broadway strews along its diag-onal path as it crosses Manhattan avenues, Fifth at Twenty-third, site of the Flatiron, and Seventh at Forty-second, site of the Times. The resulting slenderness of the two buildings, plus the absence of scientific data on wind stresses, caused the New York engineers to take special precautions. Trian-

*antenna-shaped*
   antenniform
*apple-shaped*
   maliform, pomiform
*apse-shaped*
   apsidal
*arch-shaped*
   arciform
*arm-shaped*
   brachial
*arrowhead-shaped*
   sagittate, sagittiform
*arrowhead-shaped (with flaring or spear-shaped barbs)*
   hastate
*awl-shaped*
   subulate, subulated, subuliform
*ax-shaped or cleaver-shaped*
   dolabriform, dolabrate, securiform, axiniform

*bag-shaped*
   sacciform, scrotiform, bursiform
*ball-shaped*
   conglobulate
*bark-like*
   corticiform
*barley-grain-shaped*
   hordeiform
*barrel-shaped*
   dolioform
*basin-shaped*
   pelviform
*basket-shaped (small basket)*
   corbiculate
*beak-shaped*
   rostate, rhamphoid, rostriform

gular "gusset plates" were inserted as braces, four to each joint of horizontal beam and vertical column.
JOSEPH GIES, *Wonders of the Modern World*

Later, experimenting with small and full-size gliders, he found that setting the wings at a slight dihedral (or shallow V-shaped) angle to each other gave lateral stability, and that a tail plane set behind the main wings was necessary for longitudinal stability.   ALVIN M. JOSEPHY, JR., ED.,
*The American Heritage History of Flight*

Often the edges bounding a face make up a fairly simple plane figure—a triangle, or a square, or the like. And often the faces bounding the whole crystal make up a corresponding simple solid figure—a cube, a tetrahedron, or an octahedron. . . .
ALAN HOLDEN AND PHYLIS MORRISON,
*Crystals and Crystal Growing*

These consist of cylindrical cells set together to form a palisade-like layer. . . . Each cell is polygonal in horizontal section; cuboidal cells are square in vertical section, whereas columnar cells are taller than their diameter. Commonly, microvilli are found on the free surface of such cells, providing a large, absorptive area . . . , as in the epithelium of the small intestine (columnar cells with a striated border), the gall bladder (columnar cells with a brush border) and the proximal and distal convoluted tubules of the kidney (large cells with brush borders).
PETER L. WILLIAMS AND ROGER WARWICK,
*Gray's Anatomy*

*bean-shaped*
fabiform, fabaceous

*beard-shaped*
barbate

*bell-shaped*
campaniform, campaniliform, campanular, campanulate, campanulous, caliciform (calyx)

*berry-shaped*
baccate, bacciform

*bill-shaped*
rostriform, rostate, rhamphoid

*bladder- or flask-shaped*
ampullaceous, ampulliform, lageniform, utriculate, utriculoid

*boat-shaped*
navicular, naviculiform, naviform, scaphoid, cymbiform, nautiform, hysterioid, hysteriform

*bonnet- or miter-shaped*
mitrate, mitriform

*bowed or arched*
arcuate, bandy

*bowl-shaped*
crateriform

*brain-like*
cerebriform

*branched*
furcal, furcate

*branched slightly*
furcellate

*brush-shaped*
muscariform, scopiform, scopulate, scopuliform, aspergilliform

*bubble-like*
bulliform

*buckler (or round shield)-shaped*
scutate, clypeate

We had crossed the high and relatively level sands which form the base of the Fork, and were entering the labyrinth of detached banks which obstruct the funnel-shaped cavity between the upper and middle prongs. This I knew from the chart.     ERSKINE CHILDERS, *The Riddle of the Sands*

A geometric plan of Beaux-Arts derivation organized the main exhibit area into a *rond-point* system of radiating streets and fanlike segments. Symmetrical axes led to the Fair's central theme building, the Trylon and Perisphere. The longitudinal central axis of Constitutional Mall extended from the Trylon and Perisphere eastward to the oval Lagoon of Nations and beyond, to the Court of Peace, which was flanked by foreign-sponsored pavilions and terminated by the symmetrical U.S. Government Building. Extending at 45° angles from either side of the Trylon and Perisphere were the Avenue of Patriots and the Avenue of Pioneers, both of which culminated in circular plazas—the former at Bowling Green, before the IRT and BMT entrances, and the latter at Lincoln Square.

HELLEN A. HARRISON, *Dawn of a New Day*

Skilfully formed, with flakes being removed from both faces of a flint nodule, the almond-shaped hand axes testify to the expertise of their makers.

RICHARD MUIR, *The Stones of Britain*

For the structural supports Wright devised dendriform (tree-shaped) columns with elongated tapered shafts carrying

*bud-like*
    gemmiform
*bulb-shaped*
    bulbiform, bulbous
*buttocks-like*
    natiform

*cactus-shaped*
    cactiform
*canal-like*
    canaliform
*cat-shaped*
    feliform
*caterpillar-shaped*
    eruciform
*catkin-shaped*
    amentiform
*cavity-like*
    aveoliform
*cell-like*
    celliform
*chain-like*
    catenary, catenoid, catenular, catenulate
*chisel-shaped*
    scalpriform
*chisel-shaped (primitive)*
    celtiform
*cigar-shaped*
    terete
*claw- or nail-shaped*
    unguiform
*claw- or pincer-shaped*
    cheliform
*cleaver- or ax-shaped*
    dolabriform, securiform, axiniform

broad flat disks. Forming the roof of the secretarial staff room is a forest of these columns, three stories high. . . .

Leland M. Roth,
*A Concise History of American Architecture*

The towers are separated by six arciform gates, convex to the Mississippi, and hinged in trunnion blocks secured with steel to carom the force of the river into the core of the structure.

John McPhee, *The Control of Nature*

At the other end of the series we have the cells of the hive-bee, placed in a double layer: each cell, as is well known, is an hexagonal prism, with the basal edges of its six sides bevelled so as to join on to a pyramid, formed of three rhombs.

Charles Darwin, *The Origin of Species*

To bring light into the center of the room, a portion of the roof was raised about 4 meters higher than the roof over the side sections; the columns supporting the two sections differed, with bundle papyriform columns used at the side and full-blooming open papyriform columns in a larger size standing along the central aisle.

Dora P. Crouch, *History of Architecture*

Long slats of blue-black, plankton-straining baleen hung from the roof of its mouth in a U-shaped curtain, some of the blades nearly 15 feet long.

Barry Lopez, *Arctic Dreams*

*cloud-shaped*
  nubiform

*clover-leaf-like*
  trifoliate, trifoliated, trefoil

*club-shaped*
  clavate, claviform

*club-shaped inversely*
  obclavate

*cobweb-like*
  cortinate

*coin-shaped*
  nummiform, nummular

*column-like*
  columnar, basaltiform, columniform

*column-like (small column)*
  columelliform

*comb-shaped or toothed*
  pectinate

*combs-like (series of combs)*
  cardiform

*cone-shaped*
  conical, coniform, strobile

*cord- or rope-like*
  funiform

*cow-like*
  vaccine (rare)

*crab-shaped*
  cancriform

*crater-like*
  crateriform

*crescent-shaped*
  meniscal, meniscate, meniscoid, menisciform, lunate, falcate,
  falcicular, falciculate, drepaniform, drepanoid, sickle-shaped,
  bicorn, bicornuate, bicornuous, half-moon-shaped,
  crescentiform, crescentic

The reactor room was quite large. It had to be to accommodate the massive, barrel-shaped steel vessel.

TOM CLANCY, *The Hunt for Red October*

She has twin screws; ours have one propeller. And finally, her hull is oblate. Instead of being cylindrical like ours, it is flattened out markedly top and bottom.

TOM CLANCY, *The Hunt for Red October*

It was warm in the room where around the aged chandelier, with gray little glass pendants like dirty icicles, flies were describing parallelograms, lighting every time on the same pendants. . . .

VLADIMIR NABOKOV, *King, Queen, Knave*

Peeping out through the thin curtains of the litter, which were fixed ingeniously to the bearing-pole, I perceived, to my infinite relief, that we had passed out of the region of eternal swamp, and were now travelling over swelling grassy plains towards a cup-shaped hill.

H. RIDER HAGGARD, *She*

They were much shorter than any animal he had yet seen on Malacandra, and he gathered that they were bipeds, though the lower limbs were so thick and sausage-like that he hesitated to call them legs. The bodies were a little narrower at the top than at the bottom so as to be very slightly pear-shaped, and the heads were neither round like those of *hrossa* nor long like those of *sorns,* but almost square.

C. S. LEWIS, *Out of the Silent Planet*

*crescent-shaped (small crescent)*
   lunulate

*crest-shaped*
   cristiform

*cross-shaped*
   cruciate, cruciform

*crown-shaped*
   coroniform

*cube-shaped*
   cubiform

*cucumber-shaped*
   cucumiform

*cumulus-cloud-like*
   cumuliform

*cup-shaped*
   scyphate, scyphiform, cupulate, cupuliform, cyathiform,
   calicular, caliculate, calathiform, pocilliform, poculiform

*curl-like*
   cirriform

*cushion-shaped or pad-like*
   pulviliform, pulvillar, pulvinate

*cylinder-shaped*
   cylindriform

*dart-shaped*
   belemnoid

*disc-shaped*
   disciform, discoid

*double- or two-faced*
   Janiform

*drop-shaped* (see *teardrop-shaped*)

*ear-shaped*
   auriform, auriculate

The ball was there, but where the flame-like figure should have been, a deep depression of irregular shape had been cut as if to erase it.   C. S. LEWIS, *Out of the Silent Planet*

The terrain was new to the bats but not altogether different from their Mexican home. Hungry, their flattened spade-shaped noses soaked up the animal smells on the night wind.

MARTIN CRUZ SMITH, *Nightwing*

The coyote that had ripped open the ewe had deposited two species: common Dog Fleas, rounded, with a moustachelike mouth comb; and blunt-headed, eyed Carnivore Fleas. There were two specimens of the last species. They had eyeless, helmet-shaped heads. A mouth comb like mimic teeth. Bat Fleas.   MARTIN CRUZ SMITH, *Nightwing*

The cavern wormed its way half a mile into the mountain. Its general shape was ovoid, the walls below the ridge smoothly curved to the floor, the walls above arched another hundred feet up to giant stalactites and the bat roosts.

MARTIN CRUZ SMITH, *Nightwing*

From these the cane juice runs down a wedge-shaped trough to the boiling house, where a Negro stands and rinses a little lime wash into it with a grass brush to make it granulate.   RICHARD HUGHES, *A High Wind in Jamaica*

Certainly there was nothing to remind one of Germany in the neat, rectilinear streets and the featureless, repetitive buildings.   DAVID LODGE, *Out of the Shelter*

*eel-shaped*
  anguilliform

*egg-shaped*
  ooid, oval, ovoid, oviform, ovaliform, elliptical, ellipsoidal

*egg-to-pear-like in shape*
  ovopyriform

*embryo-like*
  embryoniform

*eye-shaped*
  oculiform

*fan-shaped*
  flabellate, flabelliform, rhipidate

*feather-like*
  pinnate, pinniform, penniform, plumiform, pennaceous,
  plumaceous

*fern- or frond-shaped*
  filiciform

*fiddle- or violin-shaped*
  pandurate

*fig-shaped*
  ficiform, ficicoid, caricous

*finger-like*
  dactyloid, digitate, digitiform

*fish-shaped*
  ichthyomorphic

*flask- or bladder-shaped*
  ampullaceous, ampulliform, lageniform

*flower-like*
  floriform, floral

*flowerpot-shaped*
  vasculiform

*foot-shaped*
  pediform, pedate

The figure of each separate dwelling-house, being the segment of a circle, must spoil the symmetry of the rooms, by contracting them towards the street windows, and leaving a larger sweep in the space behind.

TOBIAS SMOLLETT, *The Expedition of Humphry Clinker*


On shelves opposite Lapham's desk were tin cans of various sizes, arranged in tapering cylinders, and showing, in a pattern diminishing toward the top, the same label borne by the casks and barrels in the wareroom.

WILLIAM DEAN HOWELLS, *The Rise of Silas Lapham*


Near to the foot of the hill arose the short spiky spears of a sweet chestnut plantation, and beyond it a little patch of woodland, where the wild cherry was but lately over, half veiled a group of conical oast houses in a blur of green.

IRIS MURDOCH, *An Unofficial Rose*


He watched a man standing in the greenish shade, raising up, holding a black cluster in one hand, taking the knife from his belt, cutting, laying the bunch in a flat boat-shaped basket.

KATHERINE MANSFIELD,
"The Man Without a Temperament"


Her face was heart-shaped, wide at the brows and with a pointed chin—but not too pointed.

KATHERINE MANSFIELD, "Prelude"

*forceps-like*
forcepiform

*forked*
forficate, furcate

*fringe-like*
fimbriate, fimbricate, lanciniform

*fringed (small fringe)*
fimbrillate

*frond- or fern-shaped*
filiciform

*fruit-shaped*
fructiform

*funnel-shaped*
infundibular, infundibuliform, choanoid, funnelform

*gill-shaped*
branchiform

*gland-like*
adeniform

*grain-like*
graniform

*granule-like*
granuliform

*grape-cluster-like*
botryose, aciniform

*grouped together*
agminate

*hair-like*
piliform, capilliform

*hammer-shaped*
malleiform

*hand-shaped*
meniform, palmate

With the lights out, the desert was gray tufted with black spots of desert growth. Here and there loomed tall columns, and one rocky mass shaped like a pipe organ.

LOUIS L'AMOUR, *The Haunted Mesa*

But it was augmented and rendered sublime by the mighty Alps, whose white and shining pyramids and domes towered above all, as belonging to another earth, the habitations of another race of beings.   MARY SHELLEY, *Frankenstein*

Then came a bust of a German soldier, very idealized, full of unfear. After this, a masterful crudity—a doughnut-bodied rider, sliding with fearful rapidity down the acute back-bone of a totally transparent sausage-shaped horse who was moving simultaneously in five directions.

E. E. CUMMINGS, *The Enormous Room*

In the distance rose the purplegray spire of a church and the irregular forms of old buildings.

JOHN DOS PASSOS, *War's Misadventures*

A dead-windowed house stared at them suddenly from a clearing; across the road a barn had collapsed in a spiral of timbers and twisted roof.   WALLACE STEGNER,
"The Sweetness of the Twisted Apples"

Gerard's face, describable as "rugged," had been better characterised by his brother-in-law the art dealer as "cubist."

*handle-shaped*
    manubrial, ansate

*hat-like*
    galericulate

*headlike at one end*
    capitate

*heart-shaped*
    cordiform, cordate

*heart (inverted)- or spade (cards)-shaped*
    obcordate, obcordiform

*helmet-shaped*
    galeiform, galeate, cassideous

*herring-shaped*
    harengiform

*hinged-joint-like*
    ginglymoid

*honeycomb-like*
    faviform, faveolate, alveolate

*hood-shaped*
    cucullate, cuculliform

*hoof-shaped*
    ungulate

*hook-shaped*
    ankyroid, ancistroid, aduncate, uncinate, unciform,
    hamiform

*horn-shaped*
    corniform, cornute

*horseshoe-shaped*
    hippocrepiform

*hourglass-shaped*
    biconical

*insect-like*
    insectiform

There were a number of strong dominant surfaces, a commanding bone structure, a square even brow, a nose that appeared to end in a blunt plane rather than a point.

IRIS MURDOCH, *The Book and the Brotherhood*

He had been dreaming, and he saw his dream in its exact form. It was, first an emerald. Cut into an octagon with two long sides, it was shaped rather like the plaque at the bottom of a painting. Events within this emerald were circular and never-ending.

MARK HELPRIN, "The Schreuderspitze"

In the jargon of his trade, this region was covered by "the semi-permanent Pacific High." He looked at it malignantly. Then he smiled, for he noticed that the High had today accidentally assumed the shape of a gigantic dog's head. Rising from the Pacific waters it looked out stupidly across the continent. The blunt nose just touched Denver; the top of the head was in British Columbia. A small circle over southern Idaho supplied an eye; three concentric ovals pointing southwest from the California coast furnished a passable ear.

GEORGE R. STEWART, *Storm*

The only end in sight was Yossarian's own, and he might have remained in the hospital until doomsday had it not been for that patriotic Texan with his infundibuliform jowls and his lumpy, rumpleheaded, indestructible smile cracked forever across the front of his face like the brim of a black ten-gallon hat. JOSEPH HELLER, *Catch-22*

*ivy-leaf-shaped*
  hederiform

*jelly-like*
  gelatiniform

*jug-shaped (one handle)*
  urceiform

*keel-shaped*
  carinate, cariniform

*keyhole-shaped*
  clithridiate

*kidney-shaped*
  reniform, nephroid

*kidney-bean-shaped*
  reniform, nephroid

*knob-like at one end*
  capitellate

*knot- or node-shaped*
  nodiform

*ladder-like*
  scalariform

*lambda-shaped (Λ)*
  lambdoid

*lance-head-shaped*
  lanceolate

*lance-shaped*
  lanciform

*lance-shaped inversely*
  oblanceolate

*lattice-like*
  clathrate, clathroid, clathrose

*leaf-shaped*
  phylliform, foliiform

Near the same tree two more bundles of acute angles sat with their legs drawn up. One, with his chin propped on his knees, stared at nothing, in an intolerable and appalling manner; his brother phantom rested its forehead, as if overcome with a great weariness; and all about others were scattered in every pose of contorted collapse, as in some picture of a massacre or a pestilence.

JOSEPH CONRAD, Heart of Darkness

The only decoration is an odd-looking piece right next to the bed: an end table made out of a slab of unevenly cut marble and thin crisscrosses of black lacquer wood for the legs. My mother puts her handbag on the table and the cylindrical black vase on top starts to wobble.

AMY TAN, The Joy Luck Club

On the prow of that stone ship in the centre of the strait, and seemingly a part of it, a shaped and geometrical outcrop of the naked rock, stood the pueblo of Malpais. Block above block, each story smaller than the one below, the tall houses rose like stepped and amputated pyramids into the blue sky. At their feet lay a straggle of low buildings, a criss-cross of walls; and on three sides the precipices fell sheer into the plain. A few columns of smoke mounted perpendicularly into the windless air and were lost.

ALDOUS HUXLEY, Brave New World

At the foot of the palatial facade was strown [*sic*], with careful art and ordered irregularity, a broad and broken heap of massive rock, looking as if it might have lain there since the

*leather-bottle-shaped*
   utriform

*lens-shaped (flattened oval)*
   lenticular, lentiform, lentoid

*lentil-shaped*
   lenticular, lenticuliform, lentiform

*lily-shaped*
   liliform

*lip-shaped*
   labial, labellate, labelloid

*lobe-shaped*
   lobate, lobular, lobiform

*loop- or sling-shaped*
   fundiform

*lotus-petal-shaped*
   lotiform

*lyre-shaped*
   lyriform

*miter- or bonnet-shaped*
   mitrate, mitriform

*moon-shaped*
   luniform

*mountain-shaped*
   montiform

*mouth-shaped*
   oriform

*mulberry-shaped*
   moriform

*mummy-like*
   mummiform

*mushroom-shaped*
   fungiform, agariciform

deluge. Over a central precipice fell the water, in a semicircular cascade; and from a hundred crevices, on all sides, snowy jets gushed up, and streams spouted out of the mouths and nostrils of stone monsters, and fell in glistening drops. . . .

NATHANIEL HAWTHORNE, *The Marble Faun*

But there were other objects of delight and interest claiming his instant attention; there were quaint twisted candlesticks in the shape of snakes, and a teapot fashioned like a china duck, out of whose open beak the tea was supposed to come. And there was a carved sandal-wood box packed tight with aromatic cotton-wool, and between the layers of cotton-wool were little brass figures, hump-necked bulls, and peacocks and goblins, delightful to see and to handle. Less promising in appearance was a large square book with plain black covers. . . .     SAKI, "The Lumber Room"

The charm of Edna Pontellier's physique stole insensibly upon you. The lines of her body were long, clean and symmetrical; it was a body which occasionally fell into splendid poses; there was no suggestion of the trim, stereotyped fashion-plate about it.     KATE CHOPIN, *The Awakening*

Shivering in terror, Meggie [*sic*] leaned forward to peer inside the doll's cranium. The inverted contours of cheeks and chin showed dimly, light glittered between the parted lips with their teeth a black, animal silhouette, and above all this

*nail- or claw-shaped*
unguiform

*narrowing at the top*
fastigiate

*navel-like*
umbiliform, umbiliciform

*neck-like*
colliform

*needle-shaped*
aciform, acicular, acerose, aciculate, styloid

*net-like*
retiform, reticular

*nipple-shaped*
mammiloid, mammiliform

*node- or knot-shaped*
nodiform

*nose-like*
nasiform, nasutiform

*nostril-like*
nariform

*nut-shaped*
nuciform

*oar- or paddle-shaped*
remiform

*oat-shaped*
aveniform

*obelisk-shaped*
obeliscoid, obeliskoid

*omega-shaped (Ω)*
omegoid

*oyster-shaped*
ostreiform

were Agnes's eyes, two horrible clicking balls speared by a
wire rod that cruelly pierced her head.

COLLEEN MCCULLOUGH, *The Thorn Birds*


He could see the bedroom, the Edwardian apartment block,
the tarred roofs of its back additions with their lopsided,
crusty cisterns, the mess of south London, the hazy curvature
of the earth.                  IAN MCEWAN, *The Child in Time*


It was box-shaped with its front door dead center, four small
windows near each corner, and constructed of the same red
bricks as The Bell. A path made out of leftover bricks made
a shallow S-shape between the gate and the front door.

IAN MCEWAN, *The Child in Time*


Eventually he saw up through the long narrow air shaft that
the stars had faded and the rhomboid of night sky had grown
gray.                         E. L. DOCTOROW, *Ragtime*


While he was using the lavatory, he began making his Evelyn Waugh face, then abandoned it in favour of one more
savage than any he normally used. Gripping his tongue between his teeth, he made his cheeks expand into little hemi-
spherical balloons; he forced his upper lip downwards into
an idiotic pout; he protruded his chin like the blade of a
shovel.                       KINGSLEY AMIS, *Lucky Jim*


Now, why was diagonal cutting better than cutting straight
across? Because the corner of a triangularly cut slice gave you

*pad-like or pillow-shaped*
  pulviliform, pulvillar

*paddle- or oar-shaped*
  remiform

*palm-shaped*
  palmate, palmiform, palmatiform

*papyrus-shaped*
  papyriform

*pea-shaped*
  pisiform

*pear-shaped*
  pyriform

*pear (upside-down)-shaped*
  obpyriform

*pebble-shaped*
  calciform, calculiform

*pencil-shaped*
  penciliform

*petal-shaped*
  petaliform

*phallus-shaped*
  phalliform

*pie-shaped*
  sectoral

*pie-shaped with a flat end rather than a point*
  segmental

*pincer- or claw-shaped*
  cheliform

*pipe- or tube-shaped*
  tubiform, fistuliform

*pitcher-shaped*
  ascidiform

*plant-shaped*
  phytoform

an ideal first bite. In the case of rectangular toast, you had to angle the shape into your mouth, as you angle a big dresser through a hall doorway: you had to catch one corner of your mouth with one corner of the toast and then carefully *turn* the toast, drawing the mouth open with it so that its other edge could clear; only then did you chomp down. Also, with a diagonal slice, most of the tapered bite was situated right up near the front of your mouth, where you wanted it to be as you began to chew. . . .

NICHOLSON BAKER, *The Mezzanine*

In home bathrooms, the toilet seats are complete ovals, while in corporate bathrooms the seats are horseshoe-shaped; I suppose the gap lessens the problem of low-energy drops of urine falling on the seat when some scofflaw thoughtlessly goes standing up without first lifting the seat.

NICHOLSON BAKER, *The Mezzanine*

Very clever were some of their productions—pasteboard guitars, antique lamps made of old-fashioned butter boats covered with silver paper, gorgeous robes of old cotton, glittering with tin spangles from a pickle factory, and armor covered with the same useful diamond-shaped bits left in sheets when the lids of tin preserve pots were cut out.

LOUISA MAY ALCOTT, *Little Women*

Make your locks as smooth as you like, and add a garland of those scarlet, star-shaped blossoms hanging from the bush

*pod-shaped*
   leguminose, leguminiform
*pouch-shaped*
   sacciform, scrotiform, bursiform
*prickle-shaped*
   aculeiform
*prop-like*
   fulciform
*pruning-knife-shaped*
   cultrate, cultriform
*pulley-shaped*
   trochleiform
*purse-shaped*
   bursiform

*radial in form*
   actiniform
*ram's-head-shaped*
   arietinous
*reed-like*
   calamiform
*rice-grain-like*
   riziform
*ring-shaped (or spirally curled)*
   circinate, cingular, annular
*rod-like*
   virgulate, bacillary, bacilliform, vergiform, baculiform
*roof-shaped*
   tectiform
*rope- or cord-like*
   funiform
*rows-of-bricks-like*
   muriform

behind you—crown yourself as you crowned old Cla-cla—
but the crazed look will remain just the same.

W. H. HUDSON, *Green Mansions*

Now, running diagonally down her leg was a series of saucer-shaped welts, the center of each puffed and purple.

MICHAEL CRICHTON, *Sphere*

In his sleep he could hear the horses stepping among the
rocks and he could hear them drink from the shallow pools
in the dark where the rocks lay smooth and rectilinear as the
stones of ancient ruins. . . .

CORMAC MCCARTHY, *All the Pretty Horses*

Building the hive, the workers have the look of embryonic
cells organizing a developing tissue; from a distance they are
like the viruses inside a cell, running off row after row of
symmetrical polygons as though laying down crystals.

LEWIS THOMAS, *The Lives of a Cell*

In one large painting he had put a bell-shaped mountain in
the very foreground and covered it with meticulously
painted trees, each of which stood out at right angles to the
ground, where it grew exactly as the nap stands out on
folded plush.    MARILYNNE ROBINSON, *Housekeeping*

Now whether it was physically impossible, with half a dozen
hands all thrust into the napkin at a time—but that some one

*S-shaped*
 sigmoid, annodated
*saddle-shaped*
 selliform
*sandal-shaped*
 sandaliform
*saucer-shaped*
 pateriform, acetabuliform
*sausage-shaped*
 allantoid, botuliform
*scimitar-shaped*
 acinaciform
*scissors-shaped*
 forciform
*shallow-depression-shaped*
 glenoid
*shark-shaped*
 squaliform, selachian
*shell-shaped*
 conchiform, conchate
*shield-shaped*
 scutiform, scutatiform, aspidate, elytriform, peltate, clypeate, clypeiform, peltiform
*shovel- or spade (implement)-shaped*
 palaceous
*sickle-shaped*
 meniscal meniscate, meniscoid, menisciform, lunate, falcate, drepaniform, drepanoid, bicorn
*sieve-like*
 cribriform, cribrose, cribral, cribrate, coliform
*sling- or loop-shaped*
 fundiform
*slipper-shaped*
 calceiform, soleiform

chestnut, of more life and rotundity than the rest, must be put in motion—it so fell out, however, that one was actually sent rolling off the table; and as Phutatorius sat straddling under—it fell perpendicularly into that particular aperture of Phutatorius's breeches, for which, to the shame and indelicacy of our language be it spoke, there is no chaste word throughout all Johnson's dictionary. . . .

LAURENCE STERNE, *Tristram Shandy*

Quite different from these nests of paper and clay are those of thickly felted vegetable hairs made by large wasps of the genus *Apoica*. Round or hexagonal in shape, five or six inches in diameter, these nests have the form of an umbrella without a handle or a stalkless mushroom.

ALEXANDER F. SKUTCH, *A Naturalist in Costa Rica*

It was in this place of astonishing miniatures that I came upon the lairs of the lions in the sunny sand—ant lions, that is. Small funnel-shaped pits dimpled the sand—inverted cones an inch or two in diameter across the top, tapering to the bottom perhaps an inch deep in the sand.

VIRGINIA S. EIFERT, *Journeys in Green Places*

Probably the best known of the moths are the sphinx or hawk moths, some of which are so large they resemble hummingbirds. The bodies of these moths are relatively stout and torpedo-shaped.

DAVID F. COSTELLO, *The Prairie World*

*snail-shell-shaped*
    cochleate, cochleiform, soleiform

*snake-shaped*
    colubriform, anguiform

*spade (implement)- or shovel-shaped*
    palaceous

*spade (cards)- or inverted-heart-shaped*
    obcordate, obcordiform

*spatula-shaped*
    spatulate

*spear-shaped or arrowhead-shaped (with flaring barbs)*
    hastate

*sphere-shaped*
    spherical, spheriform

*spike-shaped*
    spiciform, spicate

*spindle-shaped*
    fusiform

*spine- or thorn-shaped*
    aculeiform, spiniform

*spinning-top-shaped*
    strombuliform

*spoon-shaped*
    cochleariform, spatulate

*spread-fingers-like*
    digitate

*stake-shaped*
    sudiform

*stalk-like*
    stipiform

*star-shaped*
    astroid, actinoid, stellate, stellar, stelliform

*star-shaped (small star)*
    stellular

So, now, by opening the dam, he was able to fling an imposing girdle of water, a huge quadrilateral with the river as its
base, completely around the plantation, like the moat encircling a medieval city.

CARL STEPHENSON, "Leiningen Versus the Ants"

The crust of the Great Basin has broken into blocks. The
blocks are not, except for simplicity's sake, analogous to
dominoes. They are irregular in shape. They more truly
suggest stretch marks. Which they are.

JOHN MCPHEE, *Basin and Range*

Salt has a low specific gravity and is very plastic. Pile eight
thousand feet of sediment on it and it starts to move. Slowly,
blobularly, it collects itself and moves. It shoves apart layers
of rock. It mounds upon itself, and, breaking its way upward, rises in mushroom shape—a salt dome. Still rising into
more shales and sandstones, it bends them into graceful
arches and then bursts through them like a bullet shooting
upward through a splintering floor. The shape becomes a
reverse teardrop.    JOHN MCPHEE, *Basin and Range*

In the pool of light shed onto her lap, an exquisitely mani-
cured hand guides a slender gold-plated propelling pencil
across the lines of print, occasionally pausing to underline a
sentence or make a marginal note. The long, spear-shaped
finger-nails on the hand are lacquered with terracotta var-
nish. The hand itself, long and white and slender, looks almost weighed down with three antique rings in which are
set ruby, sapphire, and emerald stones.

DAVID LODGE, *Small World*

*stem-like*
  cauliform

*stirrup-shaped*
  stapediform

*stone-like (small stone)*
  lapilliform

*strap-shaped*
  ligulate, lorate

*string-of-beads-like*
  moniliform, monilioid

*sword-shaped*
  gladiate, ensate, ensiform, xiphoid, xiphiiform

*tail-like*
  caudiform

*teardrop-shaped*
  guttiform, lachrymiform, stilliform

*tendril-like*
  pampiniform

*tent-shaped*
  tentiform

*thorn- or spine-shaped*
  aculeiform, spiniform

*thread-like*
  filiform, fililose, filariform

*tongue-shaped*
  linguiform

*toothed or comb-shaped*
  pectinate

*tooth-like*
  odontoid, dentiform

*top-shaped (inversely conical)*
  trochiform, turbinate

*torpedo-shaped*
  terete

The stub of a candle, barely two inches long, lit at first attempt. The shadows of the switchboard cupboard bobbed against the wall at my approach. It looked different. The little wooden handle on its door was longer, more ornate, and set at a new angle. I was two feet away when the ornamentation resolved itself into the form of a scorpion, fat and yellow, its pincers curved about the axis of the diagonal and its chunkily segmented tail just obscuring the handle beneath. IAN MCEWAN, *Black Dogs*

. . . I could imagine how, in our absence, June's spirit, her many ghosts, might stealthily reassert possession, recapturing not just her furniture and kitchenware and pictures but the curl of a magazine cover, the ancient Australia-shaped stain on the bathroom wall, and the latent body shape of her old gardening jacket, still hanging behind a door because no one could bear to throw it out. IAN MCEWAN, *Black Dogs*

Kayerts stood still. He looked upwards; the fog rolled low over his head. He looked round like a man who has lost his way; and he saw a dark smudge, a cross-shaped stain, upon the shifting purity of the mist.

JOSEPH CONRAD, "An Outpost of Progress"

The room's one window, too high for a woman not standing on a stool to peer out of, had lozenge panes of leaded glass, thick glass bubbled and warped like bottle bottoms.

JOHN UPDIKE, *The Witches of Eastwick*

*tower-shaped*
  turriform, pyrgoidal, turrical, turricular

*tree-shaped*
  arboriform, dendritic, dendriform, dendroid, dendritiform

*triangle-shaped or delta (Δ)-shaped*
  triangular, sphenic, cuneate, cuneiform

*trumpet-shaped*
  buccinal

*tube- or pipe-shaped*
  tubular, tubiform, fistulous, fistular, fistuliform

*turnip-shaped*
  napiform, rapaceous

*turret-shaped*
  turriculate, turriculated

*two- or double-faced*
  Janiform

*U-shaped*
  hyoid, oxbow-like, hippocrepiform, parabolic

*upsilon (Υ)- or Y-shaped*
  hypsiloid, ypsiliform, hypsiliform

*valve-shaped*
  valviform

*violin- or fiddle-shaped*
  pandurate

*vortex-like*
  vorticiform

*wedge-shaped or delta (Δ)-shaped*
  triangular, sphenic, cuneate, cuneiform, deltoid

*wedge-shaped inversely*
  obcuneate, obdeltoid

*wheel-shaped*
  rotiform, rotate

Sometimes a young man appears, bearing the twin drums, the *tablas,* to help her with the necessary percussion which otherwise she provides herself with sharp little flicks of her supple fingers on the onion-shaped tamboura.

PAUL SCOTT, *The Jewel in the Crown*

The rich benignant cigar smoke eddied coolly down his throat; he puffed it out again in rings which breasted the air bravely for a moment; blue, circular—I shall try and get a word alone with Elizabeth to-night, he thought—then began to wobble into hour-glass shapes and taper away; odd shapes they take, he thought.

VIRGINIA WOOLF, *Mrs. Dalloway*

This miniature world demonstrated how everything was planned, people lived in these modern streamlined curvilinear buildings, each of them accommodating the population of a small town. . . .     E. L. DOCTOROW, *World's Fair*

A high lozenge of light told Medlar's one cracked and sleep-blurred eye that dawn had come. That dim gray oval was the porthole in the cabin trunk, opposite.

JOHN HERSEY, *Under the Eye of the Storm*

Directly across the way stood a top-heavy dockhouse, a weatherbeaten cube of pure nineteenth century raised up on out-curving supports for the purpose of enabling elderly ladies to sit out on good afternoons to watch the sailboats leaning at their work—a setting rendered completely otherday and unreal by this thick, moist air.

JOHN HERSEY, *Under the Eye of the Storm*

*wing-like*
    aliform

*X-shaped*
    decussate, chiasmal

*Y- or upsilon (ϒ)-shaped*
    hypsiloid, ypsiliform, hypsiliform

# Patterns and Edges

I can hardly believe the Angels have a need for such scarves; anyway, the ones made by the Commander's Wife are too elaborate. She doesn't bother with the cross-and-star pattern used by many of the other Wives, it's not a challenge. Fir trees march across the ends of her scarves, or eagles, or stiff humanoid figures, boy and girl, boy and girl. They aren't scarves for grown men but for children.

MARGARET ATWOOD, *The Handmaid's Tale*

Serena Joy, what a stupid name. It's like something you'd put on your hair, in the other time, the time before, to straighten it. *Serena Joy,* it would say on the bottle, with a woman's head in cut-paper silhouette on a pink oval background with scalloped gold edges.

MARGARET ATWOOD, *The Handmaid's Tale*

With such exuberant invention, the identity of the animals represented can become very obscure. Usually there are precise clues. Two prominent teeth and a rectangular cross-hatched tail among the maze of symbols indicate a beaver; a wide toothless mouth and no tail, a frog; a dorsal fin and a blow-hole, a killer whale.

DAVID ATTENBOROUGH, *The Tribal Eye*

*having a pattern or design*
  patterned, designed, figured

*having a planned and orderly design*
  schematic

*having a varied pattern*
  variegated, motley, harlequin

*having a consistent or recurrent conceptual element*
  having a motif

*represented in a simplified or symbol-like form*
  formal

*represented in a realistic or somewhat detailed form*
  naturalistic

*having markings or images that don't mean literally what they represent
(or that mean more than that)*
  symbolic, ideogramic, ideogrammic, ideogramatic,
  ideogrammatic

*having markings or images that mean what they represent*
  pictographic, hieroglyphic, glyphic

*lengthwise*
  longitudinal, axial
*widthwise*
  horizontal, transverse

*having many dots*
  punctuate

Set on a basement of "rusticated" stonework of varying tones, its principal story is built of tan brick banded with strips of gaily-floriated tiles, which parallel the lines of the basement. Then, based on the module of the square flower tile, there rises an intricately corbelled cornice, a series of chimneys and a cylindrical tower, all of which are harmoniously interrelated by patterns such as chevrons and prisms.

GEORGE R. COLLINS, *Antonio Gaudi*

Bichrome wares accompany the prevalent monochrome pottery described above, but with the addition of white-painted motifs. The primarily geometric designs include bands, circles, dots, scrolls, frets, zigzags, triangles, diamonds, chevrons, and sunbursts, either singly or in combination, although some may represent stylized animals. Common shapes are water jars, with designs painted on the vessel shoulders and handles, and tripod-supported bowls with flaring walls, often painted white on both interior and exterior surfaces.

SYLVANUS AND GEORGE BRAINERD, *The Ancient Maya*

In a painting from a Kwakiutl housefront . . . , which was made for me by an Indian from Fort Rupert, the large head with the incisors will be recognized. The scaly tail appears under the mouth. The broken lines . . . around the eyes, indicate the hair of the beaver.

FRANZ BOAS, *Primitive Art*

The entrance to this ancient place of devotion was under a very low round arch, ornamented by several courses of that

*having spots*
   spotted, speckled, dappled, menald, macular, maculose,
   pardine, flecked

*having gold dots made with a pointed tool*
   pointillé

*having colored spots or speckles*
   variegated

*having an eye-like spot or spots*
   ocellate

*having soft shadow-like small touches or spots*
   stippled

*having holes*
   holey, pierced, porous, perforated, spongeous, cribriform

*having bowl-like depressions*
   cratered

*having small depressions*
   pitted, cuppy, cavernulous, foveate

*having small fissures or chinks*
   rimulose

*having scoop-like indentations*
   chiseled, gouged

*having a structure of rows and openings*
   honeycombed, faveolate, faviform, alveolate,
   compartmentalized, chambered

*having an angular-labyrinth or straight-pathways design*
   fretted

*cavity-divided or compartmentalized*
   locular, loculate

*having a horizontal marking or strip*
   banded, barred, belted

*having a horizontally encircling band or stripe*
   crossbanded

zig-zag moulding, resembling sharks' teeth, which appears so often in the more ancient Saxon architecture.

SIR WALTER SCOTT, *Ivanhoe*

The North Rim is so deeply excavated by side canyons that in certain sections its pattern resembles a giant-toothed comb. The side canyons of the South Rim merely serrate it in gentle scallops.

ROBERT WALLACE, *The Grand Canyon*

The wall decoration contains an arabesque motif in its intersecting semicircular shapes.

LARA VINCA MASINI, *Gaudi*

Within the channels are many features, such as teardrop-shaped islands, longitudinal grooves, terraced margins, and inner channel cataracts, that are also found in regions on Earth affected by large floods.

CARY R. SPITZER, ED., *Viking Orbiter Views of Mars*

Men swore. They pushed at the wheels with long oak poles and slashed at the oxen till their backs were crosshatched with bleeding welts and their noses ran pink foam.

JOHN GARDNER, *Grendel*

Then I went out to the courtyard. The night was clear. The toothed roof-edge, the watchman with his spear and horn, stood black against the stars.

MARY RENAULT, *The King Must Die*

*having lines or stripes*
lined, striped, lineate, scored

*having spaces or interruptions rather than being continuous*
broken

*having narrow markings or irregular stripes*
streaked

*having variegated marble-like streaks*
marbled

*having fine lines*
lineolate

*having longitudinal (lengthwise) stripes*
vittate

*in sequence or in rows*
serial

*having vertical ranks*
rectiserial

*arranged in two rows or series*
biserial

*having grooves*
grooved, fluted, channeled, cannellated, chamfered, beveled, rutted

*having rectangular grooves*
dadoed

*having long furrows or grooves*
sulcated, canaliculate

*having rows of folds or ridges and grooves*
corrugated, plicate

*having minute grooves*
striated

*having raised lengthwise strips*
ridged

*having hair-like ridges*
lirate

The sparks were not a pattern on a dark ground, they were themselves the background, that of a flaming evening sky. The black lines, and stripes upon it, were the lower branches of a fir thicket; these branches were dead and bare because the growth was so dense that no light reached down here.

ISAK DINESEN, "The Caryatids, An Unfinished Tale"

When the sea is moderately calm, and slightly marked with spherical ripples, and this gnomon-like fin stands up and casts shadows upon the wrinkled surface, it may well be supposed that the watery circle surrounding it somewhat resembles a dial, with its style and wavy hour-lines graved on it.

HERMAN MELVILLE, *Moby-Dick*

The large 420-pound bongo's bright chestnut-red is also disrupted by mottled ears, a white chevron on the forehead, white cheek spots, a white crescent on the chest and, like the eland of the savanna, by ten or thirteen narrow transverse white stripes across back and sides.

RICHARD PERRY, *Life in Forest and Jungle*

They scuttled for days and days till they came to a great forest, 'sclusively full of trees and bushes and stripy, speckly, patchy-blatchy, shadows, and there they hid: and after another long time, what with standing half in the shade and half out of it, and what with the slippery-slidy shadows of the trees falling on them, the Giraffe grew blotchy, and the Zebra grew stripy, and the Eland and the Koodoo grew darker, with little wavy grey lines on their backs like bark on a tree trunk; . . .

RUDYARD KIPLING, "How the Leopard Got His Spots"

*having spiral grooves*
 rifled

*having long or row-like thin projections*
 ribbed, costate

*having cord- or tube-like trimming*
 piped

*having cracks*
 cracked, crackled, craquelé

*wound together*
 interlaced, intertwined, interwoven, entwined, plaited,
 braided, plexiform

*flourish-like curve*
 curlicue

*finely interlacing curves or floral or animal figures*
 arabesque

*having ornamental curls or plaiting*
 goffered

*having crossed lines*
 crisscross, crisscrossed, crosscut, reticulate, reticulated,
 cancellate

*having a design of crossed strips*
 latticed

*marked with two or more sets of intersecting parallel lines*
 cross-hatched

*having a net-like pattern*
 reticular, reticulated

*network of fine lines or dots (as on a postage stamp)*
 burelé, burelage

*map line representing connecting places having the same elevation*
 contour line

The tattoos were freshened by the air. Oriental dragons climbed Karp's arm, green claws splayed from his feet, ink-blue women wrapped around the columns of his thighs, and with each steamy breath the vulture picked at his heart. More vivid were the whitening scars, dead stripes on his chest, where the accusations had been burned away. Across his narrow brow spread a livid band.

MARTIN CRUZ SMITH, *Polar Star*

She had gone into the sea, touched bottom and returned with no apparent signs of corruption aside from the stillness of death. After the tension of rigor mortis all flesh became slack on the bone: breasts sagged on the ribs, mouth and jaw were loose, eyes flattened under half-open lids, the skin bore a luminous pallor mottled with bruises.

MARTIN CRUZ SMITH, *Polar Star*

Regular transverse division of black and white bands, and interchange of white and black in the spaces marked off, produce a chessboard, counterchange pattern, unless a band of foliated ornament is placed so as to alternate with the chequering. A chequered black and white stripe set against a plain black one would again lead us astray, giving the simple cross-band design shown. . . .

ARCHIBALD H. CHRISTIE, *Pattern Design*

In the first, the two series of chevrons are interlaced and the central lozenges are coloured differently from the decorated triangles which project beyond the margin into the edging lines. The second, formed with continuous angular S-figures

*map shading line to suggest relief*
  hachure

*having sharp back-and-forth turns*
  zigzag, staggered, chevroned, chevronwise, cringle-crangle

*having a pattern of uniformly spaced squares or perpendicular lines*
  grid-like, graticulated

*having a pattern of contrasting or variegated squares*
  checkered, checkerboard, chessboard, counterchanged,
  tesselated, patchwork

*having or resembling a design of inlaid pieces*
  mosaic

*having an indented checkered pattern*
  waffle, waffled

*having a pattern of unbalances or irregular squares*
  plaid

*having a pattern of varicolored diamonds*
  argyle

*painted thickly*
  pastose

*having pieces or elements overlapping*
  imbricate, imbricated, obvolute

*having a pattern of tangent or overlapping circles or semicircles*
  scaled, perulate

*having thin and flat or gill-like plates*
  lamellate, lamellated

*having several whorls*
  multispiral

*having a swirling pattern*
  marbled

*having coils or spirals*
  whorled

imposed upon themselves in reverse direction, is a pattern much used by medieval workers, both in the form given and with S-elements of normal curved shape.

ARCHIBALD H. CHRISTIE, *Pattern Design*

. . . she could only look out at the brown marshes and the million black factories and the puddly streets of towns and a rusty steamboat in a canal and barns and Bull Durham signs and roundfaced Spearmint gnomes all barred and criss-crossed with bright flaws of rain. The jeweled stripes on the window ran straight down when the train stopped and got more and more oblique as it speeded up.

JOHN DOS PASSOS, *The Morning of the Century*

They lay on a ledge high upon the sunny east slope and looked out to the north through the notch cut as sharply as a wedge out of a pie. Far below them the golden plain spread level, golden-tawny grass and golden-green wheat checkerboarded in a pattern as wide as the world.

WALLACE STEGNER, "Two Rivers"

The blossom-covered surface of the river is smooth, stretched taut from bank to bank like a polka-dotted fabric. The prow of the boat rips a passage through with a sizzling hiss.          KEN KESEY, *Sometimes a Great Notion*

The bedstead, chairs, and lounges, were of bamboo, wrought in peculiarly graceful and fanciful patterns. Over the head of the bed was an alabaster bracket, on which a

*having a pattern of worm-like curves*
vermiculate, vermiculated

*having irregular crooked or sinuous lines*
rivulose

*having wavy lines*
undé, damascened

*having a shimmering rippled or watery pattern (from two superimposed patterns)*
moiré

*showing circular continuation or movement*
rotary, rotational

*having flower-shaped or flower-like ornaments*
floriated, floral, floreted

*arranged in a pattern of rosettes*
rosular

*having an ornamentally curled design*
scrolled

*curled or coiled inward*
involute

*having star-like rays*
asteriated

*radially symmetrical*
actinoid

*having encircling parallel rings*
ringed

*showing delicately ornamental openwork*
filigreed

*puckered, blistered*
bullate, bulliform

*knobbed*
bosselated

*bulging*
bombé

beautiful sculptured angel stood, with drooping wings, holding out a crown of myrtle-leaves. From this depended, over the bed, light curtains of rose-colored gauze, striped with silver, supplying that protection from mosquitos which is an indispensable addition to all sleeping accommodation in that climate.

HARRIET BEECHER STOWE, *Uncle Tom's Cabin*

Every bed was covered with a woven mat, our only bedding during the months of constant wet heat. And the hot bricks of the courtyard were crisscrossed with bamboo paths.

AMY TAN, *The Joy Luck Club*

Where the curving hills scalloped the edge of the light-blue sky Mount Egmont soared ten thousand feet, sloping into the clouds, its sides still white with snow, its symmetry so perfect that even those like Frank who saw it every day of their lives never ceased to marvel.

COLLEEN MCCULLOUGH, *The Thorn Birds*

Later he stared at his finished work and longed to know if anyone other than Mr. Cromarty would be able to make sense of the miniature circles, dashes, and curlicues that floated freely above the lines with their sudden cruel hooks.

IAN MCEWAN, *The Child in Time*

. . . Hunt never commented on her appearance again, though a year later he gave her a present—a long, thin, limp, old silk scarf, with slanted ends and a black border and a small

*having a hammered appearance*
malleated

*having an edge of short threads or strips*
fringed, fimbriate

*having an uneven and sharp edge*
jagged

*having a rough and untrimmed edge (as a piece of paper)*
deckle-edged

*having cuts along the edge*
indented, nicked, nocked

*having vee-shaped indentations*
notched

*having teeth or notches*
toothed, saw-toothed, notched, crenelated, serrated,
serrulate, dentate, denticulate, dentelated, dentellated,
shark's-tooth, serried

*minutely toothed*
crenulate

*having deep and sharp indentations*
vandyked

*having curled indentations*
foiled

*having curled projections along the edge*
scalloped, crenate, invected, invecked

*having rounded projections*
lobed, lobate, lobular

*having small curled projections along the edge*
crenulate, crenellated

*having sharp backward projections*
barbed

*having concave indentations along the edge*
engrailed

*having a beveled or flattened edge (cut on an angle)*
chamfered

geometric pattern of green, beige and white checks and diamonds, a scarf from the thirties, which smelt faintly of age
and old-fashioned face powder and cats and sawdust.

MARGARET DRABBLE, *The Middle Ground*

He leaned over the side, gritting his teeth; a sunken brown
channel, ending in a fragment of discoloured paper, lay
across a light patch in the pattern of a valuable-looking rug.
This made him feel very unhappy, a feeling sensibly in-
creased when he looked at the bedside table. This was
marked by two black, charred grooves, greyish and shiny in
parts, lying at right angles and stopping well short of the
ashtray, which held a single used match.

KINGSLEY AMIS, *Lucky Jim*

As we drew close to the next floor, I could see a green glow
coming from under the crenellated slit where the escalator
steps disappeared. . . .

NICHOLSON BAKER, *The Mezzanine*

*having teeth along the edge*
    saw-toothed, dentate

*having small teeth along the edge*
    serrate, denticulate, dentellated

*having a notch near the edge*
    rabbeted

*having cuts on the surface*
    scratched, scarred, scored

# Surfaces and Textures

The ceiling of the companion-way which had paralleled the angle of descent now presented the only means of ascent, a slippery and precipitous slope of painted steel with lighting panels inset and flush, an unmanageable surface offering no grip or handhold of any kind.

PAUL GALLICO, *The Poseidon Adventure*

The turbid water, swollen by the heavy rain, was rushing rapidly on below; and all other sounds were lost in the noise of its splashing and eddying against the green and slimy piles.

CHARLES DICKENS, *Oliver Twist*

The mud lay thick upon the stones, and a black mist hung over the streets; the rain fell sluggishly down, and everything felt cold and clammy to the touch.

CHARLES DICKENS, *Oliver Twist*

It was a wild, cold, seasonable night of March, with a pale moon, lying on her back as though the wind had tilted her, and a flying wrack of the most diaphanous and lawny texture.

ROBERT LOUIS STEVENSON, *Dr. Jekyll and Mr. Hyde*

*flat or without varying elevation*
  plane, level, planate, tabular, tabulate
*made flat, flattened*
  applanate, planiform, complanate
*bent or twisted out of its plane*
  warped, buckled

*smooth and free of roughness*
  even, uniform, glabrous, levigate
*smooth and shiny*
  lustrous, glossy, polished, burnished, buffed, glazed,
  varnished, shellacked, lacquered, gleaming, glistening, glassy,
  suave
*like glass*
  glassy, glazed, glazy, vitreous, vitriform, hyaline
*not shiny*
  lusterless, dull, matte

*having an uneven surface*
  irregular, bumpy, humpy, hummocky, lumpy
*rough*
  coarse, prickly, scabrous, abrasive, scratchy, choppy, ragged,
  jagged, sandpapery, raspy
*rough with prominent irregularities*
  scraggly, scraggy
*having wrinkles*
  wrinkled, corrugated, rugose, crinkly, crinkled, crispate

Pseudo-Arabic minarets, dentils, and spindled galleries silhouette the outlines of furniture designed on the circle and
its parts—the arc and chord. The wooden frame was covered in chamois leather within *repoussé* metal mounts or
veneered in pewter and brass with insect-like motifs and
Middle Eastern calligraphy.

ALASTAIR DUNCAN, *Art Nouveau Furniture*

Both saw Violet-le-Duc's influence in the house's whiplash
contours.    ALASTAIR DUNCAN, *Art Nouveau Furniture*

I was to have an early breakfast, and start at dawn, for that
was the usual way; but I had the demon's own time with my
armor, and this delayed me a little. It is troublesome to get
into, and there is so much detail. First you wrap a layer or
two of blanket around your body, for a sort of cushion and
to keep off the cold iron; then you put on your sleeves and
shirt of chain mail—these are made of small steel links
woven together, and they form a fabric so flexible that if you
toss your shirt onto the floor, it slumps into a pile like a peck
of wet fishnet. . . .

MARK TWAIN, *A Connecticut Yankee in King Arthur's Court*

My horse was not above medium size, but he was alert,
slender-limbed, muscled with watch springs, and just a grey-
hound to go. He was a beauty, glossy as silk, and naked as he
was when he was born, except for bridle and ranger saddle.

MARK TWAIN, *A Connecticut Yankee in King Arthur's Court*

*having a grain-like consistency*
grainy, granular, gritty, coarse-grained, rough-grained, granulated, branny

*having a sand-like consistency*
sandy, sabulous, tophaceous, arenaceous, arenarious

*having a pushed-up surface*
raised, embossed, relief, in relief

*having rounded protuberances*
knobbed

*having small rounded protuberances*
pimpled

*having hard ornamental protuberances*
studded

*having raised (relief) patterns made by hammering the other side*
repoussé

*having a cut-into surface*
incised, engraved, tooled

*having small pits or indentations*
pitted, pocked, pockmarked

*having hammered indentations*
chased

*sharp*
acute, cutting, keen-edged, keen, knife-edged, knife-like, razor-edged, razor-like, cultrate

*having or coming to a point*
pointed, acute, acuminate, mucronate, acuate

*having sharp projections*
thorny, prickly, barbed, spiny, echinated

*not sharp*
dull, blunt, obtund, obtuse

*cut along the edge*
nicked, notched, hacked

I could not go abroad in snow—it would settle on me and expose me. Rain, too, would make me a watery outline, a glistening surface of a man—a bubble. And fog—I should be like a fainter bubble in a fog, a surface, a greasy glimmer of humanity.                    H . G . W E L L S , *The Invisible Man*

I've heard the long sigh go up, from around me, the sigh like air coming out of an air mattress, I've seen Aunt Lydia place her hand over the mike, to stifle the other sounds coming from behind her, I've leaned forward to touch the rope in front of me, in time with the others, both hands on it, the rope hairy, sticky with tar in the hot sun, then placed my hand on my heart to show my unity with the Salvagers and my consent, and my complicity in the death of this woman.
                M A R G A R E T   A T W O O D ,   *The Handmaid's Tale*

He sits me down, and sits himself down beside me. He puts an arm around my shoulders. The fabric is raspy against my skin, so unaccustomed lately to being touched.
                M A R G A R E T   A T W O O D ,   *The Handmaid's Tale*

He lets the book fall closed. It makes an exhausted sound, like a padded door shutting, by itself, at a distance: a puff of air. The sound suggests the softness of the thin oniony pages, how they would feel under the fingers. Soft and dry, like *papier poudre,* pink and powdery, from the time before, you'd get it in booklets for taking the shine off your nose, in those stores that sold candles and soap in the shapes of things: seashells, mushrooms. Like cigarette paper. Like petals.
                M A R G A R E T   A T W O O D ,   *The Handmaid's Tale*

*having a sliced opening or openings*
> slit, cut, slashed, incised, gashed, scissored

*having scratches*
> scratched, scored, abraded, scuffed, scraped, scarred

*solid*
> substantial, dense, concrete, material, palpable, intact

*hard*
> firm, unyielding, inflexible, rock-hard, stone-like, flinty, adamantine, indurate, steely

*hardened*
> toughened, indurated

*marble-like*
> marmoreal

*granite-like*
> granitic

*cement-like*
> cementitious

*diamond-like*
> adamantine

*stiff*
> rigid, starchy, inelastic, inflexible, inextensible

*tight*
> taut

*tough*
> fibrous, leathery, sinewy, ropy, stringy, gristly, chewy, coriaceous

*brittle*
> crisp

*soft*
> yielding, pliant

*limp*
> flaccid, slack, loose, baggy, droopy, loppy

*lacking solidity*
> flimsy, unsubstantial

She had a vision of her mad wet face against the sky, as she rocked on the slippery stone. She tried to catch at her habit to help her, but the stuff was slimy with wet and dirt. Then Sister Ruth seemed to fall into the sky with a scream, as she went over the railings.

RUMER GODDEN, *Black Narcissus*

A grainy, porous overlay might account for the waffling or graham-cracker appearance of much of the surface in the photos.

RICHARD S. LEWIS, *Appointment on the Moon*

The buttress merged with roof and floor in flowing and perfectly proportioned curves. And on its face was superimposed a small, delicately sculptured column, so oddly weathered that it seemed almost a decorative afterthought. The surface of this column was rounded and smooth, as if it had been sandpapered by a patient carpenter, and its fine-drawn strata stood out sharp and clear, like the grain on unstained, highly polished wood.

ERNEST BRAUN, *Grand Canyon of the Living Colorado*

But after a foot or two of this ladder-like progression they are faced either with the battering fall of white water at their left or with a smooth black stretch of rock wall in front, hit every few seconds by heavy splashes of spray. For a few feet at the bottom of this wall grows a close slimy fur of waterweed, and among its infinitesimal tendrils the elvers twine themselves and begin, very slowly, to squirm their way upwards, forming a vertical, close-packed queue perhaps two feet wide. GAVIN MAXWELL, *Ring of Bright Water*

*breakable*
> fragile, frangible, frail, crackable, crushable

*crumbleable*
> easily crumbled, friable, pulverizable

*easily cuttable or splittable*
> scissile

*rubbery, elastic*
> blubbery, resilient, springy

*yielding*
> claylike, doughy, pudding-like, pulpy, porridge-like,
> pultaceous

*flexible*
> bendable, pliable, pliant, malleable, elastic, resilient,
> moldable, fictile

*moldable*
> supple, malleable, fictile

*stretchable*
> tensile, ductile, extensible

*limp*
> loose, flaccid, floppy

*mealy*
> floury, farinaceous

*flaky*
> scaly, squamate, shivery


*without moisture*
> dry, arid, dessicated, parched, sere


*offering poor or no traction*
> slippery, slick, lubricated, glossy

*oily, greasy, fat-like*
> slick, oleaginous, unguinous, sebaceous

*soapy*
> saponaceous

. . . and the fields would be deep in that rank, hairy or slick, juicy, sticky grass which the cattle gorge on and never gets flesh over their ribs for that grass is in that black soil and no matter how far the roots could ever go, if the roots were God knows how deep, there would never be anything but that black, grease-clotted soil and no stone down there to put calcium into that grass. . . .

ROBERT PENN WARREN,  *All the King's Men*

This was the road, and when the surface of the earth became too deeply pitted and potholed with traffic the cars and trucks would deviate and choose another course.

NEVIL SHUTE,  *A Town Like Alice*

This was prudent, for in point of fact the dwarf, knowing his disposition, was lying in wait at a little distance from the sash armed with a large piece of wood, which, being rough and jagged and studded in many parts with broken nails, might possibly have hurt him.

CHARLES DICKENS,  *The Old Curiosity Shop*

I touched earth, and stones, and a slimy worm that made me start. Then I came upon moldy cloth, and a hard shape within. I pulled back my hand; it had a feel of bones.

MARY RENAULT,  *The King Must Die*

Childerique had let down her hair, still moist from the children's splashings. It was very thick and soft, and wafted round her neck and shoulders as she moved.

ISAK DINESEN,  "The Caryatids, An Unfinished Tale"

*coated*
    bedaubed, lacquered, filmy, overlayed, glossed

*sticky*
    viscous, viscid, adhesive, gummy, mucilaginous,
    agglutinative

*lying close against*
    adhering, clinging

*moist, damp, wet*
    dank, bedewed, dewy, roral, rorid, imbrued

*wet, watery*
    fluid, serous

*very wet*
    sodden, soaked, saturated, suffused

*coolly moist and sticky*
    clammy

*absorbent*
    porous, leachy

*wet and yielding*
    spongy, semiliquid, pulpy, mushy, squishy, oozy

*thick*
    clotted, grumous

*soft like nap or down*
    fluffy, downy, fleecy, cottony, feathery, lanuginous,
    lanuginose

*soft and lustrous*
    silken, satiny

*woolly*
    flocculent, lanate, lanose

*felt-like*
    pannose

*velvety*
    velutinous

A vast pulpy mass, furlongs in length and breadth, of a glancing cream-color, lay floating on the water, innumerable long
arms radiating from its centre, and curling and twisting like a
nest of anacondas, as if blindly to clutch at any hapless object
within reach.          HERMAN MELVILLE, *Moby-Dick*

From the branches of these pear trees hung carafes full of a
glutinous yellow substance for trapping insects still changed
religiously every month by the local horticultural college.
                    MALCOLM LOWRY, *Under the Volcano*

And worst of all, the old ladies ignoring their foul neighbor
munched their sandwiches and sucked on fuzzy sections of
orange, wrapping the peels in scraps of paper and popping
them daintily under the seat.
                    VLADIMIR NABOKOV, *King, Queen, Knave*

Fifty dirty, stark-naked men elbowing each other in a room
twenty feet square, with only two bathtubs and two slimy
roller towels between them all. I shall never forget the reek
of dirty feet. Less than half the tramps actually bathed (I
heard them saying that hot water is "weakening" to the
system), but they all washed their faces and feet, and the
horrid greasy little clouts known as toe-rags which they bind
round their toes.
            GEORGE ORWELL, *Down and Out in Paris and London*

They would never be like Mrs. Grandlieu's old timber
house, with its worn decorative woodwork, its internal

*pillow-like*
　cushiony, puffy

*feathery*
　plumy

*hairy*
　hirsute, bristly

*fuzzy*
　shaggy, nubby

*knobby*
　studded, lumpy, nubby, nubbly, knubbly, nubbed, noded, noduled

*very thin*
　sheer, lawny

*dense*
　compact, compacted, close-textured, thick, close-knit, consolidated, condensed

*clotted*
　congealed, coagulated

*separable*
　fissile, scissile, partable

*light and somewhat transparent*
　filmy, gauzy, gossamer, cobwebby

*powdery, dusty*
　floury, chalky, triturated, comminuted, pulverous, pulverulent, powdered

*foamy*
　frothy, spumescent

*jelly-like*
　gelatinous, colloidal

*cork-like*
　suberose

*rocky*
　petrous, calcified

arches of fretwork arabesques that caught the dust, its mahogany-stained floor springy but polished smooth, the hard graining of the floorboards standing out from the softer wood.                    V. S. NAIPAUL, *Guerrillas*

"Beate Leibowitz, ora pro me!" whispered Brother Francis. His hands were trembling so violently that they threatened to ruin the brittle documents.

WALTER M. MILLER, JR., *A Canticle for Leibowitz*

The Leibowitz print, another abstraction, appealed to nothing, least of all to reason. He studied it until he could see the whole amazing complexity with his eyes closed, but knew no more than he had known before. It appeared to be no more than a network of lines connecting a patchwork of doohickii, squiggles, quids, laminulae, and thingumbob. The lines were mostly horizontal or vertical, and crossed each other with either a little jump-mark or a dot; they made right-angle turns to get around doohickii, and they never stopped in mid-space but always terminated at a squiggle, quiggle, quid, or thingumbob.

WALTER M. MILLER, JR., *A Canticle for Leibowitz*

Far beyond, cliffs and spires of the familiar green rock rose against the dark blue sky. A moment later he saw that what he had taken for downlands was but the ridged and furrowed surface of a blue-grey valley mist—a mist which would not appear a mist at all when they descended into the *handramit*.

C. S. LEWIS, *Out of the Silent Planet*

*stony*
    pebbled, pebbly, gravelly

*covered with another material or substance*
    overlaid

*covered with a glossy surface*
    enameled

*covered with a crust*
    encrusted

In one case the entire residence unit consists of juxtaposed rectangular rooms enclosing a roughly trapezoid court.

DAVID L. CLARKE, *Spatial Archeology*

Their dark branches grow to an extraordinary extent laterally; are endlessly angled, twisted, raked, interlocked, and reach quite as much downward as upwards.

JOHN FOWLES, *The Tree*

Beneath the strongest of the lantern beams they saw that the ladder or iron staircase Scott had found leading from the next to last platform to the plating of the double bottom of the vessel had been twisted around sideways offering a not too difficult climbing angle, except that the last five steps had been sheared off, leaving a gap about level with their heads. A man could take hold of the bottom and swing himself up. Above, at the top, the light showed the gleaming silver cylinder of the propeller shaft, the entrance to the tunnel and the reversed walkway of solid piping that followed it to the stern of the ship.

PAUL GALLICO, *The Poseidon Adventure*

*large, big*
> huge, vast, great, massive, extensive, bulky, sizable,
> considerable, ample, substantial, hefty, jumbo

*very large*
> giant, gigantic, mountainous, colossal, mammoth,
> behemoth, brobdingnagian, gargantuan, stupendous,
> amplitudinous, monstrous, gross, extensive, far-ranging,
> far-reaching, enormous, titanic, humongous, immense,
> megatherian

*large in capacity*
> capacious, voluminous, roomy, spacious, comprehensive

*small, little*
> inconsiderable

*very small*
> petite, diminutive, wee, puny, teeny, teeny-weeny,
> minuscule, infinitesimal, minute

*wide*
> broad, thick, latitudinous, spread, outspread

*very wide*
> expansive, panoramic

*narrow*
> thin, slender, slim, constricted, spindly

*high, tall*
> elevated, lofty, altitudinous

*very high*
> towering, soaring

These abandoned channels are best preserved on the slip-off side of a bend—usually as a nest of crescentic loops. Artificial levees form a regular pattern and roughly parallel the course of the river. Drainage or irrigation canals are generally at right angles to the river, although lateral canals may parallel it.                              WILLIAM C. PUTNAM,
*Map Interpretation with Military Applications*

The exteriors of most Puuc-style buildings are devoid of sculptural decoration below the medial molding, the intricate mosaics being concentrated in the upper half of the facades. The Palace of the Masks, however, stands on a low platform, the face of which is decorated with a single row of mask panels; above this is a carved molding, surmounted by the lower half of the facade, which is in turn composed of three rows of mask panels running across the front of the building. Above an elaborate medial molding there are again three rows of mask panels, the topmost being surmounted by a terminal molding.
SYLVANUS MORLEY AND GEORGE BRAINERD,
*The Ancient Maya*

When I'm naked I lie down on the examining table, on the sheet of chilly crackling disposable paper. I pull the second sheet, the cloth one, up over my body. At neck level there's another sheet, suspended from the ceiling. It intersects me so that the doctor will never see my face. He deals with a torso only.                MARGARET ATWOOD, *The Handmaid's Tale*

The act of pious charity performed, Cedric again motioned them to follow him, gliding over the stone floor with a

*long*
>   lengthy, extensive, elongated

*very long*
>   endless

*short*
>   undersized, squat

*very deep*
>   profound, abyssal, bottomless, depthless, unplumbed, yawning

*related*
>   connected, interconnected, associated, affiliated, interrelated, correlated, correlative, correlational, interlinked

*in direct relation to*
>   corresponding, correlative, mutual, reciprocal, vis-à-vis

*in order*
>   ordered, systematic, grouped, arranged, arrayed, aligned, organized

*not in order, out of order*
>   disarranged, unordered, disarrayed, unaligned, jumbled

*in a line or something like a line*
>   lined up, aligned, ranged, arrayed

*in proportion*
>   proportionate, proportional

*not in proportion*
>   disproportionate, disproportional, in misproportion, ill-proportioned

*in balance*
>   balanced, equipoised, equiponderant, counterbalanced, counterweighted, counterpoised

*not in balance*
>   unbalanced, disequilibriate

noiseless tread; and, after ascending a few steps, opened with great caution the door of a small oratory, which adjoined to the chapel. It was about eight feet square, hollowed, like the chapel itself, out of the thickness of the wall; and the loop-hole which enlightened it being to the west, and widening considerably as it sloped inward, a beam of the setting sun found its way into its dark recess. . . .

SIR WALTER SCOTT, *Ivanhoe*

Away to his right was a dark, formless blur lying on the water, a blur that might have been Cape Demirci: straight ahead, across the darkly velvet sheen of the Maidos Straits, he could see the twinkle of far-away lights—it was a measure of the enemy's confidence that they permitted these lights at all, or, more likely, these fisher cottages were useful as a bearing marker for the guns at night: and to the left, surprisingly near, barely thirty feet away in a horizontal plane, but far below the level where he was standing, he could see the jutting end of the outside wall of the fortress where it abutted on the cliff, the roofs of the houses on the west side of the square beyond that, and, beyond that again, the town itself curving sharply downwards and outwards, to the south first, then to the west, close-girdling and matching the curve of the crescent harbour. Above—but there was nothing to be seen above, that fantastic overhang above blotted out more than half the sky; and below, the darkness was equally impenetrable, the surface of the harbour inky and black as night. ALISTAIR MACLEAN, *The Guns of Navarone*

An interesting point is that in this particular "ideal" theme, the fundamental diagram of the face is the same as the one of

*in balance with respect to relationship between elements or features*
proportional

*larger on or leaning to one side*
lop-sided

*heavier or larger on top*
top-heavy

*having a perfectly divisible order left and right (bilateral) or top and bottom*
symmetrical

*not symmetrical*
asymmetrical

*having radial symmetry*
actinoid, actinomorphic, actinomorphous

*north*
northern, northerly, boreal, hyperborean

*south*
southern, southerly, austral, meridional

*east*
eastern, easterly, oriental

*west*
western, westerly, occidental

*opposite*
contraposed, antipodal, counterposed, contrary

*pertaining to opposite sides*
heterolateral

*at the top*
apical, topmost

*at the bottom*
basal, bottommost

*on or to the right*
dextral

the whole body; the link between the two is that the height of the face is equal to the vertical distance between the middle of the body (intersection of the legs in "ideal" specimens) and the navel (the *minor* of the two segments in the $\Phi$ proportion determined by the navel) is equal to the distance between the tip of the medium finger (the arm hanging vertically) and the floor or horizontal level supporting the whole.      Matila Ghyka, *The Geometry of Art and Life*

The movement made to swing the left arm holding the muleta, which is crossed in front of the body, out and past the right side to get rid of the bull is called crossing. Any time the man does not make this cross he will have the bull under him. Unless he swings him far enough out the horn is certain to catch him.
                    Ernest Hemingway, *Death in the Afternoon*

Sometimes the ice is black and glossy, blasted smooth by the endless wind, with only a few swaths of snow lying on it. Sometimes it is hummocky, with drifts of snow sheltered behind the hummocks. Sometimes it is ridged and buckled from the enormous strains of the wind, the currents and the line of advancing bergs.
                    Richard Brown, *Voyage of the Iceberg*

Although on a hilltop, the fortress has a comparatively low-lying profile and is sunk into an encircling dry ditch. The towers and the revelin do not rise above the parapet of the curtain walls, so that the whole fortress appears flat-topped

*on or to the left*
  sinistral

*to or at the side*
  lateral, flanking

*on the same side*
  ipsilateral, ipselateral, homolateral

*on the opposite side*
  contralateral

*upright or up-down in direction*
  vertical, perpendicular, plumb, erect, true

*side to side in direction*
  horizontal, level, plane

*extending crosswise linearly*
  cross, transverse, athwart, diagonal

*at an angle or in a sloping direction or position (from the perpendicular)*
  angled, aslant, slanting, slanted, oblique, raked, canted,
  inclined, tilted

*from corner to opposite corner*
  diagonal

*on the outside*
  external, exterior, without, outer, outermost

*on the inside*
  internal, interior, within, inner, innermost

*center*
  core, nucleus, middle, centrum, heart, nexus

*edge*
  periphery, border, margin, marge, fringe, boundary, frontier

*extending out from a center*
  radial, radiating

*middle (linearly)*
  central, midway, medium, mean, mesial, midmost,
  middlemost

with the exception of its traditional square mastio which rises higher in the centre of the fort.

QUENTIN HUGHES, *Military Architecture*

The process begins with a simple geometric form, a triangle, positioned in three dimensional space. The midpoint of each edge of the triangle has been connected to the other midpoints dividing the original triangle into four triangles. The midpoints are deflected randomly upward or downward to give volume to the form.

RICHARD MARK FRIEDHOFF,
*Visualization: The Second Computer Revolution*

Above him Escher's head grew smaller and smaller against the bright circle of sky at the mouth of the moulin. At this depth the shaft divided into two parts like the legs of a pair of trousers. Agassiz chose the wider of the two ways but soon found it repartitioned into a number of impassable holes. Upon signaling to Escher, he was hoisted back up to the bifurcation and then allowed to descend the other passage. He was now more than 100 feet below the surface of the glacier.                                          RONALD H. BAILEY, *Glacier*

. . . detailed features are shown not by conventional signs nor by their outline ground-plans, but by pictures of their actual appearance as viewed from above at an oblique, near vertical, angle. At first sight this seems to be simply the technique of the bird's-eye view, and we might say that Varle's plan of Philadelphia is a mixture of bird's-eye view and map.

P.D.A. HARVEY, *The History of Topographical Maps*

*constituting a central line or axis*
    axial

*coming together linearly*
    meeting, converging, convergent, intersecting

*going in two different directions*
    separating, diverging, divergent, bifurcating, bifurcate,
    bifurcal, dichotomous, diffluent

*running in directional alignment without touching*
    parallel, nonconvergent, nondivergent, paradromic,
    collateral, collimated

*not with or near*
    apart, separate, individual, discrete, disjunct, detached,
    independent, asunder

*brought apart*
    detached, disconnected, unfastened, sundered, disjoined

*in pieces or parts*
    divided, partitioned, compartmentalized, segmented

*in two parts*
    bipartite, dual, double, twofold

*in three parts*
    tripartite, triple, threefold, triform

*in four parts*
    quadripartite, quadriform, fourfold

*divided into two usually equal parts*
    bisected

*divided into three usually equal parts*
    trisected

*divided into four usually equal parts*
    quadrisected

*scattered*
    dispersed, distributed, disseminated, strewn, diffused

The house, leading straight on from the stables, is in the shape of a flat dome surmounted by open work walls as in a lighthouse.          LARA VINCA MASINI, *Gaudi*

The final element of the surround was a gate. A sturdy young tree, stripped of its branches, was positioned upright at one side of an opening in the fence. A hole was dug for the base, and a mound of stones was piled up around it for support.          JEAN M. AUEL, *The Mammoth Hunters*

Some of the much-moved bluestones were reset in a circle around the five trilithons, while those that had been elegantly smoothed were arranged in a horseshoe inside the trilithons. The tallest of them was erected near the centre. A circle inside a circle, a horseshoe within a horseshoe, a central pillar.          AUBREY BURL, *Rings of Stone*

A fleet of barges were coming lazily on, some sideways, some head first, some stern first; all in a wrong-headed, dogged, obstinate way, bumping up against the larger craft, running under the bows of steamboats, getting into every kind of nook and corner where they had no business, and being crunched on all sides like so many walnut shells; . . .
          CHARLES DICKENS, *The Old Curiosity Shop*

Before lowering the boat for the chase, the upper end of the line is taken aft from the tub, and passing round the loggerhead there, is again carried forward the entire length of the boat, resting crosswise upon the loom or handle of every

*continuous*
> continual, uninterrupted, unbroken

*not continuous*
> discontinuous, interrupted, broken, disjunct

*at a point farther than*
> beyond

*having the same position or place*
> coinciding, coincident

*coinciding when superimposed*
> congruent

*lying along the same straight line*
> collinear

*even or continuous with a given surface*
> flush

*having coinciding axes (or being concentric)*
> coaxial

*of the same size*
> equivalent, equisized

*near*
> nearby, close, close by, proximal, proximate, nigh, immediate, in the area of, propinquous, propinquant, neighboring, vicinal

*next to*
> adjacent, contiguous, apposite, paradromic (parallel), bordering, side by side, juxtaposed, cheek by jowl, conterminous, coterminous, abreast, beside, by, alongside

*up against or connected to*
> abutting, adjoining, against

*distant*
> far, far away, far off, at a distance, long-range, a good way

*equally near to or far from*
> equidistant

man's oar, so that it joggs against his wrist in rowing; and also passing between the men, as they alternately sit at the opposite gunwales, to the leaded chocks or grooves in the extreme pointed prow of the boat, where a wooden pin or skewer the size of a common quill, prevents it from slipping out.                    Herman Melville, *Moby-Dick*

On the other side, to their left, Geoffrey's house came in sight, almost a bird's-eye view, the bungalow crouching, very tiny, before the trees, the long garden below descending steeply, parallel with which on different levels obliquely climbing the hill, all the other gardens of the contiguous residences, each with its cobalt oblong of swimming pool, also descended steeply toward the barranca, the land sweeping away at the top of the Calle Nicaragua back up to the pre-eminence of Cortez Palace.

Malcolm Lowry, *Under the Volcano*

He was left alone with his gray sandwich in the now spacious compartment. He munched and gazed out of the window. A green bank was rising there diagonally until it suffused the window to the top. Then, resolving an iron chord, a bridge banged overhead and instantly the green slope vanished and open country unfurled—fields, willows, a golden birch tree, a winding brook, beds of cabbage.

Vladimir Nabokov, *King, Queen, Knave*

I descended upon the glacier. The surface is very uneven, rising like the waves of a troubled sea, descending low, and interspersed by rifts that sink deep. The field of ice is almost a

*at the edge*
peripheral, border, marginal

*at or near the beginning*
initial

*at or near the end*
terminal, final

*near the point of attachment*
proximal

*at the far end from the point of attachment*
distal

*over*
above, atop, upward, higher, superior

*lying above*
superjacent, superincumbent

*placed above*
superposed

*under*
below, beneath, downward, lower, inferior

*lying below*
subjacent, underlying, surmounted

*on the surface of*
atop, superincumbent

*overhanging*
overhung, projecting, beetling, jutting, lowering, pensile

*underhanging*
underhung

*hanging from*
dependent, pendent, suspended, pendulant, dangling,
suspensory

*supporting*
bracing, buttressing, underpinning, carrying, bearing,

league in width, but I spent nearly two hours in crossing it. The opposite mountain is a bare perpendicular rock.

MARY SHELLEY, *Frankenstein*

It had been at some point, perhaps in its original construction, attached by a rough stone and brick arched passage to a closely adjacent, indefinitely ancient, stone-built cottage or cabin.      IRIS MURDOCH, *The Book and the Brotherhood*

Its main thoroughfare, an oblique continuation of National Avenue, was called Amberson Boulevard, and here, at the juncture of the new Boulevard and the Avenue, Major Amberson reserved four acres for himself, and built his new house—the Amberson Mansion, of course.

BOOTH TARKINGTON, *The Magnificent Ambersons*

The administration area in which Hungry Joe had pitched his tent by mistake lay in the center of the squadron between the ditch, with its rusted railroad tracks, and the tilted black bituminous road.      JOSEPH HELLER, *Catch-22*

Beneath them, from the base of the abrupt descent, the city spread wide away in a close contiguity of red earthen roofs, above which rose eminent the domes of a hundred churches, beside here and there a tower, and the upper windows of some taller or higher-situated palace, looking down on a multitude of palatial abodes. At a distance, ascending out of the central mass of edifices, they could see the top of

propping up, sustaining, bolstering, shoring up, girding, suspensory

*ascending*
rising, climbing, acclivous, acclivitous

*descending*
dipping, dropping, falling, declivous, declivitous

*sticking out*
projecting, protruding, protrudent, protuberant, jutting, outjutting, outstanding, extrusive, protrusive

*set back*
recessed, indented

*surrounding*
encompassing, enclosing, encircling, circumscribing, enveloping, enfolding, enwreathing, engirding, circumambient, circumjacent, circumferential

*surrounded*
encompassed, encircled, circumscribed, enveloped, enwreathed, enfolded, engirded

*enclosing*
containing, confining, closeting, cloistering, immuring, entombing, harboring

*enclosed*
contained, confined, closeted, cloistered, immured, entombed

*between*
betwixt

*between two lines*
interlinear, interlineal

*among*
amid, amidst, in the midst of, mid, midst

*in the middle or center*
central, middlemost, centralized

the Antonine column, and near it the circular roof of the Pantheon, looking heavenward with its ever-open eye.

NATHANIEL HAWTHORNE, *The Marble Faun*

Just opposite him hung a "Last Judgment": curly-headed cherubs with rotund behinds flying up into a thunderstorm, blowing trumpets. To Richard's left hung a pen drawing by a German master; Rubashov could only see a part of it—the rest was hidden by the plush back of the sofa and by Richard's head: the Madonna's thin hands, curved upwards, hollowed to the shape of a bowl, and a bit of empty sky covered with horizontal pen-lines.

ARTHUR KOESTLER, *Darkness at Noon*

The harbour lies below me, with, on the far side, one long granite wall stretching out into the sea, with a curve outwards at the end of it, in the middle of which is a lighthouse. A heavy sea-wall runs along outside of it. On the near side, the sea-wall makes an elbow crooked inversely, and its end too has a lighthouse. Between the two piers there is a narrow opening into the harbour, which then suddenly widens.

BRAM STOKER, *Dracula*

Deep between two hills was an old quarry, which we were fond of pretending we had discovered. In places the stone stood in vertical shafts, six-sided or eight-sided, the height of stools or pillars. At the center of each of them was a sunburst, a few concentric circles, faint lines the color of rust.

MARILYNNE ROBINSON, *Housekeeping*

*near the center*
    paracentral

*in between*
    interjacent, intervenient

*placed in between or among*
    inserted, interposed, interpolated, interjected, intercalated,
    sandwiched

*situated at intervals*
    spaced out, interspaced, interspersed, intervaled, intervallic

*in a space or opening*
    interstitial, interspatial

*facing directly or frontally*
    head-on

*with the side facing*
    broadside

*regarded from the end or longest dimension or with the longitudinal and
forward*
    lengthwise

*regarded from one side or with one side forward*
    sideways

*in front of*
    anterior, to the fore

*at or to the front*
    frontal, anterior, ventral, obverse, in the foreground, fore,
    vanward

*behind*
    posterior, to the rear, in the background

*at or to the back*
    rear, posterior, reverse, dorsal

*at or to the side*
    lateral, on the flank, sideward

The Mews was one of the most important parts of the castle, next to the stables and the kennels. It was opposite to the solar, and faced south. The outside windows had to be small, for reasons of fortification, but the windows which looked inward to the courtyard were big and sunny. The windows had close vertical slats nailed down them, but no horizontal ones.          T. H. WHITE, *The Once and Future King*

There was a steep wall of sand, behind which the firing could be heard. They made the people form up into short lines and led them through the gap which had been hurriedly dug in the sandstone wall. The wall hid everything from view, but of course the people knew where they were. The right bank of the Dnieper is cut by deep ravines, and this particular ravine was enormous, majestic, deep and wide like a mountain gorge. If you stood on one side of it and shouted you would scarcely be heard on the other. The sides were steep, even overhanging in places; at the bottom ran a little stream of clear water. Round about were cemeteries, woods and garden plots. The local people knew the ravine as Babi Yar.          D. M. THOMAS, *The White Hotel*

The tip of the nose of the Stansbury Mountains had been sliced off by the interstate to reveal a sheer and massive section of handsome blue rock, thinly bedded, evenly bedded, forty metres high. Its parallel planes were tilting, dipping, gently to the east, with the exception of some confused and crumpled material that suggested a snowball splatted against glass, or a broken-down doorway in an otherwise undamaged wall.          JOHN MCPHEE, *Basin and Range*

*facing*
> face-to-face, vis-à-vis

*facing or moving ahead or to the front*
> forward

*facing or moving back or to the rear*
> backward

*upside down*
> topsy-turvy, bottom up, turned over, inverted, upturned

*inside out*
> outside in, everted

*backwards*
> reversed, inverted

*back to front*
> reversed, retroverted

*turned so as to show a different surface*
> obverted

*in contact*
> touching, tangent, tangential, tangental, abutting, contactual

*joined*
> affixed, in conjunction, conjoined, bound, tied, adjoined, adjoining, connected, combined, combinative, fastened, yoked, bridged, linked, united, interlocked, dovetailed

*brought together*
> gathered, amassed, heaped, collected, accumulated, bunched, piled, stacked, conglomerate, agglomerate, glomerate, assembled, combined, cumulate, massed, conjoined, of a piece, clustered, grouped, united, conjunct, serried, integrated

*lying directly in the path of or in front of*
> athwart

*crossing one another*
> intersecting

. . . I mean, again, if I were exiled to a desert island with nothing but some pages of a men's magazine showing a nude woman on a desert island, with the arty kidney shapes of sand on the ass-cheeks and all that, I would probably break down and masturbate to it . . . what do you think of that word?                            NICHOLSON BAKER, *Vox*

After that they went on again; and now the road struck westwards and left the river, and the great shoulder of the south-pointing mountain-spur drew ever nearer. At length they reached the hill path. It scrambled steeply up, and they plodded slowly one behind the other, till at last in the late afternoon they came to the top of the ridge and saw the wintry sun going downwards to the west.
                            J.R.R. TOLKIEN, *The Hobbit*

He walked to the little porch which adjoined the kitchen and stood there gazing out. On this side of the house there was a row of cedars which bordered his property, slanting downward toward the bay. Beneath them the earth was naked of grass, shadowed, cool-looking. . . .
                    WILLIAM STYRON, *Lie Down in Darkness*

A few hundred yards to my right was the lip of the gorge, obscured by a rise in the land, and rolling away to the left and ahead was the harsher landscape of the Causse, hard parched soil, sagebrush, telegraph poles. Just past the ruined farm, La Prunarède, I turned down a sandy track on the right, and five minutes later I was at the dolmen.
                            IAN MCEWAN, *Black Dogs*

*second from the last*
  antepenultimate
*next to last*
  penultimate

*as seen from high above*
  bird's-eye (view)
*as seen (graphically) were the exterior or wall removed*
  cutaway
*as seen (graphically) were the parts shown individuated or apart*
  exploded

# Common Emblems and Symbols

The pommel in gilt brass was composed of acanthus leaves and swept forward in the French style, the guard fitting into the foremost part which was split resembling the beak of a bird.

ROBERT WILKINSON-LATHAM, *Swords in Color*

The Catherine-wheel window, and rude tracery below it, is the only portion clumsily adopted from the Lombards.

JOHN RUSKIN, "Assisi," *The Lamp of Beauty*

On another sculptured relief, showing the king, in a chariot, hunting lions, his tunic is embroidered with a disk encircled by a ring-border decorated with a palmette design, which contains a pictorial representation of a sacred tree confronted on either side by a priest, and surmounted by a winged solar disk, here a flower-like rosette.

ARCHIBALD H. CHRISTIE, *Pattern Design*

The curved radiating divisions of the isolated rosettes in this panel give these elements a swastika-like motion.

ARCHIBALD H. CHRISTIE, *Pattern Design*

# Common Emblems and Symbols

*figure of the earth*
geoid

*horizontal figure eight symbolizing infinity or eternity*
lemniscate

*circle with arrow pointed outward toward the upper right*
male symbol, Mars symbol

*circle with a suspended cross*
female symbol, Venus symbol

*seven-branched (Jewish) candelabrum*
menorah

*Hebrew symbol of life*
c'hai

*Judaic hexagram (intersecting triangles)*
Star of David, Magen of David, Shield of David

*intersecting triangles one of which is light and one dark*
Solomon's seal

*Buddhist symbol of the universe*
yin-yang symbol, mandala

*loop-topped cross ("peace symbol")*
ankh, crux ansata, key of life, key of the Nile, looped Tau
cross

*three loops interlaced into a roughly triangular form*
triquetra

*Japanese (Shinto) shrine-gate symbol*
torii

Besides the uncial writing on the convex side of the sherd
[*sic*], at the top, painted in dull red on what had once been
the lip of the amphora, was the cartouche already mentioned
as appearing on the *scarabaeus,* which we had found in the
casket.                              H. RIDER HAGGARD, *She*

The pilgrim was only a minor ingredient, as far as Francis
was concerned, in a mandala design at whose center rested a
relic of a saint.

    WALTER M. MILLER, JR., *A Canticle for Leibowitz*

Under his eyes new cities grew. Mesa Verde, Aztec,
Wupatki, Keet Seel. Each built and at the height of its pros-
perity abandoned until the people were gathered for their
last great migration into the desert itself. Into four groups
they divided themselves and in four directions they left,
making a cross over the land until more hundreds of years
passed and they wheeled right, forming a swastika. As this
swastika wheeled, they broke into smaller groups, all returning but all moving in circles until the land was a giant's
pattern of moving swastikas and serpentines. A pueblo
would live for an instant. Another group would find it and a
spiral map of their predecessors' path and then turn in the
opposite direction, one eddy twisting from another, yet always directed to the finally permanent gathering at the center of the world.       MARTIN CRUZ SMITH, *Nightwing*

All the gold, and stucco ornamentation, the cartouches of
pan-pipes and tambourines, the masks of Comedy, and the

*hooked cross*
swastika, gammadion, fylfot, crux gammata

*figure with three curved branches or legs from the same center (or a three-armed swastika)*
triskelion, triskele, triskelis

*five interlocking circles (three above two)*
Olympic symbol

*flame-shaped symbol*
flammulation

*almond-shaped object or ornament*
mandorla

*five-pointed star*
pentacle, pentagram, pentalpha

*diamond-shaped scale or plate*
mascle

*triangular or wedge-shaped symbol*
delta

*moon (first or last quarter) or sickle shape*
crescent

*three-pronged spear associated with the god of the sea*
trident

*L-shape*
gamma

*V or upside-down-V emblem*
chevron

*coiled snake on a winged staff (medical symbol)*
caduceus, kerykeion

*human skull (as a symbol of mortality)*
death's-head, memento mori

*skull and crossbones (pirate or poison symbol)*
Jolly Roger

*iris symbol (royal emblem of France)*
fleur-de-lis

*rose-like ornament*
rosette, cockade (when worn as an ornament)

upholstery in garnet plush were democratic stabs at palatial luxury; these were the palaces of the people.

ROBERTSON DAVIES, *World of Wonders*

He wore a green robe with gold patterns: tridents, crescents, and triangles. The sleeves, rolled back, bared his forearms, which were hairless and as yellow as old ivory. His beard, freshly washed, looked silky. Above his beard, his cheeks were plump as a baby's. The robe had an attached hood, which framed his face and peaked as stiffly as a wizard's conical cap.

DAVID BLACK, *Minds*

He examined the hilt. It was black, beautifully enamelled, and within a circle near the top was a small white swastika.

IRIS MURDOCH, *An Unofficial Rose*

I looked at six eyes which sat at a desk. . . . Two appertained to a splendid old dotard (a face all ski-jumps and toboggan slides), on whose protruding chest the rosette of the Legion pompously squatted.

E. E. CUMMINGS, *The Enormous Room*

They turned their faces cityward, and, treading over the broad flagstones of the old Roman pavement, passed through the Arch of Titus. The moon shone brightly enough within it to show the seven-branched Jewish candlestick cut in the marble of the interior.

NATHANIEL HAWTHORNE, *The Marble Faun*

*upward-pointing three-lobed or three-petaled (trifoliate) floral shape*
    trefoil, shamrock

*four-lobed or four-petaled floral shape*
    quatrefoil

*five-lobed or five-petaled floral shape*
    cinquefoil

*common ornament showing spread leaves or petals*
    palmette

*common ornament showing a radiating floral cluster*
    anthemion, honeysuckle ornament

*common ornament showing sprouting pointed leaves*
    lotus

*common ornament showing shapely "billowing" leaves*
    acanthus

*upright eagle with wings outstretched*
    spread eagle, heraldic eagle

*ceremonial-staff emblem of authority*
    scepter

*bundle of rods with a projecting ax blade*
    fasces

*sun surrounded by (a representation of) its rays*
    sunburst

*wheel whose spokes project beyond the rim*
    catherine wheel, spider wheel

*map's circular symbol with N, S, E, and W indicated*
    compass rose

*ornamental oval or somewhat curved frame*
    cartouche

*Egyptian beetle-like symbol or ornament*
    scarab

*stylized asp worn on ancient headdresses*
    uraeus

*symbolic or memorial cluster of weapons or armor*
    trophy

Colored red ochre, blue and tan, they paraded along the walls in that peculiar frontal way of Egyptians, with vultures on their palms, sheaves of wheat, water lilies and lutes. They were accompanied by lion, scarabs, owl, oxen and dismembered feet. E. L. DOCTOROW, *Ragtime*

*curved band (often with an inscription on it)*
 ribbon

*thin curling or spiral form like a leafless stem*
 tendril

# Light and Colors

And there I saw myself as a man might expect, except that my skin was very white, as the old fiend's had been white, and my eyes had been transformed from their usual blue to a mingling of violet and cobalt that was softly iridescent. My hair had a high luminous sheen, and when I ran my fingers back through it I felt a new and strange vitality there.

ANNE RICE, *The Vampire Lestat*

The woman's face was Chinese, brown and withered like a ginger root; she wore dark blue clothes, a necklace of turquoises and sharp little silver knives, and her hair in pigtails like two grey wires.     RUMER GODDEN, *Black Narcissus*

Framed in the pale triangle ahead, the mountain showed again, gray at first, then silver, then pink as the earliest sun rays caught the summit.     JAMES HILTON, *Lost Horizon*

"And not only paper, but cotton fibre, linen fibre, wool fibre, woody fibre, and *bone,* Kemp, *flesh,* Kemp, *hair,* Kemp, *nails* and *nerves,* Kemp, in fact the whole fabric of a man except the red of his blood and the black pigment of hair, are all made up of transparent, colourless tissue. So little

## LIGHT

*without light*
dark, dusky, unlighted, unilluminated, unlit, obscure,
tenebrous, stygian, caliginous, fuliginous, sunless
*having or showing forth little light*
dim, dingy, murky, darkish
*shadowy*
shady, gloomy, umbral, umbrageous

*giving forth light*
shining, beaming, bright, illuminated, illumined, luminous,
irradiated, radiant, lucent, lustrous, luminiferous
*very bright*
brilliant, glaring, blazing, blinding, refulgent, effulgent
*lighted*
lit, lit up, alight, aglow, irradiated

*sparkling*
glittering, scintillating, coruscating, twinkling
*sparkling or shining in a subdued way*
shimmering, shimmery
*giving off reflected light*
glinting, gleaming
*shining with reflected light*
glistening
*flashing*
fulgurant, fulgurating

suffices to make us visible one to the other. For the most part the fibres of a living creature are no more opaque than water."                    H. G. WELLS, *The Invisible Man*

The houses of the central village were quite unlike the casual and higgledy-piggledy agglomeration of the mountain villages he knew; they stood in a continuous row on either side of a central street of astonishing cleanness; here and there their pari-coloured facade was pierced by a door, and not a solitary window broke their even frontage. They were particoloured with extraordinary irregularity; smeared with a sort of plaster that was sometimes grey, sometimes drab, sometimes slate-coloured or dark brown; . . .

H. G. WELLS, "The Country of the Blind"

The advance guard of the expected procession now appeared in the great gateway, a troop of halberdiers. They were dressed in striped hose of black and tawny, velvet caps graced at the sides with silver roses, and doublets of murrey-and-blue cloth embroidered on the front and back with the three feathers, the prince's blazon, woven in gold. Their halberd staves were covered with crimson velvet, fastened with gilt nails, and ornamented with gold tassels.

MARK TWAIN, *The Prince and the Pauper*

These men who looked steadily into their platinum igniter flames as they lit their eternally burning black pipes. They and their charcoal hair and soot-colored brows and bluish-ash-smeared cheeks where they had shaven close; but their heritage showed.                    RAY BRADBURY, *Fahrenheit 451*

*flashing occasionally or fitfully*
    winking
*flashing regularly*
    blinking, stroboscopic
*flashing weakly or going out*
    fluttering, guttering, sputtering

*showing deflected light rays or distortion of image*
    refracted, refractive

*burning unsteadily or suddenly*
    flaring, blazing
*giving off flame-like light*
    flickering, wavering, lambent
*flame-colored*
    flammeous
*glowing or luminescent with absorbed radiation in a continuing way*
    phosphorescent
*glowing or luminescent with electromagnetic radiation*
    fluorescent

*visible or glowing at night*
    noctilucent

*glowing whitely with light or intense heat*
    incandescent

*giving off a reddish or golden glow*
    rutilant

*having a milky or cloudy iridescence (like an opal)*
    opalescent, opaline
*having a pearly iridescence (like a pearl)*
    nacreous, pearlescent

*transparent*
    sheer

The earth grows wan and weird, defertilized, dehumanized, neither brown nor gray nor beige nor taupe nor ecru, the no color of death reflecting light, sponging up light with its hard, parched shag and shooting it back at us. . . .

HENRY MILLER, *The Colossus of Maroussi*

Walls of daffodil yellow are broken by vermillion pylons, purple buttresses appear against rosy domes, and vistas of turquoise blue terminate in great ships' bows of ultramarine.

GUIDEBOOK TO THE NEW YORK WORLD'S FAIR, 1939/1940 (AS QUOTED IN HELEN A. HARRISON, *Dawn of a New Day*)

At Stenness, only three of an original twelve or thirteen stones survive; but the ruins remain impressive, as much because of the peculiar characteristics of the flagstone as because of the massive size of the slabs. All are more than fifteen feet tall, quite broad, but remarkably slender, one waif-like sheet being less than a foot in thickness. The Brodgar stones are of the same flagstone; changing colour according to the light, they sometimes seem a pinkish buff, but the hues are spangled with white and lemon lichen blotches, and sometimes a furry, blue-green lichen growth.

RICHARD MUIR, *The Stones of Britain*

Eventually I identified the rocks. The petrified roses were barite, probably from Oklahoma. The scratchy brown mineral was bauxite—aluminum ore. The black glass was obsidian; the booklet of transparent sheets was mica; the

*not transparent*
    untransparent, nontransparent, opaque, adiaphanous,
    impervious

*admitting the passage of (or letting show through) light*
    translucent, diaphanous, pellucid, sheer

*transparent in water or when wet*
    hydrophanous

*without color*
    colorless, hueless, achromatic, achromic, untinged

*colored*
    colorful, hued, toned, painted, chromatic, pigmented,
    tinctured (dyed or stained)

*slightly or weakly colored*
    tinged, tinted, tinctured

*having one color or hue*
    monochrome, monochromatic, monochromous,
    monochromic, monotone

*having many colors*
    many-colored, multicolored, parti-colored, variegated,
    motley, varicolored, versicolor, versicolored, polychromatic,
    polychrome, polychromic kaleidoscopic, prismatic

*rainbow-like*
    iridescent, iridian

*changeable in or showing a shift or play of color*
    iridescent

*highly or brilliantly colored*
    prismatic

*having altered or poor coloration*
    discolored

goldeny iridescent handful of soft crystals was chalcopyrite, an ore of copper. . . .

ANNIE DILLARD, *An American Childhood*

The scattered polychrome of the exterior, strewn with blobs and drops as if handfuls of coloured confetti have been thrown at it, evokes the atmosphere of a Venetian carnival with gondolas and crinolines.

LARA VINCA MASINI, *Gaudi*

The smaller man was looking around, with the air of a child just come to a birthday party—at the clumsy old island schooners tied up at the water's edge, with red sails furled; at the native women in bright dresses and the black ragged crewmen, bargaining loudly over bananas, coconuts, strange huge brown roots, bags of charcoal, and strings of rainbow-colored fish; at the great square red fort, and at the antique cannons atop its slanted seaward wall, pointing impotently to sea; at the fenced statue of Amerigo Vespucci, almost hidden in purple, orange, and pink bougainvillea; at the houses of Queen's Row, their ancient arching plaster facades painted in vivid colors sun-bleached to pastels; at the old gray stone church, and the white-washed Georgian brick pile of the Sir Francis Drake Inn.

HERMAN WOUK, *Don't Stop the Carnival*

New elements (especially prevalent in the highlands) include the first attempts at polychrome painting (black, white, red, and yellow paints applied after firing), the first bichrome slipping (for instance, red-on-cream and red-on-orange),

## Useful Color Modifiers

| | | |
|---|---|---|
| antique | dun | moderate |
| bleached-out | dusky | muted |
| bled | dusty | neon |
| bright | electric | pale |
| brilliant | faded | pastel |
| burnt | faint | phosphorescent |
| clashing | fluorescent | pure |
| cool | garish | riot (of) |
| dark | gaudy | slate |
| Day-Glo | gay | smoky |
| (fluorescent in | glowing | soft |
| daylight) | hot | streaky |
| dazzling | light | strong |
| deep | lustrous | vibrant |
| discordant | medium | vivid |
| drab | mellow | warm |
| dull | metallic | washed-out |

## Colors

*snow white*
   snowy, niveous
*white as chalk*
   chalk white, cretaceous, chalky
*white as milk*
   milky white
*white as a lily*
   lily white
*bleached-out white*
   blanched, etiolated

and the beginnings of the Usulutan tradition of resist decoration. Red, black, orange, and streaky brown slipped wares are typical; the streaky-brown pieces were often highly polished.                SYLVANUS MORLEY, *The Ancient Maya*

But above all it is the fantastic colouring of the beaches that as an image overpowers the minutiae. Above the tide-line the grey rocks are splashed gorse-yellow with close-growing lichen, and with others of blue-green and salmon pink. Beneath them are the vivid orange-browns and siennas of wrack-weeds, the violet of mussel-beds, dead-white sand, and water through which one sees down to the bottom, as through pale green bottle-glass, to where starfish and big spiny urchins of pink and purple rest upon the broad leaves of the sea-tangle.
                GAVIN MAXWELL, *Ring of Bright Water*

The picture was her final treasure waiting to be packed for the journey. In whatever room she had called her own since childhood, there it had also lived and looked at her, not quite familiar, not quite smiling, but in its prim colonial hues delicate as some pressed flower. Its pale oval, of color blue and rose and flaxen, in a battered, pretty gold frame, unconquerably pervaded any surroundings with a something like last year's lavender.        OWEN WISTER, *The Virginian*

From the basic blackness of the flesh of the tribe there broke or erupted a wave of red color, and the people all arose on the white stone of the grandstands and waved red objects, waved or flaunted. Crimson was the holy-day color of the

*not quite pure white or slightly grayish*
    off-white (e.g., oyster, cream, eggshell)

*thinly or translucently white*
    bone white

*bluish white*
    alabaster

*yellowish white*
    eggshell, cream, ivory, bone

*grayish white*
    oyster, platinum, tattletale gray

*silvery white*
    argent

*bluish white*
    pearl

*bright or vivid red*
    crimson, scarlet, vermilion, vermeil, cardinal, carmine,
    geranium, cinnabar, apple red, tomato, lobster red,
    fire-engine red, fiery

*dark red*
    wine, wine red, maroon, ruby, cranberry, garnet, currant

*moderate red*
    cherry, cerise, blood red

*brownish red*
    burgundy

*orangish red*
    poppy

*grayish or bluish red*
    strawberry

*purplish red*
    raspberry, magenta, grape, raisin, claret

*brick red*
    lateritious

*rust red*
    rufous, ferruginous

Wariri. The amazons saluted with purple banners, the king's colors. His purple umbrella was raised, and its taut head swayed.                    SAUL BELLOW, *Henderson the Rain King*


Thundery day along Greenback. All the willows standing still with their leaves pricked. Dusty green. Pale lilac shadows. Tarred road reflecting the sky. Blue to make you jump. A great cloud over on the Surrey shore. Yellow as soap and solid as a cushion. Shaped like a tower about a mile high and half a mile thick, with a little Scotch pepper pot in front. Dresden blue behind full of sunlight floating like gold dust. River roughed up with little waves like the flat side of a cheese grater. Dark copper under the cloud, dark lead under the blue. I could use that cloud in the Fall, I thought. It's a solid square. To give weight in the top left-hand corner, opposite the Tower. Salmon on pink. It's an idea worth trying.                    JOYCE CARY, *The Horse's Mouth*


The mountains were covered with a rug of trees, green, yellow, scarlet and orange, but their bare tops were scarfed and beribboned with snow. From carved rocky outcrops, waterfalls drifted like skeins of white lawn, and in the fields we could see the amber glint of rivers and the occasional mirror-like flash of a mountain lake. . . .

GERALD AND LEE DURRELL, *Durrell in Russia*


Above the field the swollen palpitating tangle of light frayed and thinned out into hot darkness, but the thirty thousand pairs of eyes hanging on the inner slopes of the arena did not look up into the dark but stared down into the pit of light,

*pink*
  rose, salmon, carnation

*yellowish pink*
  seashell, coral, flesh-colored, peach

*whitish-to-yellowish pink*
  shell

*deep pink*
  melon

*vivid or glowing pink*
  hot pink, shocking pink

*reddish orange*
  tangerine, carrot

*brownish orange*
  terra-cotta, Titian, tawny

*bright or vivid yellow*
  goldenrod, daffodil

*light yellow*
  canary

*pale yellow*
  straw yellow, flaxen, primrose, ocher

*orange yellow*
  champagne

*moderate yellow*
  brass

*greenish yellow*
  citron, lemon, mustard, lime

*grayish yellow*
  buckskin, oatmeal, parchment, honey yellow, chamois

*brownish yellow*
  amber, buff, gold

*pinkish yellow*
  apricot, peach

where men in red silky-glittering shorts and gold helmets hurled themselves gainst men in blue silky glittering shorts and gold helmets and spilled and tumbled on the bright arsenical-green turf like spilled dolls, and a whistle sliced chillingly through the thick air like that scimitar through a sofa cushion.

ROBERT PENN WARREN, *All the King's Men*

I haven't (the seeing eye), unfortunately, so that the world is full of places to which I want to return—towns with the blinding white sun upon them; stone pines against the blue of the sky; corners of gables, all carved and painted with stags and scarlet flowers and crowstepped gables with the little saint at the top; and grey and pink palazzi and walled towns a mile or so back from the sea, on the Mediterranean, between Leghorn and Naples.

FORD MADOX FORD, *The Good Soldier*

A triangle of white light was advancing from the porch into the sitting room, over the curling edge of the electric-blue carpet, which lay untacked on the terrazzo floor.

V. S. NAIPAUL, *Guerrillas*

The wind howled, piling up snow in drifts and blinding the night with ice-white dust. I walked bent over against the cold, protecting my eyes with my arms. Trees, posts, cowsheds loomed into my vision, then vanished, swallowed in white. JOHN GARDNER, *Grendel*

*bright or vivid green*
　　emerald, smaragdine

*clear light green*
　　apple green

*bluish green*
　　aquamarine, turquoise, jade

*yellowish green*
　　Kelly green, leek green, hunter green, Nile green, absinthe
　　green, pistachio, verdigris, pea green, grass green, sea green,
　　verdant green, leaf green, malachite, moss green

*dull yellow green*
　　ocher green, olive

*deep olive*
　　loden green

*grayish olive*
　　olive drab

*brilliant yellow green*
　　chartreuse

*dark green*
　　forest green, evergreen, bottle green, marine green, peacock
　　green

*grayish green*
　　sage green

*grayish yellow green*
　　celadon green

*blackish green*
　　avocado


*bright or vivid blue*
　　ultramarine

*pale blue*
　　baby blue, sky blue, aquamarine, powder blue, Persian blue,
　　Wedgwood blue, sky blue, cerulean, azure, lapis lazuli

Light, line, and color as sensual pleasures, came later and were as crude as the rest. The New England light is glare, and the atmosphere harshens color. The boy was a full man before he ever knew what was meant by atmosphere; his idea of pleasure in light was the blaze of a New England sun. His idea of color was a peony, with the dew of early morning on its petals. The intense blue of the sea, as he saw it a mile or two away, from the Quincy hills; the cumuli in a June afternoon sky; the strong reds and greens and purples of colored prints and children's picture-books, as the American colors then ran; these were ideals. The opposites or antipathies were the cold grays of November evenings, and the thick, muddy thaws of Boston winter.

HENRY ADAMS, *The Education of Henry Adams*

The pink dusty road before us, the scrub and the dark pines, lay always between these depths of blue. The sea was calm; as one looked down, it drowned the eye like a second zenith, but bluer still; bluer than lapis, or sapphire, or whatever flower is bluest; and then again, in the dark clear shadows round the deep roots of the rocks, green and grape-purple, like the ring-dove's sheen.

MARY RENAULT, *The King Must Die*

The counterpane was of patchwork, full of odd little particolored squares and triangles; and this arm of his tattooed all over with an interminable Cretan labyrinth of a figure . . . this same arm of his, I say, looked for all the world like a strip of that same patchwork quilt.

HERMAN MELVILLE, *Moby-Dick*

*greenish blue*
    turquoise, peacock blue, cobalt, Prussian blue, aqua, teal,
    china blue, Nile blue
*purplish blue*
    sapphire, moonstone blue, gentian, hyacinth, violet, marine
*deep blue*
    royal blue
*reddish blue*
    violet
*grayish blue*
    Dresden blue, shadow blue, delft blue, robin's egg, steel
    blue, Copenhagen blue, electric blue (or electric green),
    indigo
*violet blue*
    periwinkle

*light purple*
    orchid
*pale purple*
    lavender
*moderate purple*
    lilac, amethyst
*reddish lavender*
    heliotrope
*reddish purple*
    fuchsia, raspberry, plum
*bluish purple*
    mauve
*brownish purple*
    puce
*dark purple*
    aubergine, eggplant

*brown or brownish colors in general*
    earth tones

She drew a deep breath, the air had yet a hint about it of dawn, the dawn this morning at Acapulco—green and deep purple high above and gold scrolled back to reveal a river of lapis where the horn of Venus burned so fiercely she could imagine her dim shadow cast from its light on the air field, the vultures floating lazily up there above the brick-red horizon into whose peaceful foreboding the little plane of the Compania Mexicana de Aviacion had ascended, like a minute red demon, winged emissary of Lucifer, the windsock below streaming out its steadfast farewell.

MALCOLM LOWRY, *Under the Volcano*

Like a woman's wispy dress that has slipped off its hanger, the city shimmered and fell in fantastic folds, not held up by anything, a discarnate iridescence limply suspended in the azure autumnal air. Beyond the nacrine desert of the square, across which a car sped now and then with a new metropolitan trumpeting, great pink edifices loomed, and suddenly a sunbeam, a gleam of glass, would stab him painfully in the pupil.     VLADIMIR NABOKOV, *King, Queen, Knave*

Off to my left, in that vast bowl of stillness that contains the meandering river, tens of square miles of tundra browns and sedge meadow greens seem to snap before me, as immediate as the pages of my notebook, because of unscattered light in the dustless air. The land seems guileless. Creatures down there take a few steps, then pause and gaze about. Two sandhill cranes stand still by the river. Three Peary caribou, slightly built and the silver color of the moon, browse a cutbank in that restive way of deer. Tundra melt ponds, their bright dark blue waters oblique to the sun, stand out boldly

*bright or vivid brown*
  café au lait

*light or yellowish brown*
  tan, khaki, beige, fawn, caramel, sienna (raw sienna), fox,
  bistre, camel, ecru

*golden brown*
  butterscotch

*yellowish brown*
  ginger

*reddish brown*
  mahogany, umber, chestnut, bay, cinnamon, henna, russet,
  copper, sienna (burnt sienna), walnut, oxblood, roan,
  rosewood

*moderate brown*
  auburn, coffee, cocoa, saddle tan, saddle brown

*grayish brown*
  nutmeg, sepia

*metallic or greenish brown*
  bronze

*mottled brown and yellow*
  tortoiseshell

*dark brown*
  chocolate, nut brown

*pale gray*
  ash gray

*moderate gray*
  platinum

*bluish gray*
  smoke, battleship gray, steel gray, slate, Wedgwood blue,
  pearl

*purplish gray*
  gunmetal gray, dove, zinc

*brownish gray*
  smoke, mouse gray, taupe, fuscous, dun

in the plain. In the center of the large ponds, beneath the surface of the water, gleam cores of aquamarine ice, like the constricted heart of winter.

Barry Lopez, *Arctic Dreams*


If they left behind the light-streak traces they do on time-exposed film, you would see the varicolored rings stacked one atop another, parallel to the horizon, shrinking in diameter, until the last ring, less than 2° across and traced by Polaris, circled the dark spot of empty space that lies over the North Pole.

Barry Lopez, *Arctic Dreams*


The one had leaves of dark green that beneath were as shining silver, and from each of his countless flowers a dew of silver light was ever falling, and the earth beneath was dappled with the shadows of his fluttering leaves. The other bore leaves of a young green like the new-opened beech; their edges were of glittering gold. Flowers swung upon her branches in clusters of yellow flame, formed each to a glowing horn that spilled a golden rain upon the ground; and from the blossom of that tree there came forth warmth and a great light.

J.R.R. Tolkien, *The Silmarillion*


Like a rope of jewels the gorge spread beneath him, purple, sapphire blue, yellow and pinkish white, a rich and variegated inlay of wooded land and disappearing, reappearing, ubiquitous water.

C. S. Lewis, *Out of the Silent Planet*

*yellowish gray*
 sand

*dark gray*
 field gray, charcoal gray

*black*
 ebony, ebon, sable, jet, onyx, ink black, coal black,
 anthracite

*purplish black*
 sooty black

And among the various communities of the colored poor, distributed over miles and miles of indistinguishable grid, in bungalows and tenements and the clapboard huts they call shotgun houses—you could shoot a bullet easy front to back—in all that formless mass of poor Miami, tight loyal communities cluster around their origins, their friends and their cultures.     JAN MORRIS, *Journeys*

Daily, I looked at houses to rent—shotgun cottages by the rail yards, ski chalets with circular fireplaces, and a house that was built under a small hill, for energy reasons. Finally I found one I liked, a cedar A-frame cabin with a wood stove and a sleeping loft and a flower box with marigolds.

IAN FRAZIER, *Great Plains*

But not even the soft wash of dusk could help the houses. Only dynamite would be of any use against the Mexican ranch houses, Samoan huts, Mediterranean villas, Egyptian and Japanese temples, Swiss chalets, Tudor cottages, and every possible combination of these styles that lined the slopes of the canyon.

NATHANAEL WEST, *The Day of the Locust*

# Buildings and Dwellings

## Types of Structures

*relatively large structure*
edifice, building, construction, erection, construct, fabric

*structure in which to live*
dwelling, home, house, habitation, abode, residence, domicile, homestead, living quarters, lodgings, shelter, dwelling house, billet, accommodations

*structure in which people work*
office building, commercial building, workplace, shop, factory, store, plant, place of business

*structure with individual living units*
apartment house, tenement, residential building, high-rise, cooperative apartment house, co-op building, co-op, condominium, multiple-unit dwelling

*structure where lodging and usually meals are provided*
boardinghouse, guest house, pension, rooming house

*overnight lodging place*
hotel, motel, inn, hostelry, caravansary, lodge, bed-and-breakfast

*cheap lodging place*
hostel, flophouse, dosshouse, fleabag, cold-water flat

*large private dwelling (usually on spacious property)*
mansion, estate, château, country house, palace, manor, manor house, family home, ancestral home, homestead, hacienda

The house he lived in was a nondescript affair called the San Bernardino Arms. It was an oblong three stories high, the back and sides of which were of plain, unpainted stucco, broken by even rows of unadorned windows. The facade was the color of diluted mustard and its windows, all double, were framed by pink Moorish columns which supported turnip-shaped lintels.

NATHANAEL WEST, *The Day of the Locust*

Yes, there it was, the Manderley I had expected, the Manderley of my picture post-card long ago. A thing of grace and beauty, exquisite and faultless, lovelier even than I had ever dreamed, built in its hollow of smooth grass-land and mossy lawns, the terraces sloping to the gardens, and the gardens to the sea.    DAPHNE DU MAURIER, *Rebecca*

The sweet old farmhouse burrowed into the upward slope of the land so deeply that you could enter either its bottom or middle floor at ground level. Its window trim was delicate and the lights in its sash were a bubbly amethyst.

ERIC HODGINS, *Mr. Blandings Builds His Dream House*

Yetta Zimmerman's house may have been the most open-heartedly monochromatic structure in Brooklyn, if not in all of New York. A large rambling wood and stucco house of the nondescript variety erected, I should imagine, sometime before or just after the First World War, it would have faded into the homely homogeneity of other large nondescript dwellings that bordered on Prospect Park had it not been for its striking—its overwhelming—pinkness. From its second-

*impressive public or private dwelling*
   palace, palazzo

*farmhouse*
   grange

*additional or minor building*
   outbuilding, outhouse

*large or impressive building or buildings*
   pile

*tall building*
   skyscraper

*pyramidal towerlike structure with winding terraces (originally a Sumerian temple)*
   ziggurat

*group of interrelated buildings*
   complex, installation, facility, base

*luxurious country estate or retreat*
   villa (Russia: dacha)

*home of prebuilt sections or units*
   prefab, modular home, modular

*tunnel-shaped prefabricated shelter of corrugated metal (and concrete floor)*
   Nissen hut, Quonset hut

*small rural or resort-area house*
   cottage, cabin

*simple one-story house built of logs*
   log cabin

*house whose rooms lie in a line front to back*
   shotgun house

*poor or shabby dwelling*
   hut, shack, hovel, shanty, shed, hutch, cottage, cabin

*cabin with an open breezeway*
   dogtrot house

*primitive (Eskimo) domelike dwelling usually made of blocks of snow*
   igloo

floor dormers and cupolas to the frames of its basement-level windows the house was unrelievedly pink.

WILLIAM STYRON, *Sophie's Choice*

Above the treetops, the structure raised, clear against the sky's hot haze, a small dome. The dome was surmounted by a pillared cupola in whose round base four faces of the courthouse clock were set. Crowning the cupola, stiffly poised on the summit, stood a bronze effigy—Justice. The copper carbonates of time had turned this effigy greenish-blue. The epicene figure's verdigrised hands held the verdigrised sword and balance.

JAMES GOULD COZZENS, *By Love Possessed*

We found ourselves in a vast patio or court, one hundred and fifty feet in length, and upwards of eighty feet in breadth, paved with white marble, and decorated at each end with light Moorish peristyles, one of which supported an elegant gallery of fretted architecture. Along the mouldings of the cornices and on various parts of the walls were escutcheons and ciphers, and cufic and Arabic characters in high relief, repeating the pious mottoes of the Moslem monarchs, the builders of the Alhambra, or extolling their grandeur and munificence.

WASHINGTON IRVING, "The Alhambra"

The sitting-room, beside it, was slightly larger, and they both commanded a row of tenements no less degenerate than Ransom's own habitation—houses built forty years before, and already sere and superannuated. These were also

*primitive circular (Mongol) tentlike hut of hides with a conical top*
    yurt

*primitive (Native American) conical animal-skin tent*
    tepee

*primitive (Native American) matted oval or rounded hut of bark or hides*
    wigwam

*primitive (Native American) tepeelike hut of brushwood or mats*
    wickiup

*primitive (Native American) mud-covered log building of various shapes*
    hogan

*communal terraced adobe (Native American) dwelling*
    pueblo

*primitive (Native American) bark-and-wood communal dwelling of great length*
    longhouse

*house with a widely overhanging roof as well as decoratively carved supports and balconies*
    chalet

*house having a timber framework*
    frame house

*small cottage or house of one story*
    bungalow

*house whose rooms are at different one-, two-, or half-story levels*
    split-level

*luxurious one-family city house of several stories (and often of brick) and usually one of several in a row*
    town house

*house (with two entrances) designed vertically or horizontally for two families but having a common side wall*
    two-family house, duplex house, semidetached

*small house connected to an apartment building*
    maisonette

*house similar to others in a development*
    tract house

painted red, and the bricks were accentuated by a white line; they were garnished, on the first floor, with balconies covered with small tin roofs, striped in different colours, and with an elaborate iron lattice-work, which gave them a repressive, cage-like appearance, and caused them slightly to resemble the little boxes for peeping unseen into the street, which are a feature of oriental towns.

HENRY JAMES, *The Bostonians*

The Tassel House is not imposing (the facade measures 25 feet), but its design is characterized by a rhythmic fluidity which has a majesty of its own. The consoles flanking the entrance way support a corbeled loggia which links the ground and parlor floors. The completely glazed, curved bay window is supported by visible iron framework. The only ornamentation is the wrought-iron balustrade of the bay window. BERNARD CHAMPIGNEULLE, *Art Nouveau*

The portal, flanked on either side by shops, contained two seats outside for clients. The atrium, in process of being redecorated at the time of the eruption, contained a marble impluvium. Beyond, the peristyle and its adjacent chambers resembled a suburban villa, with the major difference that, being in the crowded city, it was self-contained and inward-looking. At the rear of the house, a spacious portico, with its sunken water channel, overlooked a spacious garden, containing pear, chestnut, pomegranate and fig trees. . . .

G. B. TOBEY, *A History of Landscape Architecture*

The lodge, unlike the castle, had been built in an age in which symmetry was regarded as the only means to ele-

*house that is one of a continuous line of houses all of the same general appearance*
   row house

*one-story house with a low-pitched roof*
   ranch house, ranch, rambler

*house high up on a hill or mountain*
   aerie, eyrie

*apartment suite with connecting rooms on two floors*
   duplex apartment, maisonette

*apartment with rooms in more or less a straight line*
   railroad flat, railroad apartment

*roof-level or special (and usually luxurious) upper-level apartment*
   penthouse

*ground-floor apartment having its own backyard or private garden area*
   garden apartment

*apartment with one main room (often with a high ceiling) but with kitchen and bathroom facilities*
   studio apartment, studio

*small apartment (often furnished) with a bathroom and kitchenette*
   efficiency apartment, efficiency

*building's upper story converted for use as an artist's studio or apartment*
   loft, atelier

## PARTS OF STRUCTURES

*building's upper or visible part*
   superstructure

*building's lower or unseen part*
   understructure

*main story of a house*
   bel étage

*ground floor*
   rez-de-chaussée

gance, and it consisted of four diminutive rooms, each in a kind of pygmy Gothic, disposed two on one and two on the other side of the drive.

MICHAEL INNES, *Lord Mullion's Secret*


Stretching out of sight on either side of the rod were identical semidetached houses, each with a path running down the side. They might, she thought, be architecturally undistinguished, but at least they were on a human scale. The gates and railings had been removed and the front gardens were bounded with low brick walls. The front bay windows were square and turreted, a long vista of ramparted respectability.

P. D. JAMES, *Innocent Blood*


The house itself looked, more than anything else, like an English country house. Family descended from the Normans. There was an enormous terrace skirting the tall square fieldstone house with a mansard roof. At each corner there were small round towers with tall narrow windows in them.

ROBERT B. PARKER, *A Catskill Eagle*


Ocean Street is five minutes from the motel, an extension of Sea Street, profuse with weathered shingles and blue shutters. Shepard's house was no exception. A big Colonial with white cedar shingles weathered silver, and blue shutters at all the windows. It was on a slight rise of ground on the ocean side of Ocean Street.

ROBERT B. PARKER, *Promised Land*

*intermediary and often balcony-like story*
   mezzanine, entresol

*platform outside or aound a house*
   deck

*glass or multi-windowed porch or room for enjoying maximum sunlight*
   sun porch, solarium, sun parlor, sun room

*glass structure for growing many plants*
   greenhouse, conservatory

*covered or arched and usually columned walkway open on at least one side*
   galley, arcade, loggia, cloister

*small or blind (decorative rather than structural) arcade*
   arcature

*columns in a row and usually supporting a roof or wall*
   colonnade

*colonnade encircling an open space or building*
   peristyle

*roofed outdoor passageway between buildings*
   breezeway, (of a cabin) dogtrot

*long walkway within a structure or between buildings*
   passageway

*level open grassy or paved area for walking*
   esplanade

*interior open area*
   courtyard, court, cloister

*platform-like and usually paved open recreational area alongside a house*
   terrace, patio

*depressed open area at cellar or basement level*
   areaway

*level space that encompasses a building site*
   parterre

*ornamental garden with paths*
   parterre

I found the place within a couple of minutes: a big, old, twenties Victorian with a lot of gingerbread trim on the front porch and windows that had leaded-glass borders.

BILL PRONZINI, *Bindlestiff*

I drove on past the curve that goes down into the Strip and stopped across the street from a square building of two stories of rose-red brick with small white leaded bay windows and a Greek porch over the front door and what looked, from across the street, like an antique pewter doorknob. Over the door was a fanlight and the name Sheridan Balou, Inc., in black wooden letters severely stylized.

RAYMOND CHANDLER, *The Little Sister*

It was the damndest-looking house I ever saw. It was a square gray box three stories high, with a mansard roof, steeply sloped and broken by twenty or thirty double dormer windows with a lot of wedding cake decoration around them and between them. The entrance had double stone pillars on each side but the cream of the joint was an outside spiral staircase with a stone railing, topped by a tower room from which there must have been a view the whole length of the lake.

RAYMOND CHANDLER, *The Long Goodbye*

Because it was a remnant, soon to be swept away, it was greatly favored by railway buffs. Their interest always seemed to me worse than indecent and their joy-riding a mild form of necrophilia. They were on board getting their last looks at the old stations, photographing the fluting and

*garden decoratively interspersed with rocks*
> rock garden, rockery

*walkway or arbor with vine-covered posts and trelliswork*
> pergola

*small roofed open structure in a garden or with a pleasant view*
> belvedere, gazebo, summer house, pavilion

*roofed entrance structure*
> porch, portico

*roofed and railinged platform fronting or around part of a house*
> porch, veranda

*small porch or entrance stairway*
> stoop

*screen-walled or roofed driveway (along a house entrance or to an interior courtyard) for vehicles*
> porte cochere, carriage porch

*front wall*
> facade, face

*protective or ornamental covering on the front of a building*
> facing

*projecting brace supporting a building externally*
> buttress

*low protective wall along a roof or platform*
> parapet

*defensive or decorative notched parapet topping a wall*
> battlement

*building's external angle or corner, or the stone forming it*
> quoin, cornerstone

*triangular part of a roof's end or building's projection (sometimes with a window)*
> gable

*above-the-roof gable with "steps" or setbacks*
> crowstep gable, corbiestep

floriation, the pediments and bargeboards and pilasters, the valencing on the wooden awnings, the strapwork, and—in architecture every brick has a different name—the quoins.

PAUL THEROUX, *The Kingdom by the Sea*

The house, which was painted a dark brown, stood at the end of a short grass-grown drive, its front so veiled in the showering gold-green foliage of two ancient weeping willows that Vance could only catch, here and there, a hint of a steep roof, a jutting balcony, an aspiring turret. The facade, thus seen in trembling glimpses, as if it were as fluid as the trees, suggested vastness, fantasy and secrecy.

EDITH WHARTON, *Hudson River Bracketed*

Everything about the front was irregular, but with an irregularity unfamiliar to him. The shuttered windows were very tall and narrow, and narrow too the balconies, which projected at odd angles, supported by ornate wooden brackets. One corner of the house rose into a tower with a high shingled roof, and arched windows which seemed to simulate the openings in a belfry. A sort of sloping roof over the front door also rested on elaborately ornamented brackets, and on each side of the steps was a large urn of fluted iron painted to imitate stone, in which some half-dead geraniums languished. EDITH WHARTON, *Hudson River Bracketed*

The Radley Place jutted into a sharp curve beyond our house. Walking south, one faced its porch; the sidewalk turned and ran beside the lot. The house was low, was once white with a deep front porch and green shutters, but had

*small sloping-roof or attic gable often with a window (all in all like a miniature house)*
    dormer

*low or small dormer over which the roofing curves*
    eyebrow

*horizontal frame-like (and often decorative) projection all along the top of a wall*
    cornice

*projecting block (one of many) beneath a cornice*
    dentil

*part (lower) of roof overhanging the wall*
    eave

*rounded vertical support*
    pillar, column

*square or rectangular vertical support*
    pier

*rectangular vertical support not freestanding but projecting from part of a wall*
    pilaster

*scroll-like or spiral ornamental feature*
    volute

*wall's clamp-like support (beneath a roof or overhang)*
    bracket, corbel

*ornamental scroll-like projection beneath a cornice*
    modillion

*projecting curved or foliage-like ornament high up on a building*
    crocket

*rounded (part of a sphere) rooftop structure*
    dome, cupola

*rooftop structure for observation or decoration*
    cupola, lantern, belfry, belvedere

*opening at the top of a dome*
    oculus

long ago darkened to the color of the slate-gray yard around
it. Rain-rotted shingles drooped over the eaves of the veranda; oak trees kept the sun away.

HARPER LEE, *To Kill a Mockingbird*

There was a drive, always covered with gravel, that swept
around in a beautiful curve and brought you up under a big
porte-cochere, which reminded you of horses with fly-nets,
and shiny and black closed carriages; and the house, which
was yellow and covered with shingles that overlapped with
rounded ends like scales, was an impressive though rather
formless mass of cupolas with foolscap tops, dormers with
diamond panes, balconies with little white railings and porches with Ionic columns, all pointing in different directions.

EDMUND WILSON, *Memoirs of Hecate County*

In front were the dark green glassy waters of an unvisited
backwater; and beyond them a bright lawn set with many
walnut trees and a few great chestnuts, well lit with their
candles, and to the left of that a low white house with a
green dome rising in its middle and a veranda whose roof of
hammered iron had gone verdigris colour with age and the
Thames weather. This was the Monkey Island Inn.

REBECCA WEST, *The Return of the Soldier*

The university capped a then bleak hill, its buildings evoking
the cultural aspirations of a faraway Europe of a distant past.
The centerpiece was the baroque Hall of Languages, built of
stones of two colors and partly covered with ivy. Behind it, a
bit to the west, stood the gymnasium, as Gothic as a temple

*Russian-style (ogival) bulbous dome that comes to a point*
  onion dome, imperial dome, imperial roof

*pointed tower-like construction rising from a roof*
  spire, flèche, steeple

*small spire-like ornament topping a feature of a building*
  pinnacle, finial

*octagonal spire*
  broach spire

*horizontal part of a classical building above the columns and below the eaves*
  entablature

*sculptured or in-relief band along the top of a classical building*
  frieze

*sculptural relief whose projection is slight*
  bas relief

*triangular gable-like fronting of a classical roof (or an ornamental version of this)*
  pediment

*crown-like upper end of a column, pier, or pilaster*
  capital

*supporting block at the base of a column, pier, or pilaster*
  plinth

*wedge-shaped piece at the top of an arch*
  keystone

*wedge-shaped piece in an arch or vault*
  voussoir

*ornamental part of a wall adjoining an arch or below an upper-level window*
  spandrel

*carved or otherwise shaped or designed ornamentation*
  fretwork

of sweat could hope to be, of dark brick, with high windows. Also to the west was the university library, later to become the administration building. Farther still to the west and south, on another rise overlooking the city, was the dark Gothic cathedral-like spire of Crouse College, in which Fine Arts were housed. Wooden walkways, some of them dilapidated, ran between these buildings.

JOHN HERSEY, *The Call*

It sat on a shelf between our lane and the creek, a little higher than the rest of the bottomland. Its board-and-batten sides and its shake roof were weathered silvery as an old rock. To me it has an underwater look—that barnacled silveriness, the way three big live oaks twisted like seaweed above the roof, the still, stained, sunken light.

WALLACE STEGNER, *All the Little Live Things*

At the far end of a scrubby courtyard was a sooty brick building, the shape of Monticello on the back of the nickel, a domed roof but with one difference: this one had a chimney at the rear belching greasy smoke. It was too squat, too plain, too gloomy for a church.

PAUL THEROUX, "A Real Russian Ikon"

The outlines of the house of Dr. Trescott had faded quietly into the evening, hiding a shape such as we call Queen Anne against the pall of the blackened sky.

STEPHEN CRANE, "The Monster"

*any construction or feature with openings in its design*
  openwork

*decorative grating-like features or ornamentation*
  grille, grill, grillwork

*decorative work with coiled forms*
  scrollwork

*building features of iron*
  ironwork


*roof peaking at a high angle*
  steep-pitched roof

*roof peaking at a low angle*
  low-pitched roof

*conventional ridged roof with the same angle of slope on either side*
  gable roof, saddle roof, saddleback roof

*horizontal or level roof*
  flat roof

*roof with a third face sloping down before where the two main slopes meet*
  hip roof, hipped roof

*roof that slopes downward*
  shed roof, pent roof, lean-to roof

*roof having not one but two slopes (or angles of slope) on either side of its ridge*
  curb roof

*roof only part of which is hipped (so that part of the main gable is "blunted" or truncated)*
  jerkinhead roof, hipped-gable roof

*curb roof with the lower of its two slopes the steeper one*
  gambrel roof, mansard roof, dual-pitched roof

*roof with four faces or slopes that rise to a point*
  pyramidal roof

*roof with a single downward or upward slope*
  lean-to roof, shed roof, penthouse roof, half-gabled roof

She was right about the guest house: it wasn't to everyone's taste. It was stubby and ill-proportioned, made of stucco in a pale shade of pinkish-gray, with the wooden trim and shutters at its windows painted lavender. Upstairs, at one end of it, French doors led out onto an abbreviated balcony that was overgrown with leafy vines, and from the balcony a frivolous vine-entangled spiral staircase descended to a flagstone terrace at what proved to be the front door. If you stepped back on the grass to take it all in with a single searching glance, the house had a lopsided, crudely fanciful look, like something drawn by a child with an uncertain sense of the way a house ought to be.

RICHARD YATES, *Young Hearts Crying*

The architects of the Knox Building had wasted no time in trying to make it look taller than its twenty stories, with the result that it looked shorter. They hadn't bothered trying to make it handsome, either, and so it was ugly: slab-sided and flat-topped, with a narrow pea-green cornice that jutted like the lip of a driven stake.

RICHARD YATES, *Revolutionary Road*

Through trees, Jeremy saw the facades of houses, all new, almost all in good taste—elegant and witty pastiches of Lutyens manor houses, of Little Trianons, of Monticellos; light-hearted parodies of Le Corbusier's solemn machines-for-living-in; fantastic adaptations of Mexican haciendas and New England farms.

ALDOUS HUXLEY, *After Many a Summer Dies the Swan*

*roof that is a double-gable or ridged roof (with the lowest part or "valley" in the center)*
    M roof

*roof with broad parallel indentations across its top*
    saw-tooth roof

*roof tiled in the southwestern U.S. style*
    Spanish-tiled roof, mission-tiled roof

*conventional wooden-frame (stile-and-rail) door with panels*
    panel door

*conventional door without panels or moldings*
    flush door

*door with some glass in it*
    sash door

*slatted doors*
    louvered doors

*slatted door on tracks that folds up or out horizontally*
    accordion door

*door composed of glass panes*
    French door

*door of glass that opens or closes along horizontal tracks*
    sliding glass door

*door with two sides that open or close*
    double door

*door hinged to swing in or out*
    double-swing door

*crude cellar or shed door*
    batten door

*paneling or other border-like features around a door*
    surround

*window that does not open*
    fixed window

*standard window with raisable upper and lower sashes*
    double-hung window

Then suddenly the car plunged into a tunnel and emerged into another world, a vast, untidy suburban world of filling stations and billboards, of low houses in gardens, of vacant lots and waste paper, of occasional shops and office buildings and churches—primitive Methodist churches built, surprisingly enough in the style of the Cartuja at Granada, Catholic churches like Canterbury Cathedral, synagogues disguised as Hagia Sophia, Christian Science churches with pillars and pediments, like banks.
ALDOUS HUXLEY, *After Many a Summer Dies the Swan*

Seventy-seventh Street was very wide at that point. On one side was the museum, a marvelous Romanesque Revival creation in an old reddish stone. It was set back in a little park with trees. TOM WOLFE, *The Bonfire of the Vanities*

The grassy track ran level, curved and dipped a little, emerged from the trees. The house, dazzlingly white where the afternoon sun touched it, stood with its shadowed back to me. It had been built on the seaward side of a small cottage that had evidently existed before it. It was square, with a flat roof and a colonnade of slender arches running round the south and east sides. Above the colonnade was a terrace. I could see the open french windows of a first-floor room giving access to it. JOHN FOWLES, *The Magus*

A square smug brown house, rather damp. A narrow concrete walk up to it. Sickly yellow leaves in a window with dried wings of box-elder seeds and snags of wool from the cottonwoods. A screened porch with pillars of thin painted

*window with a sash that moves right or left*
  sliding window

*window that opens on hinges*
  casement window

*window with adjustable horizontal slat-like glass panes*
  jalousie

*large fixed window dominating a room*
  picture window

*window or windows projecting or curving outward from a wall*
  bay window, bow window

*window above a door*
  transom

*bay window supported by a bracket (corbel)*
  oriel

*fixed window like a fan (or half a lemon slice) with radiating muntins
(sash bars)*
  fan window, transom window

*fixed fan-like window with muntins in the form of concentric semicircles*
  circle-head window

*window with a sash sliding left or right*
  sliding window

*window that (hinged at the top) opens out (sometimes with a crank
mechanism)*
  awning window

*window that (hinged at the top) opens in or is like an upside-down
awning window*
  hopper window

*window that (hinged at the top) opens in*
  basement transom window

*window with a sash anchored at the center of the frame that swings
around perpendicularly*
  center pivot window, pivot window

*window in a ceiling or roof*
  skylight

pine surmounted by scrolls and brackets and bums of jig-sawed wood. No shrubbery to shut off the public gaze. A lugubrious bay-window to the right of the porch.

SINCLAIR LEWIS, *Main Street*

The church was a Gothic monument of shingles painted pigeon blue. It has stout wooden buttresses supporting noth-ing. It had stained-glass windows with heavy traceries of imitation stone. It opened the way into long streets edged by tight, exhibitionist lawns. Behind the lawns stood wooden piles tortured out of all shape; twisted into gables, turrets, dormers; bulging with porches; crushed under huge, sloping roofs.

AYN RAND, *The Fountainhead*

The Frink National Bank Building displayed the entire his-tory of Roman art in well-chosen specimens; for a long time it had been considered the best building of the city, because no other structure could boast a single Classical item which it did not possess. It offered so many columns, pediments, friezes, tripods, gladiators, urns and volutes that it looked as if it had not been built of white marble, but squeezed out of a pastry tube.

AYN RAND, *The Fountainhead*

It was Roark's house, but its walls were not of red brick, its windows were cut to conventional size and equipped with green shutters, two of its projecting wings were omitted, the great cantilevered terrace over the sea was replaced by a little wrought-iron balcony, and the house was provided with an entrance of Ionic columns supporting a broken pediment, and with a little spire supporting a weather vane.

AYN RAND, *The Fountainhead*

*window with small panes separated by lead*
leaded window

*window like an archway with a lower side-window on either side (the whole looking like the frontal outline of a domed building)*
Palladian window, Diocletian window, Venetian window

*tall and narrow pointed-arch window*
lancet window

*wall opening with (usually wooden) adjustable slats for ventilation*
louver

*small round opening or window*
bull's-eye, oeil-de-boeuf, oxeye

*vertical dividing member in the middle of a window (particularly of a large Gothic window)*
mullion

## Useful Architectural Adjectives

*arranged or proportioned equivalently from the center*
symmetrical

*not symmetrical*
asymmetrical, irregular

*having a middle or central emphasis*
centralized

*configured like rays or spokes from a center*
radial

*standing alone or unsupported*
freestanding

*irregular in layout or spread*
rambling

*thrust forward*
projecting

*set back*
recessed

The building was of gray, lichen-blotched stone, with a high central portion and two curving wings, like the claws of a crab, thrown out on each side. In one of these wings the windows were broken and blocked with wooden boards, while the roof was partly caved in, a picture of ruin. The central portion was in little better repair, but the right-hand block was comparatively modern, and the blinds in the windows, with the blue smoke curling up from the chimneys, showed that this was where the family resided.

ARTHUR CONAN DOYLE,
"The Adventure of the Speckled Band"

Life radiated out from the club to the "cottages" on West and Eden Streets, large shapeless shingle structures, sometimes brightly painted, with well-mowed emerald lawns, to the cozy shops on Main Street with windows invitingly full of imported luxuries, to the woods and the long blue driveways of the more distant villas concealed by spruce and pine, yet all familiar to us, including stone castles, Italian palazzos, Georgian red brick villas, but still for the most part shingle habitations, with dark proliferating turrets and porches.

LOUIS AUCHINCLOSS, *Honorable Men*

The Ansonia, the neighborhood's great landmark, was built by Stanford White. It looks like a baroque palace from Prague or Munich enlarged a hundred times, with towers, domes, huge swells and bubbles of metal gone green from exposure, iron fretwork and festoons. Black television antennae are densely planted on its round summits.

SAUL BELLOW, *Seize the Day*

*being of the usual or typical style*
vernacular

*serving a single purpose without elaboration*
functional

*stately and sober in effect*
formal

*showing or using different elements or styles*
eclectic

*imposingly massive or grandiose*
monumental

*suggestive of ancient Greece or Rome*
classical, neoclassical

*in three parts or divisions*
tripartite

*in four parts or divisions*
quadripartite

*in six parts or divisions*
sexpartite

*impressively bulky or dense in construction*
massive

*lengthened or notably long*
elongated

*curved or opening outward*
flared

*arched and rounded*
domed

*stressing line or elongated contour*
streamlined, sleek

*relatively low or close to the ground*
low slung

*having different horizontal levels*
terraced

Behind the farm the stone mountains stood up against the sky. The farm buildings huddled like little clinging aphids on the mountain skirts, crouched low to the ground as though the wind might blow them into the sea. The little shack, the rattling, rotting barn were grey-bitten with sea salt, beaten by the damp wind until they had taken on the color of the granite hills. John Steinbeck, "Flight"

Trust Cowperwood to do the thing as it should be done. The place they had leased was a charming little graystone house, with a neat flight of granite, balustraded steps leading up to its wide-arched door, and a judicious use of stained glass to give its interior an artistically subdued atmosphere. Theodore Dreiser, *The Titan*

It was set on a little rise, a biggish box of a house, two-story, rectangular, gray, and unpainted, with a tin roof, unpainted too and giving off blazes under the sun for it was new and the rust hadn't bitten down into it yet, and a big chimney at each end. Robert Penn Warren, *All the King's Men*

In the Weiss house, stone has been built into heavy, windowless enclosures—an embodiment of strength and stability—giving a sense of protection to the living room. Wood has been made into a thin, drumlike box which floats the dining room on piers. Roof planes slant down to create a snug retreat at the central hearth, up as the living room opens to distant views. Stonework is sent skyward to create

*seemingly shortened or cut off (at the top or an end)*
   truncated, stunted

*relatively small and square*
   box-like, boxy

*extending around a corner or corners*
   wraparound

*showing decorative features*
   ornamental, embellished

*bearing shapes or decoration representing leaves*
   foliated

*checkered or mosaic-like*
   tesselated

*having a net-like pattern*
   reticulated

*having sunken (usually) square or octagonal panels (lacunars or lacunaria) in the ceiling*
   coffered

*showing segments (as of a circle) as constructional pieces*
   segmented

*having columns*
   columniated

*having columnar grooves*
   fluted

*without columns*
   astylar

*having a colonnade*
   colonnaded

*having a colonnade on all sides*
   peripteral, peristylar

*having or painted in several colors*
   polychrome, multicolor

the essential chimney stack. Even though the forms are new, Kahn's elements are a summation of home.

MARY MIX FOLEY, *The American House*

On the opposite side of the house, the living room fronts on a spectacular canyon view, breaking open with glass walls and a deep porch, recessed, however, to keep the taut wall line and provide shelter in any weather. Most striking of all is what has happened to the hipped roof, made unfamiliar by an oversized monitor skylight which creates a silhouette like a farmer's broad-brimmed hat.

MARY MIX FOLEY, *The American House*

Composite ranches feature irregular perimeter outlines. Thus they are characterized by degrees of irregular massing with L- and T-shapes the most prevalent forms. . . . Like other ranches, roofs are low-pitched except that multiple-gables, multiple-hip, and combined gable and hip roofs predominate.

JOHN JAKLE, ROBERT BASTIAN, AND DOUGLAS MEYER, *Common Houses in America's Small Towns*

The suffused light I had detected seconds before goes out in a flicker, while a second, brighter alpenglow leaks through three sets of wooden shutters. There is no glass. I stare at a room unlike any I have seen. Thirty feet above the ground floor, mountain views all around. Crafted with fancy handiwork, Tibetan dragons, filigree, and crenelation.

MICHAEL TOBIAS, *Voice of the Planet*

*having stone masonry whose edges or joints are accentuated (by beveling or rebating the blocks)*
> rusticated

*having a wall surface of wooden beams with masonry between them*
> half-timbered

*sloping backward vertically or upward (as a wall)*
> battered

*built or supported with horizontal beams*
> trabeated

*projecting horizontally beyond its stabilizing or anchoring support*
> cantilevered

*left visible although a supporting feature*
> exposed

*having vertical boards or strips as walls or siding*
> board-and-batten

*arched or hollowed (as a ceiling)*
> vaulted

*having a vaulted ceiling like a tunnel or half-cylinder*
> barrel-vaulted

*having a ceiling of intersecting vaults*
> groin-vaulted

*in disrepair or crumbling*
> dilapidated, ramshackle, rickety, tumbledown

## COMMON MODERN ARCHITECTURAL STYLES

### Greek Revival

Commonly classical-temple-like rectangular blocks with a full-width front or entry portico with rounded or square columns and a flat or low roof above a wide band of trim. Usually no arches, no roof balustrade, no dormers, and no wings or projections on the building. Front door usually surrounded by narrow sidelights. Windows are small and inconspicuous.

The ceiling design is in large coffered bays corresponding to the buttresses, which are emphasized by the *pietra serena* pilasters resting on a string-course above the tops of the desks and supporting a narrow architrave below the ceiling.

LINDA MURRAY, *Michelangelo*

The light of this southern fjord is not unlike the light of the Baltic; a pallid freshness is common to both cities; sitting snugly out of the sunlight in Sydney's Strand Arcade, all fancy balustrades and tesselated paving, sometimes I almost expect to see the shoppers shaking the snow from their galoshes, breathing in their hands to restore the circulation and ordering themselves a schnapps.

JAN MORRIS, *Journeys*

The flat roofs, *azoteas,* were protected by stone parapets, so that every house was a fortress. Sometimes these roofs resembled parterres of flowers, so thickly were they covered with them, but more frequently these were cultivated in broad terraced gardens, laid out between the edifices. Occasionally a great square or marketplace intervened, surrounded by its porticos of stone and stucco; or a pyramidal temple reared its colossal bulk, crowned with its tapering sanctuaries, and altars blazing with inextinguishable fires. The great street facing the southern causeway, unlike most others in the place, was wide, and extended some miles in nearly a straight line, as before noticed, through the centre of the city.                          WILLIAM H. PRESCOTT,

*The History of the Conquest of Mexico*

## Gothic Revival
Church-like steeply pitched roofs and cross gables, pointed (Gothic) arches, and gables with decorative vergeboards. Sometimes flat roofs with castle-like parapets and usually a one-story full-width or entry porch. Structure basically of one color.

## High Victorian Gothic
An eclectic variation of Gothic Revival, differing in being of many colors (polychrome), having details that are heavy rather than delicate or fragile in appearance, and having many overhanging or "top-heavy" gables and towers.

## Queen Anne
An asymmetrical hodgepodge style of house, usually with a pre-eminent front-facing gable, a steeply pitched but irregular roof with numerous gables or turrets, any kind of window except a pointed-arch one, and a porch that extends to at least one side wall. Upper stories commonly project over the lower ones.

## Italian Villa
An asymmetrical dwelling, and a square or octagonal, off-center or corner tower is typical, as are eaves projecting considerably, roofs that are flat or not steep, a veranda, and windows grouped in twos or threes.

## Second Empire
A high mansard (double-sloped on all sides) roof is the giveaway, as are varied dormer windows, chimneys, and ornamental brackets beneath the eaves. Sometimes there is a central cupola or off-center tower.

## Colonial Revival
There are many subtypes, and roofs vary, but common to most examples is a prominent, pedimented front porch and door with columns or pilasters and a fanlight or sidelights. The double-hung windows have many panes. Most but by no means all houses have symmetrical facades.

Keen to secure some photographs, I scaled the bank and climbed between the tensioned strands of the fence in sight on my right as I fought my way along the edge of the plantation for what I estimated to be about two hundred yards on a course roughly parallel to the road.

JOHN LISTER-KAYE, *The White Island*

The next morning we cross over a notch and wind out way through thick fog across a suspension bridge that spans a fulminant torrent.

MICHAEL TOBIAS, *Voice of the Planet*

The houses that adjoined this row of shops were small terraced cottages with front doors that opened straight into the front rooms, and a bare yard of space between the windows and the pavement. Their own house, though not much bigger, was more modern and semi-detached, with a pebble-dash facade and some decorative woodwork which his father, like their neighbours, kept brightly painted in two colours, green and cream.

DAVID LODGE, *Out of the Shelter*

Imagine to yourself, my dear Letty, a spacious garden, part laid out in delightful walks, bounded with high hedges and trees, and paved with gravel; part exhibiting a wonderful assemblage of the most picturesque and striking objects, pavilions, lodges, groves, grottoes, lawns, temples and cascades; porticoes, colonades [*sic*], and rotundos; adorned with pillars, statues, and painting. . . .

TOBIAS SMOLLETT, *The Expedition of Humphry Clinker*

### Regency

A simple, informal variety of Colonial Revival, typically a symmetrical white-painted brick two- or three-story house with a hip roof, double-hung windows (and shutters of the same size), and a chimney on one side; lacks the classical lines of the Georgian style.

### Federal (Adam)

A semicircular fanlight over the front door and windows with small panes are characteristic. Decorative moldings usually highlight the cornice. The house is most commonly a simple box, but it may also have curved or polygonal projections at the side or rear.

### Saltbox Colonial

A simple shingle or clapboard rectangular house with a steep, lean-to-like roof (showing no windows) extending far down its rear, and with a large central chimney. The double-hung windows are small-paned.

### Dutch Colonial

A one-story (or, occasionally, one-and-a-half story) dwelling with a side-gabled or side-gambreled roof that does not overhang far at the sides and small-paned double-hung windows. The entrance door a two-halved Dutch door unless replaced by a conventional door, and often an unsupported hood or roof over the entrance door.

### Tudor

Usually a fortresslike stone-and-brick house with semihexagonal bays and turrets, high chimneys, tall leaded-glass casement windows (with stone mullions), and the well-known decorative half-timbering.

### Spanish Colonial

Stucco-protected adobe brick or rubble stone is the distinctive material, and the flat or low-pitched red-tile roof is also distinctive. Small window openings have or originally had grilles and inside shutters. One or two stories. Elaborate ornamentation is

It is one of two evidently designed by the same architect who built some houses in a characteristic taste on Beacon Street opposite the Common. It has a wooden portico, with slender fluted columns, which have always been painted white, and which, with the delicate moldings of the cornice, form the sole and efficient decoration of the street front; nothing could be simpler, and nothing could be better.

WILLIAM DEAN HOWELLS, *The Rise of Silas Lapham*

The pretty Queen Anne house, with its pitted rosy-red bricks and its blunted grey stonework, stretched its bland length with a certain luxuriant confidence, surrendering itself to the garden whose proportions were perfectly attuned to its own.             IRIS MURDOCH, *An Unofficial Rose*

It was long and low built, with a pillared veranda and balcony all the way round. The soft white bulk of it lay stretched upon the green garden like a sleeping beast.

KATHERINE MANSFIELD, "Prelude"

. . . I escaped to the open country and fearfully took refuge in a low hovel, quite bare, and making a wretched appearance after the palaces I had beheld in the village. This hovel, however, joined a cottage of a neat and pleasant appearance, but after my late dearly bought experience, I dared not enter it.             MARY SHELLEY, *Frankenstein*

It was in shape oblong, about 80 feet by 40, unmistakably ecclesiastical in feeling—two rows of wooden pillars, spaced

sometimes found around openings, and a two-story building may have a pergola.

## Mission

A stucco style, lacking the sculptural ornamentation of the Spanish Colonial, with balconies, towers or turrets, and tiled roofs common. Eaves have a wide overhang, and square piers support porch roofs.

## Prairie

Two-story dwellings, with low, hipped roofs, widely overhanging eaves, one-story porches or wings, and no ornamentation— the emphasis or feeling being distinctly horizontal. The porch supports are often massive, and ribbon windows with dark-wood stripping are common.

## Stick (Carpenter Gothic)

Accenting the vertical, these buildings have a steep gabled roof, large verandas, and boldly projecting eaves. The main and other gables often have near the top an ornamental truss. Also characteristic are vertical, horizontal, or diagonal stick-work (boards) overlaid on the wall surface, to suggest exposed structural framing, and gingerbread trim.

## New England Farm House

A simple box-shaped house of (usually) white clapboard, with a steep-pitched roof and central chimney.

## Cape Cod

A simple rectangular, one-and-one-half-story house of clapboard, shingles, brick, or other material, with a low central chimney and a steep, shingled roof.

## Beaux-Arts

Double or coupled columns are the telltale feature of these imposing symmetrical buildings, which often have monumental (impressive) steps; wall surfaces with pilasters, columns, or decorative features; and sometimes sculpted classical figures at the top of the edifice.

at intervals of fifteen feet, rose to a vaulted ceiling 25 or 30 feet above the floor.

E. E. CUMMINGS, *The Enormous Room*

Next morning Johnny got up early and went round to the office of the Ocean City Improvement and Realty Company that was in a new greenstained shingled bungalow on the freshly laidout street back of the beach. There was no one there yet, so he walked round the town. It was a muggy gray day and the cottages and the frame stores and the unpainted shacks along the railroad track looked pretty desolate.    JOHN DOS PASSOS, *The Morning of the Century*

This house was the pride of the town. Faced with stone as far back as the dining-room windows, it was a house of arches and turrets and girdling stone porches: it had the first port-cochere seen in that town.

BOOTH TARKINGTON, *The Magnificent Ambersons*

Yossarian never went there to help until it was finished; then he went there often, so pleased was he with the large, fine, rambling shingled building.

JOSEPH HELLER, *Catch-22*

The cottages were mostly rambling, shingled affairs, gabled, dormered, and turreted, with screened porches and wooden walls on the inside and big stone fireplaces. Each cottage was different, yet one seemed much like another. The Aldrich cottage, where the McGhees always stayed, was one of

## Georgian Revival

Most commonly a boxlike house of one or two stories whose doors, windows, and chimney or chimneys are strictly symmetrical. The roof may have a centered gable or side gables or be either hipped or gambrel, but the cornice usually has a decorative molding of tooth-like dentils. Usually a paneled front door framed by pilasters and an entablature. The double-hung windows usually have small panes and are always symmetrically positioned, never paired.

## Shingle

The ground stories are sometimes of stone, but the upper stories are always cladded in shingles. Roofs are often of the gambrel type with moderate steepness ending in a broad gable, and there are generally several chimneys, extensive porches, and multilevel eaves. The windows have small panes.

## Modernistic

Sleekly asymmetrical. In the Art Moderne style, wall surfaces (usually of stucco) are smooth, and there is a generally horizontal emphasis accented by lines or grooves in the walls and horizontal balustrades. In the earlier and rarer Art Deco style, on the smooth stucco wall surfaces there are zigzag and other geometric designs and, above the roof line, tower-like projections.

## International Style

Asymmetrical but unlike parts are carefully balanced. There is absolutely no ornamentation around walls or windows, with surfaces smooth and uniform and roofs flat. The windows, of the metal casement type, are flush or blended into the walls and sometimes "turn the corner." Balconies and other projections are often cantilever supported.

## COMMON CONSTRUCTION MATERIALS

*earth and grass*
  sod, turf

Tommy's two favorites; it was a big log cabin—the only log cabin on the Island—with a Dutch door. The Farnsworth cottage, his other favorite, was a shingled house weathered to a silver sheen with blue trim and a round room in a high turret that Mrs. Farnsworth sometimes used to take him up to. You could see way up the river from that room.

WILLIAM MCPHERSON, *Testing the Current*

Through my glasses I saw the slope of a hill interspersed with rare trees and perfectly free from undergrowth. A long decaying building on the summit was half buried in the high grass; the large holes in the peaked roof gaped black from afar; the jungle and the woods made a background. There was no enclosure or fence of any kind; but there had been one apparently, for near the house half-a-dozen slim posts remained in a row, roughly trimmed, and with their upper ends ornamented with round carved balls.

JOSEPH CONRAD, *Heart of Darkness*

This palace was distinguished by a feature not very common in the architecture of Roman edifices; that is to say, a medieval tower, square, massive, lofty, and battlemented and machicolated at the summit.

NATHANIEL HAWTHORNE, *The Marble Faun*

There was always a little grey street leading to the stage-door of the theatre and another little grey street where your lodgings were, and rows of little houses with chimneys like the funnels of dummy steamers and smoke the same colour as the sky; and a grey stone promenade running hard, naked

*poles with interwoven branches, reeds, twigs, or the like used in primitive dwellings*
    wattle

*straw, rushes, or the like used for roofing*
    thatch

*length of unshaped timber*
    log

*bonding mixture (lime or cement or both with sand and water) used between stones or bricks*
    mortar

*clay bricks, tiles, stones, or concrete or glass blocks usually bonded with mortar or cement*
    masonry

*pulverized clay and limestone mixture*
    cement, Portland cement

*stone-like mixture of Portland cement with water and an aggregate (pebbles, shale, gravel, etc.)*
    concrete

*block of concrete*
    concrete block

*concrete strengthened with embedded metal (usually steel) strands or mesh*
    reinforced concrete

*translucent block used chiefly in walls*
    glass block

*red brick*
    redbrick

*glazed or baked brick*
    fired brick

*brick of sun-dried clay and straw*
    adobe, unfired brick

*raw or unfinished pieces of stone*
    fieldstone

*hewn or squared masonry stone*
    ashlar

and straight by the side of the grey-brown or grey-green
sea. . . .                    JEAN RHYS, *Voyage in the Dark*


Built of butter-yellow sandstone blocks hand-hewn in quarries five hundred miles eastward, the house had two stories
and was constructed on austerely Georgian lines, with large,
many-paned windows and a wide, iron-pillared veranda
running all the way around its bottom story.

COLLEEN MCCULLOUGH, *The Thorn Birds*


We lived on the first floor of a three-story brownstone
house that stood on a quiet street just off busy Lee Avenue.
The brownstone row houses lined both sides of the street,
and long, wide, stone stairways led from the sidewalks to the
frosted-glass double doors of the entrances.

CHAIM POTOK, *The Chosen*


Judge Tyler's house was one of the brick ones, with a Mansard roof and patterns in the shingles. There were dormer
windows. It was three stories high, with a double-decker
veranda, and with white painted stonework around all the
windows, which were high and narrow. The whole house
looked too high and narrow, and there were a lot of steps up
to the front door.

WALTER VAN TILBURG CLARK, *The Ox-Bow Incident*

*broken stone*
   riprap, rubble, revertment

*stone made (dressed) smooth*
   cut stone

*burnt or baked thin or curved slab or various building materials used mostly for roofs*
   tile, tiling

*mixture of gypsum or limestone with sand and water and sometimes hair used primarily for walls and ceilings*
   plaster

*boards of fiberboard, felt, or the like used in place of plaster*
   plasterboard, Sheetrock, drywall, gypsum board

*covering or overlay of one material over another in a wall*
   cladding

*weatherproof boards, sheets, or shingles used for the exposed facing of a frame building*
   siding

*exterior plaster finish (usually of Portland cement and sand)*
   stucco

*wall exterior of mortar and pressed-in pebbles*
   pebble-dash, rock-dash, roughcast

*long and thin horizontal board (with one edge thinner) used overlappingly with others for siding*
   clapboard, weatherboard

*sawed thin oblong of wood, slate, or other building material used overlappingly as roofing or siding*
   shingle

*split-log shingle (commonly of cedar)*
   shake

*polished mosaic or chip-like flooring usually of marble and stone*
   terrazo

# EARTH AND SKY

# Terrain and Landscape

Then they crossed a stone stile on to the moor, and followed a pony-trail northwards, with the screes of the mountain rising steeply on the left. Beyond a spinney of birches, they came to a barn and longhouse, standing amid heaps of broken wall.　　BRUCE CHATWIN, *On the Black Hill*

We now come abreast of the gap on the right, and it ends the tedium of the reach upriver. It is a broad window into stands of cypress, their wide fluted bases attached to their reflections in still, dark water.

JOHN MCPHEE, *The Control of Nature*

The coast for the fifty miles west of Bognor was full of pleats and tucks—harbors, channels, inlets, and Southampton Water, and the bays of Spithead.

PAUL THEROUX, *The Kingdom by the Sea*

We were at the edge of the New Forest, and the heather and gorse and its flatness gave it the look of a moor.

PAUL THEROUX, *The Kingdom by the Sea*

*aspect or conformation of land*
 landscape

*particular extensive locale of land*
 area, region, tract, expanse

*plant growth or life*
 vegetation, foliage

*visibly green plant life or trees*
 greenery, verdure

*grassy (or nonwoody) vegetation*
 herbage

*greenery as cover or food for deer*
 vert

*region abounding in trees*
 forest, woods, woodland, forestland

*extensive tropical wet woodland with tall trees that form a light-blocking canopy*
 rain forest

*extensive area of barren and arid land*
 desert

*extensive area of treeless grassland (with tall grasses)*
 prairie (South America: pampa)

*extensive area of treeless grassland (with short grasses) and less rainfall than a prairie*
 steppe

The path, a rather dubious and uncertain one, led us along the ridge of high bluffs that border the Missouri; and by looking to the right or to the left, we could enjoy a strange contrast of opposite scenery. On the left stretched the prairie, rising into swells and undulations, thickly sprinkled with groves, or gracefully expanding into wide grassy basins, of miles in extent; while its curvatures, swelling against the horizon were often surmounted by lines of sunny woods. . . .

FRANCIS PARKMAN, JR., *The Oregon Trail*

We entered at length a defile which I never have seen rivalled. The mountain was cracked from top to bottom, and we were creeping along the bottom of the fissure, in dampness and gloom, with the clink of hoofs on the loose shingly rocks, and the hoarse murmuring of a petulant brook which kept us company.

FRANCIS PARKMAN, JR., *The Oregon Trail*

We shook hands with our friends, rode out upon the prairie, and clambering the sandy hollows that were channelled in the sides of the hills, gained the high plains above.

FRANCIS PARKMAN, JR., *The Oregon Trail*

Immediately in front of the recess, or cave, was a little terrace, partly formed by nature, and partly by the earth that had been carelessly thrown aside by the laborers. The mountain fell off precipitously in front of the terrace, and the approach by its sides, under the ridge of the rocks, was difficult and a little dangerous.

JAMES FENIMORE COOPER, *The Pioneers*

*steppe with scattered trees and shrubs (especially in Africa)*
  veld, veldt

*extensive grazing grassland with scattered trees and shrubs*
  savanna, savannah, campo

*extensive treeless plain in the southeastern U.S.*
  savana, savannah

*extensive plain with few trees in the southwestern U.S.*
  llano

*extensive northern (subarctic) evergreen forest that is moist*
  taiga, boreal forest

*extensive northern (arctic and subarctic) treeless plain with mucky soil*
  tundra

*tundra treeless because of elevation (rather than latitude)*
  alpine tundra

*alpine forest having stunted trees*
  krummholz, elfinwood

*level area of terrain*
  flatland, flats

*extensive area of flat open terrain*
  plain, champaign, campagna

*grass-covered tract of level land*
  meadow

*green tract of grassland*
  sward, greensward, turf

*grassland tract for grazing or hay*
  pasture, lea

*tract of open and rolling land with poor soil*
  moor, heath, moorland

*high moor or barren field*
  fell

*barren land*
  waste, wasteland, barrens

*tract of sandy ground where topsoil has been blown away by the wind*
  sandblow

A dark spot of a few acres in extent at the southern extremity of this beautiful flat, and immediately under the feet of our travelers, alone showed by its rippling surface and the vapors which exhaled from it that what at first might seem a plain, was one of the mountain lakes, locked in the frosts of winter.

JAMES FENIMORE COOPER, *The Pioneers*

The traveler from the coast, who, after plodding northward for a score of miles over calcareous downs and corn-lands, suddenly reached the verge of one of these escarpments, is surprised and delighted to behold, extended like a map beneath him, a country differing absolutely from that which he has passed through. Behind him the hills are open, the sun blazes down upon fields so large as to give an unenclosed character to the landscape, the lanes are white, the hedges low and plashed, the atmosphere colourless. Here, in the valley, the world seems to be constructed on a smaller and more delicate scale; the fields are mere paddocks, so reduced that from this height their hedgerows appear a network of dark green threads overspreading the paler green of the grass.

THOMAS HARDY, *Tess of the D'Urbervilles*

Returning from one of these dark walks they reached a great gravel-cliff immediately over the levels, where they stood still and listened. The water was now high in the streams, squirting through the weirs, and tinkling under culverts; the smallest gullies were all full; there was no taking short cuts anywhere, and foot-passengers were compelled to follow the permanent ways.

THOMAS HARDY, *Tess of the D'Urbervilles*

*extensive area of uncultivated and little-populated terrain*
   wilderness, the bush, backcountry, wilds (Australia: outback)

*land covered by grass*
   grassland

*grassland for grazing*
   pasture, pastureland, pasturage

*municipal tract of public and usually park-like land*
   common

*tract of grass-covered ground cultivated or mowed*
   lawn

*long strip of terrain*
   swath, swathe

*yard or field used as a household kitchen garden or for a few farm animals*
   croft (British)

*low terrain*
   bottom, bottomland

*high terrain*
   heights

*geological fracture in the earth's crust*
   fault, rift

*opening or recession in terrain*
   hole, cavity, depression, hollow, basin, pan

*open longitudinal depression*
   trench, ditch

*small and nestled (usually wooded) valley*
   dell, glen, dingle

*deep and narrow valley*
   hollow, combe, coomb, coombe

*deep and steep-sided valley (often with a river)*
   canyon, cañon

*small and narrow steep-sided valley (often with a stream)*
   gorge, ravine, flume, gulch, clough (South Africa: kloof)

Behind and over us towered Sheba's snowy breasts, and below, some five thousand feet beneath where we stood, lay league on league of the most lovely champaign country. Here were dense patches of lofty forest, there a great river wound its silvery way. To the left stretched a vast expanse of rich, undulating veldt or grass land, on which we could just make out countless herds of game or cattle, at that distance we could not tell which.

H. RIDER HAGGARD, *King Solomon's Mines*

The lane debouched into a close-bitten field, and out of this empty land the farm rose up with its buildings like a huddle of old, painted vessels floating in still water.

D. H. LAWRENCE, *The White Peacock*

So we went along by the hurrying brook, which fell over little cascades in its haste, never looking once at the primroses that were glimmering all along its banks. We turned aside, and climbed the hill through the woods. Velvety green sprigs of dog-mercury were scattered on the red soil. We came to the top of a slope, where the wood thinned. . . . There was a deep little dell, sharp sloping like a cup, and a white sprinkling of flowers all the way down, with white flowers showing pale among the first inpouring of shadow at the bottom.        D. H. LAWRENCE, *The White Peacock*

From the windmill the ground sloped westward, down to the barns and granaries and pig-yards. This slope was trampled hard and bare, and washed out in winding gullies by the rain. Beyond the corncribs, at the bottom of the shallow

*divide between valleys or side of a valley*
> coteau

*small ravine sometimes having rainwater flowing in it*
> gully, clough, draw, coulee nullah, wash, wadi (South Africa: donga)

*flat-bottomed gulch or gully sometimes having rainwater flowing in it*
> arroyo

*long hollow or depression*
> trough

*deep drop or hollow*
> gulf, abyss, chasm

*chasm formed by receding ice*
> randkluft

*valley*
> vale, dale

*drainage depression or hollow*
> sinkhole, sink, swallow, swallowhole, dolina, doline

*limestone sinkhole with a pool or deep natural well*
> cenote

*flat-floored and steep-walled depression with no outflowing stream*
> polje

*extensive or deep mucky or mossy basin*
> mudhole, muskeg

*ground that slants upward or downward*
> slope, incline, grade

*upward slope*
> acclivity, rise

*downward slope*
> declivity

*gentle slope*
> glacis

*precipitous slope*
> steep

draw, was a muddy little pond, with rusty willow bushes growing about it.                    WILLA CATHER, *My Antonia*

I followed a cattle path through the thick underbrush until I came to a slope that fell away abruptly to the water's edge. A great chunk of the shore had been bitten out by some spring freshet, and the scar was masked by elder bushes, growing down to the water in flowery terraces.

WILLA CATHER, *My Antonia*

Dark spruce forest frowned on either side of the frozen waterway. The trees had been stripped by a recent wind of their white covering of frost, and they seemed to lean toward each other, black and ominous, in the fading light. A vast silence reigned over the land.                    JACK LONDON, *White Fang*

For a while the country was much as it had been; then, climbing all the time, we crossed the top of a Col, the road winding back and forth on itself, and then it was really Spain. There were long brown mountains and a few pines and far-off forests of beech-trees on some of the mountainsides. The road went along the summit of the Col and then dropped down. . . . We came down out of the mountains and through an oak forest, and there were white cattle grazing in the forest. Down below there were grassy plains and clear streams . . .

ERNEST HEMINGWAY, *The Sun Also Rises*

The DC-8 took off again and the sea fell away behind it; it climbed over a floor of rain forest and cleared the wall of the

*describing a tree or forest with foliage that falls off annually*
deciduous

*describing a tree or forest with foliage that stays and remains green throughout the year*
evergreen

*area of dense trees*
wood, woods, forest

*small group or grouping of trees (usually without undergrowth)*
grove

*cluster of shrubs or small trees*
shrubbery, thicket

*patch of thick or twisted growth*
tangle

*grove or thicket of small trees*
copse, coppice, arbustum (British: spinney)

*shrubs and other low vegetation in a forest*
underbrush, brush, undergrowth

*leafy tree-enclosed nook or recess*
arbor, bower

*dense thicket of shrubs or dwarf trees*
chaparral

*group of planted fruit or nut trees*
orchard

*growth or array of one type of tree (or plant) in an area*
stand

*tract of shrubby and uncultivated open land*
heath

*area of low trees and bushes*
scrub

*thicket where game hide*
covert

*thicket of cane*
canebrake

cordillera—range after range broken by sunless valleys over which the clouds lowered, brown peaks laced with fingers of dark green thrust up from the jungle on the lower slopes. And in less than an hour—in a slender valley refulgent and shimmering—the white city of Compostela, on twin hills, walled in by snow peaks and two spent volcanoes.

ROBERT STONE, *A Flag for Sunrise*

He slowed down to make the road last longer. He had passed the big pines and left them behind. Where he walked now the scrub had closed in, walling in the road with dense sand pines, each one so thin it seemed to the boy it might make kindling by itself. The road went up an incline. At the top he stopped. The April sky was framed by the tawny sand and the pines.

MARJORIE KINNAN RAWLINGS, *The Yearling*

We traveled on, past the settlement that lay behind Santa Rosa, the sloping shacks and the huts on stilts and the rows of overturned canoes on the riverbank. We passed the gate-like entrance of a green lagoon, and pushed on, struggling in the river that brimmed at our bow. It was hotter here, for the sun was above the palms and the storm clouds had vanished inland. There were no mountains or even hills. There was nothing but the riverbank of palms and low bushes and yellow-bark trees, and the sky came down to the treetops. The high muddy river had flooded the bushes on the bank.

PAUL THEROUX, *The Mosquito Coast*

I looked off at the blue forms of the mountains, growing less transparent and cloudlike, shifting their positions, rolling

*narrow tree- or branch-covered pathway*
    tunnel

*tree-bordered or hedged and park-like walk*
    alley

*planned or mall-like alley whose trees are at least twice as high as the route's width*
    allée

*moist land*
    wetland, wetlands

*tract of low and wet or spongy ground*
    marsh, bog, fen, swamp, wash, slough, marshland

*swampy grassland with branching waterways*
    everglade

*low land subject to flood tides*
    tideland, tidelands

*flat and usually muddy tideland*
    tidal flat

*flat land having brackish water*
    salt marsh

*area under water that is shallow*
    shallows

*rough or marshy tract of land with one kind of vegetation (shrubs or ferns)*
    brake, bracken

*sunken and wet tract of land*
    swale

*moist low-lying land (usually pineland)*
    flatwoods

*clump of grass*
    tussock

*country having few or no trees*
    open country

from side to side off the road, coming back and centering in our path, and then sliding off the road again, but strengthening all the time. We went through some brush and then out across a huge flat field that ran before us for miles, going straight at the bulging range of hills, which was now turning mile by mile from blue to a light green-gold, the color of billions of hardwood leaves.

JAMES DICKEY, *Deliverance*

The sun fell behind the right side of the gorge, and the shadow of the bank crossed the water so fast that it was like a quick step from one side to the other. The beginning of darkness was thrown over us like a sheet, and in it the water ran even faster, frothing and near-foaming under the canoe.

JAMES DICKEY, *Deliverance*

It lay in the blue Pacific like a huge left-handed gauntlet, the open wristlet facing westward toward the island of Oahu, the cupped fingers pointing eastward toward Maui. The southern portion of Molokai consisted of rolling meadow land, often with gray and parched grasses, for rainfall was slight, while the northern portion was indented by some of the most spectacular cliffs in the islands.

JAMES MICHENER, *Hawaii*

At our backs rose the giant green and brown walls of the sierras, the range stretching away on either hand in violet and deep blue masses. At our feet lay the billowy green and yellow plain, vast as ocean, and channelled by innumerable streams, while one black patch on a slope far away showed us

*country that is level and low in altitude*
  lowland, lowlands

*country that is elevated or mountainous*
  highland, highlands, upland, uplands

*high point*
  elevation, eminence

*top of a hill*
  hilltop, rise

*projection at the top of a hill*
  brow

*small and rounded hill*
  knoll, hillock, hummock, monticule, monticle, mound
  (England: barrow)

*hill with a broad top*
  loma

*lower hills beneath mountains*
  foothills

*narrow or oval hill*
  drumlin

*rounded elevation*
  swell

*rounded solitary hill usually with steep sides*
  knob

*mound in permafrost terrain*
  pingo

*African veld's small and scrubby hill*
  kopje, koppie

*open upland of rolling hills or open country*
  wold

*rolling grassy upland with few trees*
  down, downs

*one of successive indentations (from slumping soil) on a hillside*
  catstep, terracette

that our foes were camping on the very spot where they had
overcome us.            W. H. HUDSON, *The Purple Land*


Three men were standing in the narrow opening of the
bush. One of them was the man with the huge gilded palm
hat. They stood for a while rather bewildered, seeing the
place bare and no sign of a human being near. They called
back to the other men coming into the clearing. It seemed
they had left their horses on a little plateau, located some
hundred and fifty feet below on the road, where there was a
bit of thin pasturage.

B. TRAVEN, *The Treasure of the Sierra Madre*


Corrugated slopes of lava, bristling lava cliffs, spouts of metallic clinkers, miles of coast without a well or rivulet; scarce
anywhere a beach, nowhere a harbour: here seems a singular
land to be contended for in battle as a seat for courts and
princes.

ROBERT LOUIS STEVENSON, *In the South Seas*


It is here that an overhanging and tip-tilted horn, a good
sea-mark for Hatiheu, burst naked from the verdure of the
climbing forest, and breaks down shoreward in steep taluses
and cliffs.

ROBERT LOUIS STEVENSON, *In the South Seas*


Winged by her own impetus and the drying breeze, the
*Casco* skimmed under cliffs, opened out a cove, showed us a
beach and some green trees, and flitted by again, bowing to

*high and craggy hill or rocky peak*
> tor

*colossal single rock or rock formation*
> monolith

*oddly or fantastically shaped (eroded) rock column*
> hoodoo

*single rock or boulder carried to where it is by a glacier*
> erratic

*rounded or hump-like natural formation*
> dome

*notably arched or bridge-like formation*
> natural bridge, arch

*prominent isolated or bare rock*
> scar

*smooth and slippery rock*
> slickrock

*tree deformed by wind*
> wind cripple

*parapet-like natural formation atop a wall*
> battlement

*projecting or support-like natural formation*
> buttress

*extensive flat-topped land elevation that rises steeply on at least one side*
> plateau, tableland

*small and isolated plateau*
> mesa

*small mesa*
> mesilla

*isolated steep hill or small mountain (flat, rounded, cone-like, or pointed)*
> butte

*solitary and fragmentary mountain*
> inselberg

*series of mountains*
> range, chain

the swell. The trees, from our distance, might have been hazel; the beach might have been in Europe; the mountain forms behind modelled in little from the Alps, and the forest which clustered on their ramparts a growth no more considerable than our Scottish heath. Again the cliff yawned, but now with a deeper entry; and the *Casco*, hauling her wind, began to slide into the bay of Anaho.

ROBERT LOUIS STEVENSON, *In the South Seas*

High up on the plateau at the foot of the Blue Ridge Mountains, she saw rolling red hills wherever she looked, with huge outcroppings of the underlying granite and gaunt pines towering somberly everywhere. It all seemed wild and untamed to her coast-bred eyes accustomed to the quiet jungle beauty of the sea islands draped in their gray moss and tangled green, the white stretches of beach hot beneath a semitropic sun, the long flat vistas of sandy land studded with palmetto and palm.

MARGARET MITCHELL, *Gone with the Wind*

A world of uneven ground, of treeless hills and mist-filled hollows, of waterlogged past and heather-clad slopes, of high tors capped with broken granite, of hut circles and avenues of stones left by ancient peoples, Dartmoor extends over an area of between 200 and 300 square miles.

EDWIN WAY TEALE, *Springtime in Britain*

The primitive track we followed led toward Nab End along the great chasm of Yew Cogar Scar. When we stopped and walked to the edge of the gorge, our glance plunged down

*system of mountain chains (sometimes parallel)*
  cordillera

*chain of mountains with sawtooth-like peaks*
  sierra

*chain of hills or mountains*
  ridge, chine

*ridge dividing drainage directions and regions*
  watershed, divide

*area at the foot of a mountain range*
  piedmont

*slope of a mountain*
  mountainside, versant (of a mountain chain or region)

*slope of a hill*
  hillside

*right or left side of a formation or mountain*
  flank

*top of a mountain*
  peak, summit, pike

*exposed rock surface*
  face

*pyramidal peak usually with concave faces (where three or more arêtes meet)*
  horn

*elevation overlooking other terrain*
  heights

*elevated place*
  aerie, eyrie

*high and rugged mountain*
  alp

*mountain range section or mass*
  massif

*projection laterally or on an angle from a mountain*
  spur

the great dropoffs of the sheer walls into the depths of the narrow limestone valley.

EDWIN WAY TEALE, *Springtime in Britain*

On the other side, what seems to be an isolated patch of blue mist floats lightly on the glare of the horizon. This is the peninsula of Azuera, a wild chaos of sharp rocks and stony levels cut about by vertical ravines. It lies far out to sea like a rough head of stone stretched from a green-clad coast at the end of a slender neck of sand covered with thickets of thorny scrub.

JOSEPH CONRAD, *Nostromo*

Then, as the midday sun withdraws from the gulf the shadow of the mountains the clouds begin to roll out of the lower valleys. They swathe in sombre tatters the naked crags of precipices above the wooded slopes, hide the peaks, smoke in stormy trails across the snows of Higuerota. The Cordillera is gone from you as if it had dissolved itself into great piles of grey and black vapours that travel out slowly to seaward and vanish into thin air all along the front before the blazing heat of the day.

JOSEPH CONRAD, *Nostromo*

The sand bar of Eastham is the sea wall of the inlet. Its crest overhangs the beach, and from the high, wind-trampled rim, a long slope well overgrown with dune grass descends to the meadows on the west. Seen from the tower at Nauset, the land has an air of geographical simplicity; as a matter of fact, it is full of hollows, blind passages, and amphitheatres in which the roaring of the sea changes into the far roar of a cataract.

HENRY BESTON, *The Outermost House*

*mountain or hill protuberance*
  buttress

*area near the top or to the side of a mountain*
  shoulder

*rugged and sharp-crested mountain ridge*
  arête, hogback

*short mound or ridge*
  kame

*winding ridge that is gravelly or sandy*
  esker

*cliff formation or line of cliffs*
  scarp, escarpment, palisade, palisades

*jagged glacial ridge or pinnacle (as in an ice fall)*
  serac

*precipitous place*
  steep, precipice

*very steep descent or wall*
  drop-off

*steep vertical facing*
  wall, cliff, bluff, crag

*small space like a recess in a wall*
  niche

*projection of rock*
  outcrop, outcropping

*weathered quarry face*
  rock face

*steep and bare rocky outcrop or cliff*
  scar

*flat layer of rock*
  shelf

*narrow level space along or projecting from a cliff or slope*
  ledge, shelf

*cliff or wall projection viewed from below*
  overhang

Viewed from the seaward scarp of the moors, the marsh takes form as the greener floor of a great encirclement of rolling, tawny, and treeless land. From a marsh just below, the vast flat islands and winding rivers of the marsh run level to the yellow bulwark of the dunes, and at the end of the vista the eye escapes through valleys in the wall to the cold April blue of the North Atlantic plain.

HENRY BESTON, *The Outermost House*

From the verge of the water the land rises uniformly on all sides, with green and sloping acclivities, until from gently rolling hillsides and moderate elevations it insensibly swells into lofty and majestic heights, whose blue outlines, ranged all around, close in the view.

HERMAN MELVILLE, *Typee*

The glen of Tior will furnish a curious illustration of this. The inhabited part is not more than four miles in length, and varies in breadth from half a mile to less than a quarter. The rocky vine-clad cliffs on one side tower almost perpendicularly from their base to the height of at least fifteen hundred feet; while across the vale—in striking contrast to the scenery opposite—grass-grown elevations rise one above another in blooming terraces.

HERMAN MELVILLE, *Typee*

Following the ridge, which made a gradual descent to the south, I came at length to the brow of that massive cliff that stands between Indian Cañon and Yosemite Falls, and here the far-famed valley came suddenly into view throughout

*pointed rock formation*
  pinnacle

*long narrow opening*
  fissure, cleft, rift

*deep cleft through a mountain ridge*
  gap, notch

*channel or scoop-like depression between mountains*
  pass, col, saddle

*narrow pass between hills or cliffs*
  defile, gorge

*mountainside gorge or gully*
  couloir

*cleft that is steep and narrow in a cliff or mountain face*
  chimney

*bowl-like mountain basin with steep walls*
  cirque, cum, corrie, corry

*steep wall of a cirque*
  headwall

*roughly circular or oval flat area enclosed at one end by a curve of higher ground*
  amphitheater

*glacial fissure or crevice that is deep*
  crevasse, bergschrund

*series of crevasses*
  bergschrund

*granular or ice-like mountain (glacial) snow*
  névé, firn

*ledge-like plain above a river or body of water*
  terrace

*rocky detritus (debris) on a mountain slope*
  scree

almost its whole extent. The noble walls—sculptured into an endless variety of domes and gables, spires and battlements and plain mural precipices—all a-tremble with the thunder tones of the falling water. The level bottom seemed to be dressed like a garden—sunny meadows here and there, and groves of pine and oak; the river of Mercy sweeping in majesty through the midst of them and flashing back the sunbeams.        JOHN MUIR, *My First Summer in the Sierra*

They were in the hills now, among pines. Although the afternoon wind had fallen, the shaggy crests still made a constant murmuring sound in the high sere air. The trunks and the massy foliage were the harps and strings of afternoon; the barred inconstant shadow of the day's retrograde flowed steadily over them as they crossed the ridge and descended into shadow, into the azure bowl of evening, the windless well of night; the portcullis of sunset fell behind them.
                    WILLIAM FAULKNER, *The Hamlet*

To the east, under the spreading sunrise, are more mesas, more canyons, league on league of red cliff and arid tablelands, extending through purple haze over the bulging curve of the planet to the ranges of Colorado—a sea of desert.
                    EDWARD ABBEY, *Desert Solitaire*

Along the canyon walls are the seeps and springs that feed the stream, each with the characteristic clinging gardens of mosses, ferns and wildflowers. Above and beyond the rimrock, blue in shadow and amber-gold in light, are alcoves, domes and royal arches, part of the sandstone flanks of Navajo Mountain.        EDWARD ABBEY, *Desert Solitaire*

*rocky detritus beneath a cliff*
  talus

*slope formed of rocky detritus*
  talus

*glacial deposit of boulders and stones*
  moraine

*wall-like ridge or rocks, ice, debris, etc.*
  rampart

*sloping area of jumbled glacial ice blocks*
  icefall

*mountain (with a crater) formed by ejected material*
  volcano

*wide volcano crater (formed by eruptions or rim collapse)*
  caldera

*volcanic vapor hole*
  fumarole

*spring that at times throws up jets of hot water or steam*
  geyser

*extinct volcano crater often containing a lake or marsh*
  maar

*vast moving or spreading mass of ice*
  glacier

*vertical shaft (worn by falling surface water through a crack) in a glacier*
  moulin

*mantle of perennial ice and snow*
  ice cap, ice sheet

*sheet of floating ice*
  floe

*large floe*
  ice field

*mountain-like mass of floating ice*
  iceberg

Over your head Mount Davidson lifted its gray dome, and before and below you a rugged canyon clove the battlemented hills, making a sombre gateway through which a soft-tinted desert was glimpsed, with the silver thread of a river winding through it, bordered with trees which many miles of distance diminished to a delicate fringe; and still further away the snowy mountains rose up and stretched their long barrier to the filmy horizon—far enough beyond a lake that burned in the desert like a fallen sun, though that, itself, lay fifty miles removed.

MARK TWAIN, *Roughing It*


On either side rocks, cliffs, treetops and a steep slope: forward there, the length of the boat, a tamer descent, treeclad, with hints of pink: and then the jungly flat of the island, dense green, but drawn at the end to a pink tail. There, where the island petered out in water, was another island; a rock, almost detached, standing like a fort, facing them across the green with one bold, pink bastion.

WILLIAM GOLDING, *The Lord of the Flies*


Now the sea would suck down, making cascades and waterfalls of retreating water, would sink past the rocks and plaster down the seaweed like shining hair; then, pausing, gather and rise with a roar, irresistibly swelling over point and outcrop, climbing the little cliff, sending at last an arm of surf up a gully to end a yard or so from him in fingers of spray.

WILLIAM GOLDING, *The Lord of the Flies*


A part of the land towards the north rises more than a thousand feet perpendicularly from the sea. A tableland at this

*massed array of ice formations at sea*
   ice pack

*mass of ice fragments*
   brash

*fragment of thin ice near shore*
   pan

*submarine (undersea) mountain*
   seamount

*flat-topped seamount*
   guyot

*underground or rock-walled chamber*
   cave, cavern, grotto

*icicle-like formation hanging in a cave*
   stalactite, dripstone

*icicle-like formation on the floor of a cave*
   stalagmite, dripstone

*country route or path*
   trail, lane, track

*zigzagging path or road*
   switchback

*place suitable for crossing or zigzagging*
   traverse

*raised path or road across water or a marsh*
   causeway

*land arm almost completely surrounded by water*
   peninsula, chersonese

*land formation jutting into the sea or other large body of water*
   cape

*tongue (of land)*
   neck

*land tip or projection*
   point

height extends back nearly to the center of the island, and from this tableland arises a lofty cone like that of Teneriffe. The lower half of this cone is clothed with trees of good size, but the upper region is barren rock, usually hidden among the clouds, and covered with snow during the greater part of the year. There are no shoals or other dangers about the island, the shores being remarkably bold and the water deep. On the northwestern coast is a bay. . . .

EDGAR ALLAN POE,
*The Narrative of Arthur Gordon Pym of Nantucket*

The island in sight was Flores. It seemed only a mountain of mud standing up out of the dull mists of the sea. But as we bore down upon it, the sun came out and made it a beautiful picture—a mass of green farms and meadows that swelled up to a height of fifteen hundred feet, and mingled its upper outlines with the clouds. It was ribbed with sharp, steep ridges, and cloven with narrow canons [*sic*], and here and there on the heights, rocky upheavals shaped themselves into mimic battlements and castles; and out of rifted clouds came broad shafts of sunlight, that painted summit, and slope, and glen, with bands of fire, and left belts of sombre shade between.                MARK TWAIN, *Roughing It*

There was no bold mountainous shore, as we might have expected, but only isolated hills and mountains rising here and there from the plateau. The country is an archipelago of lakes,—the lake-country of New England.

HENRY DAVID THOREAU, *The Maine Woods*

*crescent-shaped arm of land*
   horn

*elevated land area jutting over the sea or other large body of water*
   headland, promontory, ness, naze

*neck or strip joining two larger masses of land*
   isthmus, neck

*strip of land (sometimes prehistoric or submerged) between two relatively large landmasses*
   land bridge

*land along the sea temporarily covered by tides or saturated during floods*
   tideland

*level area sometimes covered by water*
   tidal flat, mud flat

*land along a river subject to flooding*
   floodplain

*bordering terrain along a river*
   riverbank

*flat area encrusted with salt*
   salt flat

*narrow projection of sandy or gravel terrain*
   spit

*river mouth's (debouchment's) often fan-shaped sedimentary plain*
   delta, alluvial plain

*river (alluvial) land between a levee and its lower-water stage*
   batture

*sandbar connecting two islands or an island and its mainland*
   tombolo

*small jutting of sand or gravel at water's edge*
   spit, sandspit, reach

*flat place suitable for landing goods from a boat*
   landing

*channel or passage that runs beneath cliffs from the shore inland*
   gat

What is most striking in the Maine wilderness is the con-
tinuousness of the forest, with fewer open intervals or glades
than you had imagined. Except for the few burnt lands, the
narrow intervals on the rivers, the bare tops of the high
mountains, and the lakes and streams, the forest is uninter-
rupted.

HENRY DAVID THOREAU, *The Maine Woods*


These grass islands are a feature of the Amazon. They look
like lush pastures adrift. Some of them are so large it is difficult to believe they are really afloat till they come alongside. Then, if the river is at all broken by a breeze, the
meadow plainly undulates.

H. M. TOMLINSON, *The Sea and the Jungle*


In the northern cliff I could see even the boughs and trunks;
they were veins of silver in a mass of solid chrysolite. This
forest had not the rounded and dull verdure of our own
woods in midsummer, with deep bays of shadow. It was a
sheer front, uniform, shadowless, and astonishingly vivid.

H. M. TOMLINSON, *The Sea and the Jungle*


Passing between an isolated rock and the cape at the eastern
extremity of the cove, the canoe skirted the foot of a small
wooded valley, where huge old trees rose above an undergrowth of ferns and flowering shrubs.

CHARLES NORDHOFF AND
JAMES NORMAN HALL, *Pitcairn's Island*


It was an impressive lookout point. To the eastward the
main valley lay outspread. On the opposite side the land fell

*sea's juncture with a river's mouth*
  estuary

*sea inlet or arm*
  estuary, firth, frith

*shallow arm of the sea or of a river*
  wash

*connecting passage between two large bodies of water*
  strait, fretum

*wide strait or navigable connecting waterway*
  channel

*shoreline indentation*
  inlet

*shoreline indentation that is sheltered*
  cove, creek, hole, basin

*pool of water left after the tide recedes*
  tidal pool, tide pool

*pool of water between two beaches*
  beach pool

*shallow pond near a body of water*
  lagoon

*long lagoon near the sea*
  haff

*sea inlet that is extensive*
  gulf

*sea inlet smaller than a gulf*
  bay, embayment

*sea inlet or creek shallower inland*
  ria

*bay at a coastal bend*
  bight

*sea inlet that is long or separates an island from a mainland*
  sound

*sea inlet that is narrow and has steep slopes or cliffs*
  fjord, fiord

away in gullies and precipitous ravines to the sea. Several small cascades, the result of recent heavy rains, streamed down the rocky walls, arching away from them, in places, as they descended. Small as the island was, its aspect from that height had in it a quality of savage grandeur, and the rich green thickets on the gentler slopes, lying in the full splendour of the westering sun, added to the solemnity of narrow valleys already filling with shadow, and the bare precipices that hung above them.    CHARLES NORDHOFF AND

JAMES NORMAN HALL, *Pitcairn's Island*

Mombasa has all the look of a picture of Paradise painted by a small child. The deep Sea-arm round the island forms an ideal harbour; the land is made out of whitish coral-cliff grown with broad green mango trees and fantastic bald grey Baobab trees. The Sea at Mombasa is as blue as a cornflower, and, outside the inlet to the harbour, the long breakers of the Indian Ocean draw a thin crooked white line, and give out a low thunder even in the calmest weather.

ISAK DINESEN, *Out of Africa*

There is no trail up this gray valley, only dim paths that lose themselves in bogs and willow flats and gravel streams. Several hours pass before we come to the rock outwash of a chasm in the northern walls where the torrent comes down from the ice fields of Kang La. Even at midday the ravine is dark, and so steep and narrow that on the ascent under hanging rocks the torrent must be crossed over and over.

PETER MATTHIESSEN, *The Snow Leopard*

*shallow area of water*
  shallows

*land body surrounded by water*
  island, isle

*large group or chain of islands (or their ocean area)*
  archipelago

*small island*
  islet, ait, eyot

*low coral island or visible reef*
  cay, key

*ring-like coral island or reef surrounding a lagoon*
  atoll

*land border along water*
  coast, coastline, shore, shoreline, seaboard, littoral

*sandy margin along water*
  beach, strand, playa, lido

*pebbled or stony beach*
  shingle

*swampy coastline*
  maremma

*mound of accrued or windblown sand*
  dune

*crescent-like dune that shifts*
  barchan, barchane, barkhan

*shallow place in a sea or river*
  shoal

*submerged (or partly so) bank of sand or gravel obstructive to navigation*
  bar, sandbar, sandbank, shoal, reef

*coral ridge-like growth usually near the surface in warm seas*
  reef

In the bright September light and mountain shadow—steep foothills are closing in as the valley narrows, and the snow peaks to the north are no longer seen—the path follows a dike between the reedy canal and the green terraces of rice that descend in steps to the margins of the river. Across the canal, more terraces ascend to the crests of the high hills, and a blue sky.    PETER MATTHIESSEN, *The Snow Leopard*

My father and I began going down Fire Hill, the longer, and less steep, of the two hills on the road to Olinger and Alton. About halfway down, the embankment foliage fell away, and a wonderful view opened up. I saw across a little valley like the background of a Dürer. Lording it over a few acres of knolls and undulations draped with gray fences and dotted with rocks like brown sheep, there was a small house that seemed to have grown from the land.

JOHN UPDIKE, *The Centaur*

This solitary stone peak overlooks the whole of my childhood and youth, the great Salinas Valley stretching south for nearly a hundred miles, the town of Salinas where I was born now spreading like crab grass toward the foothills. Mount Toro, on the brother range to the west, was a rounded benign mountain, and to the north Monterey Bay shone like a blue platter.    JOHN STEINBECK, *Travels with Charley*

There were miles of pastures and tens of miles of wasted, washed-out land abandoned to the hardier weeds. The train cut through deep green pine forests where the ground was covered with the slick brown needles and the tops of the

*sea rock opening through which water intermittently spouts*
blowhole, gloup

*any flowing line of fresh water*
watercourse, course, channel, waterway, stream (archaic: freshet)

*junction of two rivers*
watersmeet

*inland-flowing course of fresh water smaller than a river*
stream, brook, creek

*small stream*
streamlet, brooklet, rivulet, rill, runnel, burn

*winding stream*
meander, serpentine

*winding stream dividing around a neck of land*
oxbow

*river or stream feeding a larger river*
tributary, feeder

*open stretch of river*
reach

*river's upper tributaries*
headwaters

*onrushing or raging stream*
torrent

*turbulent and rock-obstructed part of a river*
rapid, rapids

*steep rapids*
cataract

*abrupt or steep river descent*
chute

*narrow channel or strait with swift and dangerous waters*
euripus

*dangerously cross-currented or turbulent patch of water*
rip

trees stretched up virgin and tall into the sky. And farther, a long way south of the town, the cypress swamps—with the gnarled roots of the trees writhing down into the brackish waters, where the gray, tattered moss trailed from the branches, where tropical water flowers blossomed in dankness and gloom. Then out again into the open beneath the sun and the indigo-blue sky.

CARSON McCULLERS, *The Heart Is a Lonely Hunter*


He crawled up a small knoll and surveyed the prospect. There were no trees, no bushes, nothing but a gray sea of moss scarcely diversified by gray rocks, gray lakelets, and gray streamlets.    JACK LONDON, "Love of Life"


A film of mist hung over the inlet. A family of red-fronted geese rippled the water, and at the first gate more geese stood by a puddle. I passed along the track that led up into the mountains. Ahead was Harberton Mountain, black with trees, and a hazy sun coming over its shoulder. This side of the river was rolling grass country, burned out of the forest and spiked with charred trees.

BRUCE CHATWIN, *In Patagonia*


Above the tongue is North Otter Bay, which is deep; below it is South Otter Bay, so shoal as to be dangerous, in spots, to anything but a canoe. It was through the shallows of South Otter Bay that we dragged our boats ashore on the tongue of land along which the river pours itself into the lake; and it was across this tongue of land that we were obliged to carry the boats in order to get to the northward of the French.

KENNETH ROBERTS, *Northwest Passage*

*river or stream channel in a mountain ridge gap*
    water gap

*trough for water*
    run

*shallow area of water that can be waded across*
    ford

*inland body of (usually) fresh water*
    lake, loch, mere

*small lake or standing body of water*
    pond, lakelet, pondlet, pool, water hole

*artificial lake*
    reservoir

*small mountain lake with steep banks*
    tarn

*artificial pond subject to the tides of a river or stream*
    tidal basin

*stagnant pool*
    stagnum

*ocean, sea*
    the deep, the briny deep, blue water

*water moving in an inward (centripetal) circle*
    whirlpool, maelstrom, gurge, vortex

*small whirlpool*
    eddy

*waterfall*
    cataract, cascade

*dam in a stream*
    weir

*embankment to prevent river flooding*
    levee

*beach or harbor protective structure offshore*
    breakwater, mole

No sooner had we left the northern end of Missisquoi Bay that morning than we entered a spruce bog. The water was a foot deep, and in places even deeper, where the current had hollowed out channels like running brooks, into which we sometimes stumbled and sometimes fell full length.

KENNETH ROBERTS, *Northwest Passage*


Slowing on the current, I drifted past a hundred-yard gap in the false shore on the west side; it was no more than a sliver of woodland on a bar. Beyond it a watery stump field stretched away as far as I could see, the low stumps arranged with infinite regularity, like the flat tombstones in a Muslim graveyard.    JONATHAN RABAN, *Old Glory*


The river was squeezed into a twisty crevice between high bluffs, and the wind, thickened with sand from the bars, went scouring into every cranny and backwater. The forest came down sheer into the water on both sides, broken by outcrops of ribbed limestone, staring out of the solid cliffs of green like the faces of Easter Island statues.

JONATHAN RABAN, *Old Glory*


Now, after fourteen hours in the stream, a night of naps, and a soaking rain, we stand in the outlet of Allagash Lake. The most distant point we can see is perhaps four miles away—a clear shot down open water past a fleet of islands. The lake is broad in all directions, and is ringed with hills and minor mountains. Its pristine, unaltered shoreline is edged with rock—massive outcroppings, sloping into the water, inter- rupting the march of the forest.

JOHN MCPHEE, *The Survival of the Bark Canoe*

*pertaining to or like land*
    terrestrial

*pertaining to or like the ocean*
    oceanic, marine, pelagic, thalassic

*pertaining to the ocean depths or bottom*
    benthic, benthonic

*pertaining to or like a lake*
    lacustrine

*pertaining to or like a river*
    riverine, fluvial, amnic

*pertaining to or like a riverbank*
    riverain

*pertaining to or like a shore*
    littoral, riparian

*pertaining to or like a swamp*
    swampy, marshy, quaggy, boggy, paludal

*pertaining to or like a plain or field*
    campestral

*pertaining to or like a mountain*
    montane

*pertaining to or like an island*
    insular


*pertaining to a shore region moist but always above water*
    supralittoral

*pertaining to a shore region between the high-water and low-water line*
    littoral

*pertaining to an ocean zone from the low-water line to the edge of the continental shelf*
    sublittoral, neritic

*pertaining to an ocean zone from the continental shelf to a depth of some 13,000 feet (4,000 meters)*
    bathyal, bathypelagic

The canyon is a rudimentary steep *V,* the walls clay and silt. The river within looks slender and white from the air, but the damaged area is like an artillery range, pitted with boulders, heaped with khaki-colored debris.

EDWARD HOAGLAND, "River-Gray, River-Green"

We circled the lake, slipping into each estuary and up Soper Brook, then up Snare Brook. . . . The brooks were silty but the wetland grasses were a tender light-green.

EDWARD HOAGLAND, "Fred King on the Allagash"

As Ice Ages came and went and glaciers repeatedly advanced and retreated, a distinctive, fiercely-glaciated landscape was created. Valley troughs were deepened, smoothed and straightened; at the heads of the valleys, basin-like corries—the lofty nurseries of the glaciers—were slowly scooped out; knife-sharp arretes were honed as the steep corrie backwalls retreated and met; hummocks of ground-up rock debris were then dumped as moraine when the glaciers began to recede; and in the aftermath of glaciation, lakes formed in the hollows which the ice had gouged in the valley bottoms. Gradually, the deposition of river silts is filling up the lake basins, and eventually the lakes will disappear.

RICHARD MUIR, *The Stones of Britain*

The sheer flanks of the cañon descended in furrowed lines of vines and clinging bushes, like folds of falling skirts, until they broke again into flounces of spangled shrubbery over a broad level carpet of monkshood, mariposas, lupines, poppies, and daisies.

BRET HARTE, "The Youngest Miss Piper"

*pertaining to an ocean zone from some 13,000 feet (4,000 meters) to 20,000 feet (6,500 meters)*
    abyssal

*pertaining to an ocean zone deeper than 20,000 feet (6,500 meters)*
    hadal

# Climate

This was the manner of its coming. Before it, there was clear sky, and the sun shining upon new-fallen snow, a soft breeze from the west, moist and not cold. Then to the north was a line of high-banked, slate-gray cloud, and the mutter of thunder. Next, suddenly, the clouds darkened sun and sky, the north wind struck frigidly, and the air was thick with furious snow.                     GEORGE R. STEWART, *Storm*

Hour by hour the cloud-deck grew lower and thicker and darker; swift-blown scud sped beneath the low stratus, seeming to skim the wave-crests.

GEORGE R. STEWART, *Storm*

Blowing across the sky away from us is a cloud resembling a black wing, torn from the shoulder, pulling along behind it an immense dark pubic fleece.

EDMUND WHITE, *Forgetting Elena*

Above the whole valley, indeed, the sky was heavy with tumbling vapors, interspersed with which were tracts of blue, vividly brightened by the sun; but, in the east, where the tempest was yet trailing its ragged skirts, lay a dusky

*characterized by good weather*
   fair, clear, pleasant, lovely, balmy, halcyon, temperate

*characterized by bad weather*
   nasty, dirty, foul, inclement

*sunny*
   bright, cloudless, glorious, sunshiny

*intensely bright*
   glary, glaring, dazzling, blinding

*cloudy*
   cloud-covered, nebulous

*overcovered or blanketed with clouds*
   overcast, lowering, gray, gloomy, clouded up

*foggy*
   misty, thick, murky, vaporous, brumous

*windy*
   gusty, blowing, blowy, howling, roaring, turbulent,
   blustering

*breezy*
   airy, zephyrous

*stormy*
   tempestuous, raging, angry

*threatening*
   lowering, darkening, looming, black

region of cloud and sullen mist, in which some of the hills appeared of a dark-purple hue.

NATHANIEL HAWTHORNE, *The Marble Faun*


To-day is a grey day, and the sun as I write is hidden in thick clouds, high over Kettleness. Everything is grey—except the green grass, which seems like emerald amongst it; grey earthy rock; grey clouds, tinged with the sunburst at the far edge, hang over the grey sea, into which the sand-points stretch like grey fingers. The sea is tumbling in over the shallows and the sandy flats with a roar, muffled in the sea-mists drifting inland. The horizon is lost in a grey mist. All is vastness; the clouds are piled up like giant rocks, and there is a "brool" over the sea that sounds like some presage of doom.                          BRAM STOKER, *Dracula*


Sometimes, when they came down from the cirrus levels to catch a better wind, they would find themselves among the flocks of cumulus—huge towers of modelled vapour, look-ing as white as Monday's washing and as solid as meringues. Perhaps one of these piled-up blossoms of the sky, these snow-white droppings of a gigantic Pegasus, would lie before them several miles away.

T. H. WHITE, *The Once and Future King*

*damp*
> humid, muggy, dank, steamy, moist

*rainy or wet*
> precipitating, drizzly, drippy, torrential, showering, pouring

*dewy*
> roric, roriferous

*wet and cold*
> raw, bleak

*dry*
> arid, parched, dessicated, bone-dry, desert, waterless

*very warm*
> hot, torrid, burning, blazing, scorching, blistering, broiling, baking, searing, roasting, tropical, pitiless

*hot and humid*
> sultry, sweltering

*cold*
> chilly, nippy, sharp, algid

*very cold*
> biting, piercing, bone-chilling, freezing

*cool*
> chill, chilly

*refreshingly cool or chill*
> crisp, bracing, brisk

*snowing*
> snowy, niveous, nival

*frosty*
> rimy, hoary

*icy or frozen*
> frigid, freezing, gelid

# Clouds

. . . the train is rolling eastward and the changing wind veers for the moment from an easterly quarter, and we face east, like Swedenborg's angels, under a sky clear save where far to the northeast over distant mountains whose purple has faded, lies a mass of almost pure white clouds, suddenly, as by a light in an alabaster lamp, illumined from within by gold lightning, yet you can hear no thunder. . . .

MALCOLM LOWRY, *Under the Volcano*

When the sky was furrowed with whispy [*sic*] bands of altostratus cloud the colour ranged from the most delicate pearl-pinks to the deepest fiery red. Sometimes it was so breathtakingly beautiful that Donald and I rushed for our cameras to capture its ephemeral glory.

JOHN LISTER-KAYE, *The White Island*

It was a cloudy evening and as we arrived the sun disappeared into a glowing velvet bank of high cumulus cloud which obliterated Raasay from our view.

JOHN LISTER-KAYE, *The White Island*

It was quieter than the quietest night. And the clouds drifted across the sky with the same terrible, icy, inhuman slowness.

*Note: For remembering these Latinate cloud classifications (introduced in 1803 by English chemist Luke Howard), it is helpful to know the meanings of the key affixes:* cumulo-, *heap or pile;* strato-, *cover or layer;* cirro-, *curl or hair;* alto-, *high; and* nimbo-, *rain cloud.*

## (LOW-ELEVATION CLOUDS)

*stratus*
> cloud mass like a formless gray horizontal sheet, from which may come drizzle; the sky looks heavy and leaden; bases and tops of clouds are uniform.

*cumulus*
> separate, distinctively shaped puffs or fleecy domed or towered piles of cloud, brightly white in sunlight with darker base; upper parts often like cauliflower.

*stratocumulus*
> grayish, rounded, roll-like masses forming an extensive layer; often look like altocumulus but are lower.

*cumulonimbus*
> mountainously high and often dark storm cloud (or thunderheads) with swellings or "towers" and frequently a flattened, anvil-like top plume; often with ragged cloudlets underneath.

Also there were changes of colour. The scene became tinted with mauve. She watched cumulus gather on the horizon; saw it break into three, and with continuous changes of shape and colour the clouds started their journey across the sky.            D.M. THOMAS, *The White Hotel*

Ragged edges of black clouds peeped over the hills, and invisible thunderstorms circled outside, growing like wild beasts. . . . Before sunset the growling clouds carried with a rush the ridge of hills, and came tumbling down the inner slopes. Everything disappeared; black whirling vapours filled the bay, and in the midst of them the schooner swung here and there in the shifting gusts of wind.
            JOSEPH CONRAD, "Karain: A Memory"

At the base of this cliff of atmosphere cumulus clouds, moments ago as innocuous as flowers afloat in a pond, had begun to boil, their edges brilliant as marble against the blackening air.            JOHN UPDIKE, *The Witches of Eastwick*

Down river, from Andy's Landing, a burned-off cedar snag held the sun spitted like an apple, hissing and dripping juices against a grill of Indian Summer clouds. All the hillside, all the drying Himalaya vine that lined the big river, and the sugar-maple trees farther up, burned a dark brick and over-lit red.            KEN KESEY, *Sometimes a Great Notion*

## (Middle-Elevation Clouds)

*altostratus*
> a gray and smooth, sometimes striated or fibrous (string-like) uniform veil of grayish or bluish cloud through which the sun may palely shine (as if through frosted glass).

*altocumulus*
> cloud mass of various shapes, disconnected lumps or patches or a jumble of billowing cloudlets white or gray or both; sometimes lining up in parallel bands; sometimes with "towers," resembling cumulus.

*nimbostratus*
> an amorphous gray or dark cloud layer, blotting out the sun and often unseen because rain or snow is falling from it; sometimes with ragged clouds below.

## (High-Elevation Clouds)

*cirrus*
> delicate white wisps or filaments of cloud sometimes with a silky look; or like fibrous threads with hooks at the end; often seem to converge at a point on the horizon.

*cirrostratus*
> a thin, smooth, fibrous whitish cloud with which one often sees a halo effect around (but not obscuring) the sun; contourless and transparent, with no shadows cast on the ground.

*cirrocumulus*
> a thin white layer of cloud, with no shading and with a ripple or other regular pattern; usually too thin to cause shadows below; often known as "mackerel clouds" or "mackerel sky."

# ANIMALS

# Animals

The brown, or grizzly, bear (*Ursus arctos*) has a massive head and a concave facial profile. Its high shoulders produce a sloping back, emphasizing the animal's robust build. The polar bear has a more aristocratic profile—a long neck tapering to a smaller, V-shaped head. It carries itself low to the ground, out of the wind and out of sight.

JAMES SHREEVE, *Nature: The Other Earthlings*

In the Sunderbans, the tiger's favorite prey is the chital. This is a beautiful, gracefully proportioned deer, reddish brown in color, with one black stripe along its spine. Each white spot on its flanks is swept backward, hazy on the edges, giving the impression that the animal is speeding away even when it stands quite still.

JAMES SHREEVE, *Nature: The Other Earthlings*

In fact the koala is not a bear at all, but merely suggests one—a bear divested of danger, smaller, cuter, altogether a more predictable fellow. It has the slanted, beady eyes of a fearsome martinet, but they are rendered comical by bushy ears sprouting up like two enormous cowlicks. The koala's mouth is a tight and stubborn slit, but its severity is wholly undone by what appears to be a black rubber nose. The com-

*alligator*
    loricate

*ant*
    formic

*anteater*
    vermilingual

*ape*
    australopithecine, anthropoid

*ass*
    asinine

*baboon*
    cynocephalous

*badger*
    meline

*barracuda*
    sphyraenoid

*bat*
    verpertilian

*bear*
    ursine, arctoid

*beaver*
    casteroid

*bee*
    apian

*beetle*
    coleopterous, coleopteral

plete effect suggests an attempt at an authoritative demeanor that has turned out rather less than one had hoped—a dour schoolteacher proceeding through the geography lesson, unaware that his toupee is all askew.

> J A M E S   S H R E E V E ,   *Nature: The Other Earthlings*

Among the tenants of the eucaplytus [*sic*] trees are the marsupial gliders. These shy creatures are primarily nocturnal in their habits, and their moist, protuberant eyes gives [*sic*] them a characteristically wistful expression.

> J A M E S   S H R E E V E ,   *Nature: The Other Earthlings*

The herring gulls come first, to the biggest island, where the lighthouse stands. . . . Among them are two or three pairs of great black-backed gulls, massive, hoarse-voiced and vulturine.

> G A V I N   M A X W E L L ,   *Ring of Bright Water*

The waterfalls of the Sierra are frequented by only one bird,—the Ouzel or Water Thrush (*Cinclus Mexicanus,* Sw.). He is a singularly joyous and lovable little fellow, about the size of a robin, clad in a plain waterproof suit of bluish gray, with a tinge of chocolate on the head and shoulders. In form he is about as smoothly plump and compact as a pebble that has been whirled in a pot-hole, the flowing contour of his body being interrupted only by his strong feet and bill, the crisp wing-tips, and the up-slanted wren-like tail.

> J O H N   M U I R ,   *The Mountains of California*

Just as surprised as I, he stood up. He must have construed the sounds of my advance to be those of another sheep or

*bird*
> avian, avine, volucrine

*bison*
> bisontine, bisonic

*buffalo*
> buteonine

*bull*
> bovine, taurine

*butterfly*
> lepidopteral, lepidopteran, lepidopterous, papilionaceous, pierid, rhopalocerous

*buzzard*
> buteonine

*calf*
> vituline

*camel*
> cameline

*cat*
> feline, feliform

*catfish*
> silurid, siluroid

*centipede*
> myriapodous, myriapodan

*chameleon*
> vermilingual

*chipmunk*
> spermophiline

*cobra*
> cobriform

*cod*
> gadoid

*cow*
> vaccine

*crab*
> carcinomorphic, arthropodous, arthropodal

goat. His horns had made a complete curl and then some; they were thick, massive and bunched together like a high Roman helmet, and he himself was muscly and military, with a grave-looking nose. A squared-off, middle-aged, trophy-type ram, full of imposing professionalism, he was at the stage of life when rams sometimes stop herding and live as rogues.

EDWARD HOAGLAND, *Walking the Dead Diamond River*

It was a biped; its almost globular body was poised on a tripod of two froglike legs and a long thick tail, and its fore limbs, which grotesquely caricatured the human hand, much as a frog's do, carried a long shaft of bone, tipped with copper. The colour of the creature was variegated; its head, hands, and legs were purple; but its skin, which hung loosely upon it, even as clothes might do, was a phosphorescent grey. And it stood there blinded by the light.

H. G. WELLS, "In the Abyss"

It was the head of a veritable sea monster, so huge and so hideous that, if the Old Man of the Sea himself had come up, he could not have made such an impression on us. The head was broad and flat like a frog's, with two small eyes right at the sides, and a toadlike jaw which was four or five feet wide and had long fringes drooping from the corners of the mouth. Behind the head was an enormous body ending in a long thin tail with a pointed tail fin which stood straight up and showed that this sea monster was not any kind of whale. The body looked brownish under the water, but both head and body were thickly covered with small white spots.

THOR HEYERDAHL, *Kon-Tiki*

*crane*
> grallatory

*cricket*
> grillid, grilline

*crocodile*
> loricate, crocodilian, emydosaurian

*crow*
> corvine

*cuckoo*
> cuculine

*deer*
> cervine

*dinosaur*
> dinosaurian, dinosauric

*diving bird*
> urinatorial

*dog*
> canine, cynoid

*dolphin*
> delphin

*dove (also, pigeon and dodo)*
> columbine

*dragonfly*
> odonatous, libelluloid

*duck*
> anatine

*dugong*
> sirenian

*eagle*
> aquiline

*earthworm*
> lumbricoid

*eel*
> anguilliform

The grizzly is set apart from other bears not only by its light-colored shaggy coat but by its high shoulder hump, formed by a mass of powerful muscles that drive the front legs. Its head is massive, its ears small and its forehead high—all of which combine to give its face a concave, or "dished," profile.

PETER FARB, *The Land and the Wildlife of North America*

Lo and behold, here in the creek was a silly-looking coot. It looked like a black and gray duck, but its head was smaller; its clunky white bill sloped straight from the curve of its skull like a cone from its base. I had read somewhere that coots were shy. They were liable to take umbrage at a footfall, skitter terrified along the water, and take to the air. But I wanted a good look. So when the coot tipped tail and dove, I raced towards it across the snow and hid behind a cedar trunk. As it popped up again its neck was as rigid and eyes as blank as a rubber duck's in the bathtub.

ANNIE DILLARD, *Pilgrim at Tinker Creek*

When I lose interest in a given bird, I try to renew it by looking at the bird in either of two ways. I imagine neutrinos passing through its feathers and into its heart and lungs, or I reverse its evolution and imagine it as a lizard. I see its scaled legs and that naked ring around a shiny eye; I shrink and deplume its feathers to lizard scales, unhorn its lipless mouth, and set it stalking dragonflies, cool-eyed, under a palmetto.

ANNIE DILLARD, *Pilgrim at Tinker Creek*

*elephant*
elephantine, pachydermoid, proboscidian

*elk*
alcine

*falcon*
falconine, falconoid

*fish*
ichthyoid, piscial, piscine

*flamingo*
phoenicopterous

*flea*
pulicid, pulicous

*fly*
muscid

*fowl (chicken, turkeys, etc.)*
gallinaceous, galline

*fox*
vulpine, vulpecular, alopecoid

*frog*
ranine, raniform, batrachian

*giraffe*
giraffine, camelopardine

*goat*
hircine, culiciform, capric, caprine

*goose*
anserine

*gopher*
spermophiline

*gorilla*
gorilloid, gorilline, gorillian

*grasshopper (also, cricket)*
orthopterous

*gull*
larine, laridine

Newts are the most common of salamanders. Their skin is a lighted green, like water in a sunlit pond, and rows of very bright red dots line their backs. They have gills as larvae; as they grow they turn a luminescent red, lose their gills, and walk out of the water to spend a few years padding around in damp places on the forest floor. Their feet look like fingered baby hands, and they walk in the same leg patterns as all four-footed creatures—dogs, mules, and, for that matter, lesser pandas.    ANNIE DILLARD, *Pilgrim at Tinker Creek*

By then (March 1961) Chaka (a leopard cub) was two months old. He had a beautiful glossy coat and well-defined rosettes on his golden yellow body. His snow-white belly had distinct black spots. The black and white stripes on his coat were very clear, setting off to perfection his immaculate white chin.    VIVIAN J. WILSON, *Orphans of the Wild*

His captor had been clearing grass for a new maize garden when he disturbed an adult serval. He found a single male kitten in a nest in the tall grass. It had a long, fluffy, soft coat—a pale sandy-brown color—very closely spotted over the dorsal surface. His eyes were open but he could not really see well. The little ears were already erect, very black, and with a dull, dirty-white crossbar.
VIVIAN J. WILSON, *Orphans of the Wild*

Caracals flicking their long sharp-tipped and slender ears are a delight to watch. They are often pitch-black with a long tassel of hair. The outside of the ears is covered with silver hair while the inside is light grey. A black spot on either side

*hare*
> leporine, lagomorphic

*hawk*
> acciptrine

*hedgehog*
> erinaceous

*hen*
> gallinaceous

*hermit crab*
> pagurian

*heron*
> grallatory

*herring*
> clupeoid

*hippopotamus*
> hippopotamic

*hog*
> suilline

*horse*
> equine, caballine, chevaline

*housefly*
> muscid, musciform

*hyena*
> hyenic, hyaenic

*insect*
> entomologic, insectaean, insectival

*jellyfish*
> acalephan

*kangaroo*
> macropodine, macropoid

*king crab*
> limuloid

*lamb*
> agnine

of the face near the muzzle, and a black line from the eye to the nose, with some white on the chin and at the base of the ear, make the caracal's face one of the most beautiful of the African felines.

VIVIAN J. WILSON, *Orphans of the Wild*

A litter of cone-flakes on a forest path betrays the red squirrel sleeping on a branch above. With its tufted ears and tail of fine hairs curled over its back and projecting an inch in front of its face, it resembles a large hairy fir cone.

RICHARD PERRY, *Life in Forest and Jungle*

The 4-foot-long tree pangolins are almost exclusively arboreal, descending to the ground only infrequently at night. Pangolins—those elongated armadillos—have been described as mammals disguised as saurians, for their bodies and very long tails are armored with horny, leaf-shaped, sharp-edged and overlapping scales inserted into the skin by one edge and erectable like a bird's feathers; only the face and narrow toothless muzzle, the ventral parts and the inner surface of the feet are unprotected.

RICHARD PERRY, *Life in Forest and Jungle*

With rounded muzzle, short neck, backward-pointing horns and low forequarters, a duiker (the Africaans [*sic*] "diver") slips through the shrubbery with a minimum of effort, eluding the hunting leopard by agility rather than speed, twisting and turning as it weaves through the densest undergrowth, a barely detectable gray or brown form.

RICHARD PERRY, *Life in Forest and Jungle*

*leech*
> hirudinoid, bdelloid

*lemur*
> lemurine, lemuroid

*leopard*
> pardine, feline

*lion*
> leonine

*lizard*
> lacertilian, lacertine, lacertian, saurian

*lobster*
> crustacean, macrural, homarine, homaroid

*lynx*
> lyncian

*mackerel*
> scombrid, scombroid

*manatee*
> sirenian, manatine, trichechine

*mite, tick*
> acaridal, acarine

*mole*
> talpine

*mongoose*
> herpestine

*monkey*
> simian, simioid, simious, pithecoid, pithecan

*mosquito*
> culicine, culicid

*moth*
> heterocerous

*mouse*
> murine, murid

*octopus*
> octopean, octopine, cephalopodous

Rich reddish-brown or vivid orange in color, with white ear-tassels, dorsal ridges of white and black hair, and short razor-sharp tusks capable of disemboweling a leopard, bushpigs are the most spectacular of their kind.

RICHARD PERRY, *Life in Forest and Jungle*

The carrier, more especially the male bird, is also remarkable from the wonderful development of the carunculated skin about the head, and this is accompanied by greatly elongated eyelids, very large external orifices to the nostrils and a wide gape of mouth.

CHARLES DARWIN, *The Origin of Species*

For instance, the several species of the Chthamalinae (a subfamily of sessile cirripedes) coat the rocks all over the world in infinite numbers: they are all strictly littoral, with the exception of a single Mediterranean species, which inhabits deep water and has been found fossil in Sicily, whereas not one other species has hitherto been found in any tertiary formation. . . .

CHARLES DARWIN, *The Origin of Species*

The golden hamster hardly ever climbs, and gnaws so little that he can be allowed to run freely about the room where he will do no appreciable damage. Besides this, this animal is externally the neatest little chap, with his fat head, his big eyes, peering so cannily into the world that they give the impression that he is much cleverer than he really is, and the gaily coloured markings of his gold, black and white coat. Then his movements are so comical that he is ever and again

*ostrich*
struthious, struthionine

*otter*
lutrine

*owl*
strigine

*oyster*
ostreoid, ostriform

*panther*
pantherine

*parrot*
psittacine, psittaceous

*parrot fish*
scaroid

*peacock*
pavonine

*penguin*
spheniscine, impennate

*pig*
porcine, suine

*pigeon*
peristeronic

*poisonous snake*
thanatophidian

*porcupine*
hystricoid, hystricine

*porpoise*
phocaenine

*pouched animal*
marsupial, didelphian

*python*
pythonic

*rabbit*
cunicular

the source of friendly laughter when he comes hurrying, as though pushed along, on his little short legs, or when he suddenly stands upright, like a tiny pillar driven into the floor and, with stiffly pricked ears and bulging eyes, appears to be on the look-out for some imaginary danger.

KONRAD LORENZ, *King Solomon's Ring*

Like penguins, the water-shrews looked rather awkward and ungainly on dry land but were transformed into objects of elegance and grace on entering the water. As long as they walked, their strongly convex underside made them look pot-bellied and reminiscent of an old overfed dachshund.

KONRAD LORENZ, *King Solomon's Ring*

Wild dogs visited the pool, first two, then the whole pack. The strange bat-eared creatures circled around behind the car with curiosity, emitting that odd grunt-bark of alarm that contrasts so strangely with their birdlike twitterings of greet-ings and contentment. These were all good-looking animals, with shining black masks and brindle on the nape and shoul-ders, glossy black and yellow-silver bodies, irregularly splotched, and alert clean white-tipped tails.

PETER MATTHIESSEN, *Sand Rivers*

The lead bull had imposing horns, which glinted in the sun like horns of buffalo, but such horns are ill-suited to a long sad face with odd ginger eyebrows. The wildebeest has a goat's beard and a lion's mane and a slanty back like a hyena; the head is too big and the tail too long for this rickety thing, and Africans say that the wildebeest is a collection of the

*raccoon*
  procyanine
*ram*
  arietine
*rat*
  murine, murid
*rattlesnake*
  crotaline
*ray*
  batoid
*reindeer*
  rangiferine
*reptile*
  reptilian, reptiloid, herpetiform
*rodent*
  glirine, gliriform, rodential
*seacow*
  sirenian
*seal*
  sphragistic, phocine, pinnepedian, otarine
*shark*
  squaloid, squaliform, selachian
*sheep*
  ovine
*shrew*
  soricine, soricoid
*shrimp*
  caridoid
*skunk*
  mephitine
*sloth*
  edentate
*slug*
  limacine

parts that were left over after God had finished up all other creatures.                    PETER MATTHIESSEN, *Sand Rivers*

Though her ears are high, the rhinoceros makes no move at all, there is no twitch of her loose hide, no swell or raising of the ribs, which are outlined in darker gray on the barrel flanks, as if holding her breath might render her invisible. The tiny eyes are hidden in the bags of skin, and though her head is high, extended toward us, the great hump of the shoulders rises higher still, higher even than the tips of those coarse dusty horns that are worth more than their weight in gold in the Levant. Just once, the big ears give a twitch; otherwise she remains motionless, as the two oxpeckers attending her squall uneasily, and a zebra yaps nervously back in the trees.                    PETER MATTHIESSEN, *Sand Rivers*

The Virginia opossum is a large rat-shaped creature, much be-whiskered, with an untidy shaggy coat, button eyes and a long naked tail which it can wrap round a branch with sufficient strength to support its own weight for a little time at least. It has a large mouth that it opens alarmingly wide to expose a great number of small sharp teeth.

DAVID ATTENBOROUGH, *Life on Earth*

The most arboreal of all the lemurs—it hardly ever comes down to the ground—is a close relation of the sifaka, the indri. It is the biggest of all living lemurs with a head and body nearly a metre long. It is boldly marked with a variable black and white pattern and its tail is reduced to a tiny stump in its fur. Its legs are even longer in proportion than those of

*snail*
> gastropodous

*snake*
> ophidian, sinerous, anguine, anguineous, serpentine, anguiform

*songbird*
> oscine

*spider*
> arachnoid, araneiform

*squirrel*
> sciuroid, sciurine, spermophiline

*starfish*
> asteroidal

*stork*
> ciconine, herodian, herodionine

*swan*
> cygnine

*tapeworm*
> taeniid, taenial

*tick, mite*
> acaridal, acarine

*tiger*
> tigerish, tigrine, tigerine, feline

*tortoise*
> testudinal

*turtle*
> chelonian

*viper*
> viperine

*vulture*
> vulturine, vulturial

*wading bird*
> grallatory

*walrus*
> pinniped

a sifaka, the big toes are widely separated from the rest and about twice the length, so that each foot resembles a huge caliper with which the animal can grasp even thick trunks.

DAVID ATTENBOROUGH,  *Life on Earth*

The smallest of the group is the mouse lemur, with a snub nose and large appealing eyes, that scampers through the thinnest twigs. The indri has a closely related noctural equivalent, the avahi, very similar in appearance and size except that its fur, instead of being black and white is grey and woolly. Oddest and most specialised of all is the aye-aye. Its body is about the size of that of an otter, it has black shaggy fur, a bushy tail and large membranous ears. One finger on each hand is enormously elongated and seemingly withered, so that it has become a bony articulated probe.

DAVID ATTENBOROUGH,  *Life on Earth*

Late in the afternoon a pod of twenty or so gleaming-black pilot whales, their bulbous foreheads and sickle-shaped dorsal fins unmistakable even at a distance, lazed with indifference near the *Arctic Endeavour*.

LES LINE,  *The Audubon Wildlife Treasury*

Averaging perhaps twenty pounds, the wildcat seems to be a miniature cross between a tiger and a leopard, with a bit of mountain lion thrown in. Its rust-brown coat shows spots and flecks above and a suggestion of dark stripes below, blending into a white belly. Heavy lines on its wide-flaring cheek fur break up the outline of its face so it can see without being seen. A little tuft of hair on each ear serves as an

*wasp*
   vespine

*weasel*
   musteline

*whale*
   cetacean, cetaceous

*wild boar*
   aprine

*wolf*
   lupine

*woodpecker*
   piciform, picine

*worm*
   vermicular, vermiform, vermian

*zebra*
   zebrine, hippotigrine

antenna which is sensitive to sounds or air currents. Its whiskers, bedded in delicate nerves, may lie back—or reach out to determine if a certain opening will admit its body.

LES LINE, *The Audubon Wildlife Treasury*

The medieval monster was more massive than any dog, with a disproportionately large head that was wedge-shaped and elongated, ending in a pig's snout. The body was at its highest behind the head, diminishing toward the hindquarters, from which a short, tufted, and upturned tail projected. This great mass was supported on relatively short, sticklike legs. The whole was clothed in thick coarse hair, black and white mixed to make gray—except that the feet and ears were black, as was a mane that rose like a crest from the top of the forehead to the middle of the back.

LES LINE, *The Audubon Wildlife Treasury*

The alligator when full grown is a very large and terrible creature, and of prodigious strength, activity and swiftness in the water. I have seen them twenty feet in length, and some are supposed to be twenty-two or twenty-three feet. Their body is as large as that of a horse; their shape exactly resembles that of a lizard, except their tail, which is flat or cuneiform, being compressed on each side, and gradually diminishing from the abdomen to the extremity, which with the whole body is covered with horny plates or squammae, impenetrable. . . .

WILLIAM BARTRAM, *Bartram's Travels*

The bulky body of the Muskrat is about a foot long and is covered with two kinds of hair: a short beautiful undercoat

*single-celled or acellular animal*
  protozoon

*organism without a spinal column*
  invertebrate

*organism with a spinal column*
  vertebrate

*animal with hair that nourishes young with milk*
  mammal, mammalian

*animal in family Hominidae (or that of man)*
  hominid

*animal in superfamily of primates (man and apes)*
  hominoid

*hoofed and usually horned herbivorous animal*
  ungulate

*cud-chewing and even-toed animal*
  ruminant

*animal with an abdominal pouch for the young*
  marsupial

*animal feeding on refuse or carrion*
  scavenger

*animal usually with a shell and jointed limbs*
  arthropod

*small and large members of the cat family*
  felines

of soft and silky brown fur and a long coat of coarser hair. Its stout naked tail—almost as long as its body—is vertically flattened to aid in propulsion and steering when the animal is swimming. Its hind feet are partially webbed as another aid to progress in the water.

JOHN KIERAN, *Natural History of New York City*

My first mountain beaver had gone head-first into a trap set at its burrow mouth by my cousin, Mary V., on her parents' ranch above the Oregon coast. It was a grayish, unprepossessing-looking creature about a foot long, weighing two to five pounds. The appearance, to my five-year-old eyes, was grotesque: squinched slits where the eyes should be; crinkly, bare ears; no tail worthy of the name; toes splayed out exactly like those in illustrations of dinosaurs (but otherwise no similarity to the giant reptiles); four curving teeth stained as if from eons of conscientious tobacco chewing.

IRVING PETITE, *The Elderberry Tree*

Among these insectivores it is possible to distinguish various standard forms. Thus the "shrew" type comprises animals that are usually small, with a long muzzle, short, five-toed feet and a fairly long tail. Most are plantigrades, scurrying through the dense undergrowth and feeding on tiny invertebrates.    AUGUSTO TAGLIANTI, *The World of Mammals*

Despite being arboreal the gibbons of the subfamily Hylobatinae are the only monkeys that spontaneously adopt the bipedal stance when on the ground. Their walk is, however, rather odd and clumsy. The gibbons are also note-

*squirrels and other relatively small gnawing animals*
 rodents

*seals and other flippered aquatic animals*
 pinnipeds

worthy for their exceptionally long arms and legs, especially the former, and for the absence of a tail.

AUGUSTO TAGLIANTI, *The World of Mammals*

The diet of tree-shrews is largely insectivorous and partly frugivorous, but in fact they are omnivorous and will eat anything that is digestible.

M. F. ASHLEY MONTAGU,
*An Introduction to Physical Anthropology*

The muskox has a single living relative, the takin of northern Tibet, a calflike animal of ponderous build with a bulging snout like a saiga antelope's, short, stout legs, and small, swept-back horns, showing the same montane sheep/goat ancestry in its conformation and movements as the modern muskox.         BARRY LOPEZ, *Arctic Dreams*

Where the brown bear is broad-shouldered and dish-faced, the polar bear is narrow shouldered and Roman-nosed. His neck is longer, his head smaller. He stands taller than the brown bear but is less robust in the chest and generally of lighter build. The polar bear's feet are larger and thickly furred between the pads. The toes are partially webbed, the blackish-brown claws sharper and smaller than the brown bear's. It lacks the brown bear's shoulder hump and more expressive face, with its prehensile lips, well suited to stripping bushes of their berries.

BARRY LOPEZ, *Arctic Dreams*

*Note: Most of the following categorized terms, simple and in common usage, are presented here as a kind of checklist for the writer. They reflect the plain idiom used in most guides identifying different species of animals, and are included here to help remind the writer which aspects of an animal should not be forgotten in attempting to describe it.*

*Size*
very large, massive, giant
large
greater
medium, intermediate
lesser
small
very small, pygmy

*General Behavior*
active
dormant

solitary, reclusive
gregarious, social

sedentary, settled
nomadic, migrating

*Development*
full-grown, mature
young, immature

The havtagai which, like domestic camels, have long lashes to shade their eyes from the sun's glare, nostrils that can be closed against wind-driven sand, and two toes linked by pads that spread their weight over the shifting sand, differ from them in being uniformly sandy-colored, whereas domestic camels may also be dark brown, black, or even white. They differ also in their longer though fine-boned legs (lacking callosities) and small feet and pads that leave a footprint about half the size of a domestic camel's, in the thinner texture of their coats and the absence of mane and beard, and in their humps, which are small pointed cones and invariably firm, in contrast to those of domestic camels, which vary in size and condition according to their owner's health.

RICHARD PERRY, *Life in Desert and Plain*

Go to the meatmarket of a Saturday night and see the crowds of live bipeds staring up at the long rows of dead quadrupeds. Does not that sight take a tooth out of the cannibal's jaw?    HERMAN MELVILLE, *Moby-Dick*

Adults may reach a length of six feet, excluding the stumpy tail, and weigh over 300 pounds. The thick, woolly coat is white, the legs, ears and patches around the eyes are black, and a black band reaches from the forelegs across the shoulders. The head is massive, and the skull provided with large ridges to which are attached the jaw muscles.

NOEL SIMON AND PAUL GEROUDET, *Last Survivors*

The snub-nosed (or golden) monkey is related to the langurs, but separated from them by an absence of cheek

*Body*
long-bodied
short-bodied
heavy-bodied, stocky, stubby, chunky
low-slung
sleek-bodied, slender

*Coloration*
plain
colorful

marked
unmarked

regular (markings)
irregular
uniform
variable
alternating
dense
scattered

tinged, tinted, tipped, ringed (spots)

buff
tawny
dusky
grizzled

*Areas of Body*
above
below
on the back or top side, dorsal
on or along the side, lateral
on the stomach or underside, ventral

upperpart
underpart

front, anterior
hind, posterior

pouches and other anatomical differences. The species is distinguished by the thick-set body and sturdy limbs, with arms only a little shorter than the legs. The most distinctive external features are the long golden coat, which becomes denser and more brightly coloured with advancing age, and the bizarre snub-nose, which in adult males is so preposterously upturned that its tip reaches almost to the forehead.

NOEL SIMON AND PAUL GEROUDET, *Last Survivors*

The monkey-eating eagle of the Philippines has a striking appearance with a superb "mane" of long tapering feathers covering its head and the nape of its neck, which it bushes out or raises at will and which, when excited, it wears like a warlike head-dress. Its bluish eyes and enormous curved beak, flattened on the sides, gives it an expression of extreme ferocity. The two sexes are alike, clad in dark brown plumage, striped with paler edges and whitish on the upper part.

NOEL SIMON AND PAUL GEROUDET, *Last Survivors*

The Asiatic and African elephants are easily distinguishable. The Asiatic species is the smaller; the curvature of its back is convex; its skin is smooth and marked with white or pink depigmentation spots, which become more numerous with age; its ears are small and triangular-shaped; its forehead is prominently domed; its trunk is tipped with only a single finger-like protuberance; the female is tuskless, or more accurately, the tusks are so small that they do not protrude beyond the lips—and tuskless males are common.

NOEL SIMON AND PAUL GEROUDET, *Last Survivors*

close together
widely spaced
joined
webbed
separated

near the attachment point, proximal
in the middle, mesial
at the end or extremity, distal, terminal

*Parts of Body*
well-developed
poorly developed
undeveloped or no longer used as a body part, vestigial

prominent, conspicuous
projecting, bulbous
distinguishing
sharply defined

protective
humped
armored
mantled (fold-like or hood-like)

elongate, elongated
broad
narrow

widening
tapering
flattened
curved upward, recurved
curved downward

sharp, pointed
blunt, rounded
angular, squarish, flattened

enlarged
reduced

The snow leopard, or ounce, is slightly smaller than the common leopard, and among the most attractive of all the great cats. In winter coat the fur [*sic*], particularly on the lower parts, is unusually long, with thick woolly under-fur. This, in conjunction with the short muzzle, has the effect of making the head appear disproportionately small. The general ground colour is pale charcoal, faintly tinged with cream: the under parts up to the chin are milk white. The black rosettes are large, irregularly shaped, and randomly distributed. The markings on the head, along the spine, and on the upper part of the tail are well defined, but where the fur is long they are somewhat blurred: the pattern is more distinct in summer coat. The tail is long and densely furred, with large rosettes on the upper surface, white beneath, and black-tipped.

NOEL SIMON AND PAUL GEROUDET, *Last Survivors*


Suddenly the water heaved and a round, shining, black thing like a cannon-ball came into sight. Then he saw eyes and mouth—a puffing mouth bearded with bubbles. More of the thing came up out of the water. It was gleaming black. Finally it splashed and wallowed to the shore and rose, steaming, on its hind legs—six or seven feet high and too thin for its height, like everything in Malacandra. It had a coat of thick black hair, lucid as seal-skin, very short legs with webbed feet, a broad beaver-like or fish-like tail, strong forelimbs with webbed claws or fingers, and some complication half-way up the belly which Ransom took to be its genitals. It was something like a penguin, something like an otter, something like a seal; the slenderness and flexibility of the body suggested a giant stoat. The great round head, heavily whiskered, was mainly responsible for the suggestion

erect
trailing

stiff
loose

legless
limbless

long-legged
short-legged

long-tailed
short-tailed
bushy-tailed
keeled (upright and ridge-like)

odd-toed
even-toed

opposable (thumb)

long-snouted
short-snouted

long-necked
short-necked

lidded
lidless

fixed (upper or lower jaw)
movable

long-eared
short-eared

branched horns
unbranched horns

with claws
without claws

smooth
wrinkled

of seal; but it was higher in the forehead than a seal's and the mouth was smaller.

C. S. LEWIS, *Out of the Silent Planet*

I am not a naturalist, nor have we on board a book of zoology, so the most I can do is to describe him. He is almost my height (nearly five feet ten inches) and appears to be sturdily built. Feet and hands are human in appearance except that they have a bulbous, skew, arthritic look common to monkeys. He is muscular and covered with fine reddish-brown hair. One can see the whiteness of his tendons when he stretches an arm or leg. I have mentioned the sharp, dazzling white teeth, set in rows like a trap, canine and pointed. His face is curiously delicate, and covered with orange hair leading to a snow-white crown of fur. My breath nearly failed when I looked into his eyes, for they are a bright, penetrating blue.

MARK HELPRIN, "Letters from the *Samantha*"

The eyes of the buffalo were glazing over, his tongue stuck out, and blood was streaming into the dry ground. Round and round the dead beast Clint walked, looking again and again at the great black head with its short shiny dark horns, the shaggy shoulders and breast, the tufts of hair down the forelegs.

ZANE GREY, *Fighting Caravans*

The smallest of the tree flocks consisted of about fifteen gobblers. They were huge, wary birds. They were the most beautiful wild things that he had seen. Most were dark, purple-breasted, with a long beard, and a small cunning red

light-furred
dark-furred
bushy, shaggy, luxuriant
fringed
barbed

glossy
dull
silky
velvety
cottony
leathery

light-plumaged
dark-plumaged

head, dark in the back, flecked with brown, and they had a spread of reddish-white tail that dazzled Clint.

ZANE GREY, *Fighting Caravans*

Adela Pingsford said nothing, but led the way to her garden. It was normally a fair-sized garden, but it looked small in comparison with the ox, a huge mottled brute, dull red about the head and shoulders, passing to dirty white on the flanks and hind-quarters, with shaggy ears and large blood-shot eyes.

SAKI, "The Stalled Ox"

Fearsome lizards five or six feet long pounded over the ground and leaped lithely for high tree branches, as at home off the earth as on it; they were goannas. And there were many other lizards, smaller but some no less frightening, adorned with horny triceratopean ruffs about their necks, or with swollen, bright-blue tongues.

COLLEEN McCULLOUGH, *The Thorn Birds*

No coral snake this, with slim, tapering body, ringed like a wasp with brilliant colors; but thick and blunt with lurid scales, blotched with black; also a broad, flat murderous head, with stony, ice-like, whity-blue eyes, cold enough to freeze a victim's blood in its veins and make it sit still, like some wide-eyed creature carved in stone, waiting for the sharp, inevitable stroke—so swift, at last, so long in coming.

W. H. HUDSON, *Green Mansions*

Sometimes King Pellinore could be descried galloping over the purlieus after the Beast, or with the Beast after him if

# Zoological (Technical) Terminology

*warm-blooded*
    endothermic, homoiothermic
*cold-blooded*
    ectothermic, poikilothermic

*active during daylight*
    diurnal
*active at night*
    nocturnal
*active at dawn or twilight*
    crepuscular

*passing the winter in a lethargic and low-metabolic state*
    hibernating
*passing the summer in a lethargic and low-metabolic state*
    aestivating

*two-legged*
    bicrural
*two-footed*
    biped
*four-footed*
    quadruped, tetrapod
*many-footed*
    polyped
*having no feet*
    apodal

they happened to have got muddled up. Cully lost the vertical stripes of his first year's plumage and became greyer, grimmer, madder, and distinguished by smart horizontal bars where the long stripes had been.

T . H . W H I T E ,   *The Once and Future King*

The straw-coloured fruit-bat, called *abu regai* or *el hafash* by the Baggara Arabs and *ko-jok* by the Nuba, is a very handsome creature for a bat. It is readily recognized by the orange-yellow ruff, brown back and blackish wings but otherwise straw-yellow body. Large specimens have a wingspan of nearly two and a half feet and a body about eight inches long. With tall pointed ears, long foxy face and large, dark, intelligent eyes it is an attractive animal.

R . C . H .   S W E E N E Y ,   *Grappling with a Griffon*

The tadpoles in the quiet bay of the brook are now far past the stage of inky black little wrigglers attached by their two little sticky pads to any stick or leaf, merely breathing through their gills, and lashing with their hair-fine cilia. A dark brown skin—really gold spots mottling the black— now proclaims the leopard frogs they will become.

D O N A L D   C U L R O S S   P E A T T I E ,   *An Almanac for Moderns*

The cottonmouth (*Agkistrodon piscivorus*) may grow 6 feet long, though the average is about half that size. It is brown with indistinct black bands; its yellow belly may have dark markings as well, and a dark band runs from the eye to the corner of the mouth. It is distinguished from nonpoisonous water snakes by its deep spade-shaped head, light lips and white mouth.   P H I L I P   K O P P E R ,   *The Wild Edge*

*having hand-like feet*
  pedimanous, pedimane

*having arms*
  brachiate
*two-handed*
  bimanous
*having nails or claws*
  unguiculate

*having feathered feet*
  plumiped, braccate
*web-footed*
  palmiped

*capable of grasping*
  prehensile
*capable of being extended*
  protractile, protrusile
*capable of being drawn back*
  retractile

*scratching the ground for food*
  rasorial

*having ears*
  aurated

*having a tail*
  caudate
*having no tail*
  anurous
*having a tail with colored bands*
  ring-tailed

*having horns*
  corniculate

In contrast, the common dolphin (*Delphinus delphis*) often leaps from the water and plays in the bow waves of boats. Its taller dorsal fin has a curved trailing edge. Also called the saddleback, Delphinus has a black back, white belly and distinctive crisscross pattern along the sides.

PHILIP KOPPER, *The Wild Edge*

With renewed enthusiasm I dug on and was soon rewarded by the sight of the inhabitant—a gopher tortoise. Reaching into the tunnel, I grasped one stubby foreleg and tried to pull it out but found that it had apparently wedged itself so tightly in the narrow passage that I was forced to dig again. Eventually I dug around the specimen and hauled the struggling creature out. It was an adult, about eight inches across and slate-black in color. Its feet were elephant-like and bore blunt claws instead of toes, an ideal arrangement for digging. Its dome-like carapace was set with diamond-shaped plates in which the yearly growth rings or zones could clearly be discerned.     ROSS E. HUTCHINS, *Island of Adventure*

Weighing only about seven pounds, the southern gray fox is smaller than the better-known red fox. Its grizzled, salt-and-pepper-gray body, with rusty red along the sides and neck, is about two feet long; the black-tipped bushy gray tail, with a black streak along its top, adds another twelve or fourteen inches to the fox's length. He stands not much more than a foot above the ground at the shoulders, and when he trots, his paw marks along his trail are about eleven inches apart.

JOHN K. TERRES, *From Laurel Hill to Siler's Bog*

*having no horns*
    acerous

*having two teeth*
    bidentate

*having no teeth*
    edentate

*having two antennae or tentacles*
    dicerous

*not adapted to flying*
    flightless

*having wings*
    pennate, alate

*having no wings*
    apterous

*having feathers*
    plumaged, plumose

*having a beak*
    rostrate, rhamphoid

*having scales*
    squamate, squamous, squamose

*shedding or peeling off scales*
    desquamate

*having a bony or horny shell-like case*
    loricate

*having gills*
    branchiate

*having a thick hide*
    pachydermatous

But this was not a beaver. Although its fur, like a beaver's, was rich brown and glossy, I could see that the animal was smaller. Besides, I knew muskrats on sight, having trapped them when I was a boy. This one weighed about three pounds—they weigh from one and a half to four pounds—and it was about twenty inches long from the tip of its moist black nose to the end of its naked tail. The nine-inch tail, had I any doubt of what the animal was, identified it for me: a black, slender, thinner-then-high tail; not the wide, flat, boardlike tail of a beaver.

JOHN K. TERRES, *From Laurel Hill to Siler's Bog*


Barred owls are beginning to call as the raccoons first look out of their tree hollows at oncoming night. Their rounded furry ears point forward then back, catching every sound—the snap of a twig under a deer's hoof, the far baying of a distant hound, the lightest tread of a passing fox, the faintest squeak of a shrew or a mouse. As they peer dark-eyed from their black-masked faces, they lift their slender muzzles to sniff the night.

JOHN K. TERRES, *From Laurel Hill to Siler's Bog*


But hold it I did, and looked it over well, for it isn't often I can close my hands on such an exquisite minikin. Its snippet of a buff nose came to a rounded point under high-perched eyes brightly edged in gold. One brown polka-dot marked the space between each two lines of its cross, and narrow bands of brown decorated its frantically springing thighs. The soft skin of its underparts was finely granular, beigey-white with a hint of greenish, and its wrinkled throat was lightly touched with yellow. No webbing at all between its

*having a rough skin with sharp points*
    muricate

*having no hair*
    naked, hairless

*having fur (pelage)*
    furred, furry

*having shiny fur*
    sleek-furred

*having soft hair*
    pilose

*having bristles or spines*
    spiny, hispid, setaceous

*covered with bristles or spines*
    echinate

*covered with small bristles of spines*
    echinulate

*divided into defined segments or sections*
    segmented

*of two colors*
    bicolored

*of three colors*
    tricolored

*having stripes*
    striped, banded

*having long markings or somewhat uneven stripes*
    streaked

*having longitudinal stripes*
    vittate

*having transverse or crosswise stripes*
    cross-banded, cross-barred

long fingers and only a trace between its toes. Fingers and toes so delicate, so fine, and the climbing discs upon them infinitesimal but distinct. The whole adult peeper so minute it hid itself completely under the end of my thumb.

MARY LEICESTER, *Wildlings*

There is almost no way to explain a takin. Part this, part that, it looks as if it humbly adopted all the attributes that other goats and antelopes refused. Ponderous and unwieldy, its heavy body sits on fat, stubby legs, and is covered with a dingy, drab coat. Its horns look like a cross between those of the gnu and musk ox, and its face seems to have suffered a terrible accident, while the expression of its droopy lips makes one think it has been sucking a mixture of lemon and garlic.    EDWARD W. CRONIN, JR., *The Arun*

Now—the date being October 21, 1945—I hold in the hollow of my hand the body of a little bird killed last night in its migration by flying against a railing atop the roof. I saw it lying in the sunlight on the tarred roof this morning, when I went up there, a creature hardly larger than a mouse, with flaming gold breast streaked with black, and gold elsewhere or russet blending into brown and black. It has a slender, pointed black bill. Its fragile, polished black feet simply hang from it, the toes grasping nothing. You would be surprised, holding it in your hand, at how soft and thick is its coat of feathers. The plumage is most of the bird, for the body is simply a small hard core at the center which you feel with your fingers pinching through the downy mass.

LOUIS J. HALLE, *Spring in Washington*

*having spots of color (or black and white)*
spotted, mottled, maculate, liturate

*having small spots of color (or black and white)*
flecked, freckled, speckled, specked, stippled, irrorate

*having large and irregular spots*
blotched

*having black-and-white blotches*
piebald

*having patches of white and a color not black*
skewbald

*having a mask-like facial marking or coloration*
masked

*having a visibly collar-like part or marking*
collared, ruffed

*having a tuft or ridge-like formation on the head or back*
crested

*having a fin along the back*
fin-backed

*having a highly developed sense of smell*
macrosmatic

*having a weakly developed sense of smell*
microsmatic

*having virtually no sense of smell*
anosmatic

*imitative in color or form*
apatetic

*warning off by colors or changes in the body*
aposematic

*serving to conceal*
cryptic

*imitating other things by using something as a covering*
allocryptic

The possums are dark brown all over, as large as a domestic cat, and have long tails, bushy to their very tips. They are unmistakably Brush-tipped Ringtails. A male sits lower in the tree than the rest of the group and the strong spotlight reveals his features. He has broad, well muscled shoulders covered in a mantle of inch-long silky fur, much silkier than that of any other possum. His large dark brown eyes too are different from those of most possums; they are set more to the front of the face. His broad naked nose and deep jaw gives a chunky look to his profile.

STANLEY AND KAY BREEDEN,
*Wildlife of Eastern Australia*

Two kinds of geckoes live in these highlands. On the tree trunks lives the Leaf-tailed Gecko. In day-time he is a mere mottled green smudge as he lies flattened against a giant tree trunk and is virtually invisible. His fringed sides and broad tail do not even cast a tell-tale shadow and his huge lidless eyes are a maze of green and black squiggles which also match his surroundings. No bird or other predator has sight keen enough to detect him. As long as he does not move he is safe.

STANLEY AND KAY BREEDEN,
*Wildlife of Eastern Australia*

Only a Lumholtz Tree Kangaroo moves in the crown of a tall tree. He shuffles along a horizontal branch on his thickly padded, black feet and feeds on a branch which he has pulled towards him with his powerful arms. He eats first the leaves then rips off strips of bark with his strong teeth. He is sombre coloured; his round face, limbs and underside of the tail are black, his back is grey with patches of orange-fawn on the

*giving birth to young rather than producing eggs*
  viviparous

*laying eggs*
  oviparous

*laying eggs but retaining them until hatching time*
  ovoviviparous

*widely distributed around the globe*
  cosmopolitan

*dwelling in a particular region*
  endemic

*dwelling in the same region or overlapping regions*
  sympatric

*dwelling in different regions*
  allopatric

*dwelling in the air*
  aerial

*dwelling on the ground*
  terrestrial, terricolous

*dwelling (insects) at or near the ground's surface*
  epigeal

*dwelling underground*
  subterranean, hypogeous

*dwelling in caverns*
  cavernicolous

*dwelling in burrows*
  cunicular

*dwelling (insects) under a stone*
  lapidicolous

*dwelling in a tube*
  tubicolous

*dwelling in mud*
  limicolous

*dwelling in dung*
  coprophilous, coprozoic, stercoricolous

flanks, arms and underside. While eating he squats low on the branch, a powerful dark figure in the shadowless early light.                    STANLEY AND KAY BREEDEN,
*Wildlife of Eastern Australia*


Although very light birds, they are fairly large, with a wing-span of about seven feet; when sitting they cross their wings swallowlike over their backs. Although their feet are small, unwebbed, and useless for walking or swimming, frigates can perch with great ease on twigs and branches, either with two toes forward and two back, or three forward and one back. The beak is about four inches long, strongly hooked, and has a sharp tip. It is perfectly adapted for snatching fish from just below the surface, picking up floating organic de-bris, or lifting twigs from the ground or from another bird, while in full flight.    IAN THORNTON, *Darwin's Islands*


The shrew is a ferocious and deadly little animal. If it were larger—it is less than the size of a mouse—it would perhaps be one of the most feared animals in the world. It has a narrow, tapering snout; close, dark, sooty-velvet fur; and needle teeth. A poison gland in its mouth sends venom into its victim when it bites, and its prey dies quickly.
VIRGINIA S. EIFERT, *Journeys in Green Places*


The pronghorns are distinctive in other ways. Both sexes may have horns, but the horns of the female never exceed the length of the ears. The horns are composed of fused hairs which cover a bony core. The horn sheath is shed annually. The rump patch, which resembles a huge powder puff when

*dwelling in the desert*
deserticolous

*dwelling (or burrowing) in sand*
arenicolous

*dwelling in meadows or fields*
practicolous, arvicoline

*dwelling in woodlands*
silvicolous

*dwelling in trees*
arboreal

*dwelling in hedges*
sepicolous

*dwelling in mountains*
montane

*dwelling in rocks*
petricolous, saxicolous

*dwelling on land and in water*
amphibian

*dwelling in water*
aquatic

*dwelling in fresh water*
freshwater

*dwelling in the sea*
oceanic, pelagic, marine, maricolous

*dwelling in active or moving waters*
lotic

*dwelling in still or slow-moving waters*
lentic

*dwelling along the seacoast*
littoral, orarian, limicoline

*dwelling in rivers or streams*
riverine, riparian, riparial, riparious, riparicolous

the hairs are erected, acts as an alarm device. When the white hairs are erected they reflect a large amount of light.

DAVID F. COSTELLO, *The Prairie World*

About half the bulk and weight of thar, chamois are natives of European and Asian alps. For their handsome appearance, golden brown in summer with dark facial stripe between the sharply pointed ears and muzzle, black legs and short upright horns curved backwards at the tops to form semicircular hooks, they were considered 'royal' beasts, being also a challenge to hunt, good to eat, and providing buckskin.

BETTY BROWNLIE AND RONALD LOCKLEY, *The Secrets of Natural New Zealand*

I have even mentioned White-footed mice. Yes, it is a *kind* of mouse, with—giving a splendid boost to the good sense of name-givers—white feet. It (this mouse) also has a white belly and a bi-colored tail, the under half of which is white all down its length. He eats whatever mice eat (which is not at all cheese, but native seeds, roots, and some small insects), and has white whiskers and a line of demarcation between the expansive white belly and his back which is a soft, fawn-colored brown (generally). He has large ears, two cutting incisors above and two below, and large coal-black eyes, and his name is *Peromyscus*. He is clean, noninfectious, industrious, and thoroughly American. And, as I say, he has white feet.     RUSSELL PETERSON, *Another View of the City*

We had just climbed over a high dune, when we saw a strange-looking creature moving along the top of a ridge

*dwelling in marshes*
palustrine, helobious, paludicolous, paludous

*dwelling in estuaries*
estuarine

*dwelling in the deep sea*
autopelagic

*dwelling in deep water but coming at times to the surface*
spanipelagic

*dwelling on the bottom of a body of water or of the sea*
benthic, benthonic

*migrating from fresh water to the sea to spawn*
catadromous

*migrating from the sea to streams to spawn*
anadromous

*nest-building*
nidificant

*staying in the nest for a period after hatching*
nidicolous

*leaving the nest soon after hatching*
nidifugous

*dwelling in or sharing a nest with another animal*
nidicolous

*dwelling in the nest of another species*
inquiline

*helpless when hatched and needing parental care for a considerable time*
altricial

*independently active to a considerable degree after hatching*
precocial

*eating one type of food*
monophagous

*eating virtually everything*
omnivorous

ahead of us. It appeared to be a rat and had very long back legs, and a long tail ending in a bushy tuft. Its body was upright and its small forelegs were tucked under its chin. It walked along on its hind legs like a kangaroo. Then it caught sight of us with its massive saucer eyes, or sensed our presence with its lengthy moustache hairs. Its great ears twitched and it turned its head to look at us for a brief moment.

VICTOR HOWELLS, *A Naturalist in Palestine*

The lizard's tail was curled up behind while it walked, being uncurled only when angered. It had a flattened head with a lifted-up projection on top, pointed backwards over its body, to give the animal a most fearsome and yet comic aspect. Its comic appearance was added to by its most peculiar eyes. Each eye was fixed deep in a horny cone that protruded out from either side of the head. . . . This lizard was of course the well-known chameleon. . . .

VICTOR HOWELLS, *A Naturalist in Palestine*

The smaller one was flattened against the ground, front legs tensed, ready to spring. Its mate circled slowly to the left, keeping its distance, until it was only possible to hold them both in her field of vision by letting her eyes flicker between them. In this way she saw them as a juddering accumulation of disjointed details: the alien black gums, slack black lips rimmed by salt, a thread of saliva breaking, the fissures on a tongue that ran to smoothness along its curling edge, a yellow-red eye and eyeball muck spiking the fur, open sores on a foreleg, and, trapped in the V of an open mouth, deep in the hinge of the jaw, a little foam, to which her gaze kept

*eating living organisms*
    biophagous

*eating few types of food*
    stenophagous

*eating a moderate variety of foods*
    polyphagous

*eating a wide variety of foods*
    euryphagous, pantophagous

*animal- and vegetable-eating*
    omnivorous, amphivorous

*flesh-eating*
    carnivorous, amophagous, creophagous

*feeding on other animals*
    predatory, predaceous, raptorial

*eating its own kind*
    cannibalistic

*eating human flesh*
    anthropophagous

*eating horse flesh*
    equivorous

*plant-eating*
    herbivorous, vegetarian

*plant-eating (insects and lower animals)*
    phytophagous, phytivorous

*fish-eating*
    piscivorous, ichthyophagous

*fruit-eating*
    frugivorous, fructivorous

*insect-eating*
    insectivorous

*carrion-eating*
    necrophagous, scavenging

*dung-eating*
    coprophagous

returning. The dogs had brought with them their own cloud
of flies.                                   IAN MCEWAN, *Black Dogs*

There were three kittens at the end of a strange new passageway, three kittens with their blue-gray eyes but a few days
open, peering up at him from a mossy, hair-lined nest. Except for the nub of a tiny tail, and the tassels of hair at the tip
of each tiny ear, they looked much the same as barn kittens
that Henry drowned by the sackful every summer.

KEN KESEY, *Sometimes a Great Notion*

On his knees, and with his chin level with the top of the
table, Stephen watched the male mantis step cautiously towards the female mantis. She was a fine strapping green
specimen, and she stood upright on her four back legs, her
front pair dangling devoutly; from time to time a tremor
caused her heavy body to oscillate over the thin suspending
limbs, and each time the brown male shot back. He advanced lengthways, with his body parallel to the table-top,
his long, toothed, predatory front legs stretching out tenta-
tively and his antennae trained forwards: even in this strong
light Stephen could see the curious inner glow of his big oval
eyes.                      PATRICK O'BRIAN, *Master and Commander*

Solid black except for a white belly mark between the flippers, the pothead or pilot whale has a globular forehead as
round as an antique iron kettle. The sloping dorsal fin, much
wider at its base than at the top, has a deeply curved trailing
edge.                                PHILIP KOPPER, *The Wild Edge*

*feeding on decomposing matter*
saprophagous

*grass-eating*
graminivorous

*grain-eating*
granivorous

*berry-eating*
baccivorous

*nut-eating*
nucivorous

*rice-eating*
oryzivorous

*leaf-eating*
phyllophagous

*worm-eating*
vermivorous

*bone-eating*
ossivorous

*wood-eating*
hylophagous

*egg-eating*
oophagous

*seed-eating*
seminivorous

*feeding on ants*
myrmecophagous

*feeding on flowers*
anthophilous, anthophagous

*capable of movement*
motile

*"sitting" or not capable of movement*
sessile

*walking with the body erect*
orthograde

A popular prototype, the common and justly famous Atlantic blue crab is green on top and whitish below. The female's claws are tipped with red while the male's have bright azure highlights. Gender (and in the female, maturity) can also be told by the shape of a structure on the bottom shell called "apron" by diners or "abdomen" by biologists. The male's resembles the stem of a champagne glass, its foot aligned with the back edge of the shell. In the virginal female or "she-crab" the apron is an isosceles triangle. The sexually mature (and almost invariably pregnant) "sook" wears a semicircular apron with a small triangular point during the last stage of her life.   PHILIP KOPPER, *The Wild Edge*

Like all sharks, the dogfish lacks gill covers. Instead it has gill slits rather like straightened chevrons on a policeman's collar. The shape and number are characteristic for each species. Its skin is rough due to pointed triangular scales that look like microscopic teeth and are composed of similar material.
PHILIP KOPPER, *The Wild Edge*

The cottonmouth (*Agkistrodon piscivorus*) may grow 6 feet long, though the average is about half that size. It is brown with indistinct black bands; its yellow belly may have dark markings as well, and a dark band runs from the eye to the corner of the mouth. It is distinguished from nonpoisonous water snakes by its deep spade-shaped head, light lips and white mouth.   PHILIP KOPPER, *The Wild Edge*

*walking with the body virtually horizontal*
    pronograde

*walking on the sole of the foot*
    plantigrade

*walking with the back part of the foot raised*
    digitigrade

*walking on hoofs*
    unguligrade

*walking by fins or flippers*
    pinnigrade

*walking backward*
    retrograde

*moving sideways*
    laterigrade

*creeping*
    reptant, repent

*creeping like a worm*
    vermigrade

*climbing*
    scansorial

*wading*
    grallatorial

*burrowing*
    fossorial

*moving by swinging the arms*
    brachiating

*slow-moving*
    tardigrade

it while foraging in the open. In contrast, the rufous-sided towhee has striking plumage of black, white, and rusty red, and rarely forages in the open, preferring to search for seeds among the dense litter of forest brush or chaparral, where its varicolored coat blends into the dappled light and shade.

STEPHEN WHITNEY,
*A Sierra Club Naturalist's Guide to the Sierra Nevada*

Chipmunks, however, are smaller, less plump and have stripes along the sides of their heads, which the ground squirrel lacks. The stripes down the backs of both the golden-mantled ground squirrel and chipmunks serve to camouflage the animals from their numerous predators, blending with the irregular textures and broken patterns of light characteristic of the forest floor.

STEPHEN WHITNEY,
*A Sierra Club Naturalist's Guide to the Sierra Nevada*

Black-chinned nectar hunters hovered now before the crimson of a mallow, now before the blue of a morning-glory. One rufous hummingbird perched on the same twig during periods of rest for three days in a row. According to the angle of the light, its tail appeared rufous or cinnamon-hued. Turning in the sun, a female Anna's hummingbird, larger than a ruby-throat, flashed on and off like the beam of a lighthouse, a dazzling red spot that shone jewellike at its throat. Once Connie pointed out the slightly decurved bill and deeply forked tail of a lucifer hummingbird.

EDWIN WAY TEALE, *Wandering through Winter*

# PEOPLE

A lean face, pitted and scarred, very thick black eyebrows, and carbon-black eyes with deep grainy circles of black under them. A heavy five o'clock shadow. But the skin under all was pale and unhealthy-looking.

E. L. DOCTOROW, *Loon Lake*

He was a large heavy man. He was bearded. His hair was overgrown and unkempt. His eyes were blue and set in a field of pink that suggested a history of torments and conflicts past ordinary understanding. His weight and size seemed to amplify the act of breathing, which took place through his mouth. His nose looked swollen, a web of fine purple lines ran up his cheeks from the undergrowth, and all the ravage together told of the drinker.

E. L. DOCTOROW, *Loon Lake*

Webb is the oldest man of their regular foursome, fifty and then some—a lean thoughtful gentleman in roofing and siding contracting and supply with a calming gravel voice, his long face broken into longitudinal strips by creases and his hazel eyes almost lost under an amber tangle of eyebrows. He is the steadiest golfer, too. The one unsteady thing about him, he is on his third wife; this is Cindy, a plump brown-

*attractive or beautiful*
>pretty, handsome, comely, prepossessing, becoming, lovely, appealing, beauteous, exquisite, adorable, gorgeous, cute, pulchritudinous, ravishing, stunning, good-looking, fair, well-favored, pleasing, breathtaking, bonny

*ordinary*
>nondescript, plain, undistinguished, unremarkable

*unattractive*
>unbecoming, unappealing, ugly, homely, unprepossessing, unsightly, hideous, repugnant, repellent, repulsive, unlovely, ill-favored, ill-featured

backed honey still smelling of high school, though they have
two little ones, a boy and a girl, ages five and three. Her hair
is cut short and lies wet in one direction, as if surfacing from
a dive, and when she smiles her teeth look unnaturally even
and white in her tan face, with pink spots of peeling on the
roundest part of her cheeks; she has an exciting sexually
neutral look, though her boobs slosh and shiver in the triangular little hammocks of her bra.

JOHN UPDIKE, *Rabbit Is Rich*

Janice is thickening through the middle at the age of forty-
four but her legs are still hard and neat. And brown. She was
always dark-complected and with July not even here she has
the tan of a savage, legs and arms almost black like some little
Polynesian in an old Jon Hall movie. Her lower lip bears a
trace of zinc oxide, which is sexy, even though he never
loved that stubborn slotlike set her mouth gets. Her still-wet
hair pulled back reveals a high forehead somewhat mottled,
like brown paper where water has been dropped and dried.

JOHN UPDIKE, *Rabbit Is Rich*

And he saw her, with the dumb, pale, startled ghosts of joy
and desire hovering in him yet, a thin, vivid, dark-eyed girl,
with something Indian in her cheekbones and her carriage
and her hair; looking at him with that look in which were
blended mockery, affection, desire, impatience, and scorn;
dressed in the flamelike colors that, in fact, she had seldom
worn, but that he always thought of her as wearing.

JAMES BALDWIN, *Go Tell It on the Mountain*

*of average or medium size or height*
average, medium, middling, normal

*having a smooth body*
hairless
*having a hairy body*
hirsute, shaggy
*having a solid build*
stocky, thickset, heavyset, chunky, heavy-built, bulky, compact, beefy
*muscular*
sinewy, well-built, solid, athletic, brawny, burly, husky, mesomorphic, sturdy, robust, muscle-bound

*having a relatively straight frame*
angular

*having a flexible body*
limber, supple, lithe, lithesome, lissome, pliant, rubbery

*not erect or upright*
bent, stopped, bent over, slumped, hunched over
*having the shoulders bent forward*
round-shouldered, stoop-shouldered

*large or big*
hulking, giant, strapping, oversized, hefty, massive, elephantine, heavy-bodied, lumpish, looming, monstrous, a colossus, a goliath

I looked at the mouth of the boy Jody had wanted me to meet. His lips were thick and pink and a baby face nestled under the silk of white-blond hair.

SYLVIA PLATH, *The Bell Jar*

Winnie was barely into her thirties but she had a sane and practiced eye for the half-concealed disasters that constitute a life. A narrow face partly hidden by wispy brown ringlets, eyes bright and excited. She had the beaky and hollow-boned look of a great wading creature. Small prim mouth. A smile that was permanently in conflict with some inner stricture against the seductiveness of humor.

DON DELILLO, *White Noise*

Herr Landauer was a small lively man, with dark leathery wrinkled skin, like an old well-polished boot. He had shiny brown boot-button eyes and low-comedian's eyebrows—so thick and black that they looked as if they had been touched up with burnt cork.

CHRISTOPHER ISHERWOOD, *Goodbye to Berlin*

Otto has a face like a very ripe peach. His hair is fair and thick, growing low on his forehead. He has small sparkling eyes, full of naughtiness, and a wide, disarming grin, which is much too innocent to be true. When he grins, two large dimples appear in his peach-blossom cheeks.

CHRISTOPHER ISHERWOOD, *Goodbye to Berlin*

*small or little*
> slight, petite, diminutive, tiny, undersized, small-boned, wee, a shrimp, a snip, a pipsqueak

*small and supple*
> wiry

*rounded in form*
> plump, chubby, rotund, tubby, blubbery, roly-poly, round-bodied, well-rounded, pyknic, endomorphic, having embonpoint

*fat*
> obese, stout, corpulent, overweight, portly, adipose, fattish, stoutish, fleshy, bloated, gross, a blimp, a tub of lard

*fat and short-winded*
> pursy

*having loose or limp flesh*
> flabby, flaccid, soft, slack, irresilient, quaggy

*having hanging flesh*
> pendulous, baggy, loppy, drooping, droopy, nutant

*thin*
> slim, slender, slight, spare, skinny, ectomorphic, thin as a rail, bony, reedy, underweight

*thin and fit*
> trim, lean

*elegantly or sleekly thin*
> willowy, svelte, lissome

*thin and large-framed*
> rawboned

*thin and worn-looking*
> haggard, gaunt, emaciated, shriveled, underfed, scrawny, scraggy

*delicately thin*
> wraith-like, sylph-like, fragile, wispy, undernourished, skin and bone

His face was not as square as his son's and, indeed, the chin, though firm enough in outline, retreated a little, and the lips, ambiguous, were curtained by a moustache. But there was no external hint of weakness. The eyes, if capable of kindness and good-fellowship, if ruddy for the moment with tears, were the eyes of one who could not be driven. The forehead, too, was like Charles's. High and straight, brown and polished, merging abruptly into temples and skull, it had the effect of a bastion that protected his head from the world.            E. M. FORSTER, *Howards End*

She was one of those women who are middle-aged too soon, her skin burned into the colors of false health. Thin, nervous, her face was screwed tight, and in those moments when she relaxed, the lines around her forehead and mouth were exaggerated, for the sun had not touched them. Pale haggard eyes looked out from sun-reddened lids. She was wearing an expensive dress but had only succeeded in making it look dowdy. The bones of her chest stood out, and a sort of ruffle fluttered on her freckled skin with a parched rustling movement like a spinster's parlor curtain.

NORMAN MAILER, *The Deer Park*

He was a tall heavy man with silver hair and a red complexion, but even with his white summer suit and hand-painted tie he was far from attractive. Underneath the sun tan, his features were poor; his eyes were small and pouched, his nose was flat, and his chin ran into the bulge of his neck. He had a close resemblance to a bullfrog.

NORMAN MAILER, *The Deer Park*

*deathly thin*
> spectral, cadaverous, skeletal, consumptive, wasted away

*tall*
> tallish, long-limbed

*tall and thin*
> gangling, gangly, rangy, long-limbed, loose-jointed, spindly, slab-sided, a beanpole

*short*
> undersized, runty, runtish, dwarfish, bantam

*short and fat*
> a butterball

*short and heavy*
> squat, pudgy, fubsy (British), stumpy, like a fireplug

*shapelessly short and thick*
> dumpy

*broad-shouldered*
> square-shouldered, square-built

*having a broad upper torso*
> barrel-chested

*having a large belly*
> pot-bellied, paunchy, abdominous, swag-bellied, ventripotent, gorbellied (obsolete), beer-bellied

*having a proportionally short upper body (or high waistline)*
> short-waisted

*having large hips*
> wide in the middle, broad in the beam, hippy

*having thin hips*
> slim-hipped, narrow-hipped

*having long arms and legs*
> long-limbed

*having long legs*
> leggy

She was one of those pudgy-faced Victorian children with little black beads for eyes; an endearing little turnip with black hair.

JOHN FOWLES,    *The French Lieutenant's Woman*

Suddenly she looked at Charles, a swift sideways and upward glance from those almost exophthalmic dark-brown eyes with their clear whites: a look both timid and forbidding.

JOHN FOWLES,    *The French Lieutenant's Woman*

It was the French Lieutenant's Woman. Part of her hair had become loose and half covered her cheek. On the Cobb it had seemed to him a dark brown; now he saw that it had red tints, a rich warmth, and without the then indispensable gloss of feminine hair oil. The skin below seemed very brown, almost ruddy, in that light, as if the girl cared more for health than a fashionably pale and languid-cheeked complexion. A strong nose, heavy eyebrows . . . the mouth he could not see.

JOHN FOWLES,    *The French Lieutenant's Woman*

The Syrian graduate student Mrs. Beaty had been expecting turned out to be Mr. Sadek Abdul Meheen, from Damascus, and Levin made his acquaintance the day he arrived. He was a short young man with a fluff of curly black hair on a balding brown skull, and a delicate Semitic nose that sniffed in the direction of vagrant odors. His moist black eyes were gently popped.    BERNARD MALAMUD, *A New Life*

*having beautiful buttocks*
    callipygous, callipygian

*having lardy buttocks*
    steatopygic, steatopygous

*(of a woman) having an imposing and stately beauty*
    statuesque, Junoesque, goddess-like

*(of a woman) large and strong*
    Amazonian

*(of a woman) attractively or gracefully thin*
    svelte, willowy

*(of a woman) large and rounded*
    full-figured, developed, ample, opulent, full-blown

*(of a woman) attractively rounded*
    pleasingly plump, Rubensian

*(of a woman) having large breasts*
    large-breasted, big-breasted, big-chested, bosomy,
    big-bosomed, buxom, busty, top-heavy, stacked, well-built,
    built, full-bosomed

*(of a woman) having a flat chest*
    flat-chested

*(of a woman) having a full and shapely body*
    voluptuous, shapely, pneumatic, curvaceous, zaftig

*(of a woman) having a small waist*
    wasp-waisted, having an hourglass figure

The author of the paper, Albert O. Birdless, nineteen, from Marathon, Cascadia, was majoring in vocational education. His build reminded Levin of a young tugboat. He was stocky, with a short neck, heavy shoulders and legs, and stubby feet in square-toed shoes. His longish crewcut appeared to have gone to seed. On his head he usually wore a freshman beanie.    BERNARD MALAMUD, *A New Life*

Brinker looked the standard preparatory school article in his gray gabardine suit with square, hand-sewn-looking jacket pockets, a conservative necktie, and dark brown cordovan shoes. His face was all straight lines—eyebrows, mouth, nose, everything—and he carried his six feet of height straight as well.    JOHN KNOWLES, *A Separate Peace*

Phineas had soaked and brushed his hair for the occasion. This gave his head a sleek look, which was contradicted by the surprised, honest expression which he wore on his face. His ears, I had never noticed before, were fairly small and set close to his head, and combined with his plastered hair they now gave his bold nose and cheekbones the sharp look of a prow.    JOHN KNOWLES, *A Separate Peace*

Across the room, a fat beetle-browned girl in a dirty serape stared at him in anger. There was a fourth girl too, a skinny redhead with prominent teeth and a corpselike complexion who was playing with a dark wig.

ROBERT STONE, *Dog Soldiers*

*having regular and distinct features*
　clean-cut

*having angular features*
　sharp-featured

*having well-defined or shapely facial features*
　fine-featured, chiseled, delicately sculptured, sculpturesque

*having thick (or thickened) features*
　blunt, coarse, heavy, gross

*having thick features with wide lips and large eyes*
　frog-like

*free of facial hair*
　clean-shaven

*adolescent facial hair*
　peach fuzz

*looking crisply clean*
　well-scrubbed

*having a long face*
　horse-faced, horsey

*having a round face*
　moon-faced

*having a small and pretty face*
　doll-faced

*having a thin face with sharp features*
　hatchet-faced, sharp-faced, gaunt, hollow-cheeked

He had a hungry face; in it Marge detected a morphology she recognized. The bones were strong and the features spare but the lips were large and frequently in motion, twisting, pursed, compressing, being gnawed.

ROBERT STONE, *Dog Soldiers*

Journalist First Class Mac Lean was a small round-bellied man wearing parts of a Seabee uniform with a forty-five holstered on his guard belt. His arms were freckled and thickly tattooed; he had a pink boozer's face adorned with a sinister goatee and wraparound sunglasses.

ROBERT STONE, *Dog Soldiers*

Most Indian women have a rope of muscle over their hips that gives them a high-waisted, mis-shapen look, thin, bunchy legs, and too much breast-works. She had plenty in that line, but her hips were round, and her legs had a soft line to them. She was slim, but there was something voluptuous about her, like in three or four years she would get fat. All that, though, I only half saw. What I noticed was her face. It was flat, like an Indian's but the nose broke high, so it kind of went with the way she held her head, and the eyes weren't dumb, with that shiny, shoe-button look. They were pretty big, and black, but they leveled out straight, and had kind of a sleepy, impudent look to them. Her lips were thick, but pretty, and of course had plenty of lipstick on them.

JAMES CAIN, *Serenade*

He is much to my liking—I could throw my arms around him. A sharp character—no youth as I feared—a Faubourg

*having a flat and round face*
   pie-faced

*having a fat and expressionless face*
   pudding-faced

*having a hook nose and protruding chin*
   having a nutcracker face

*having wrinkles*
   wrinkled, lined, wizened, furrowed

*having heavy or drooping cheeks*
   jowly

*having a pink or reddish face*
   pink-faced, rosy-faced, ruddy, florid, flushed, rosy-cheeked,
   rubicund, rubescent, suffused

*ruddy in a coarse way*
   blowzy, blowsy

*having an open and guileless face*
   fresh-faced, sweet-faced

*having a vacant face*
   blank, unreadable, deadpan, inscrutable, mask-like,
   expressionless, impassive, empty, poker-faced

*having a face showing pain or a difficult life*
   pinched, hard-bitten

*having a worn face*
   weather-beaten, weathered, haggard

*having an interestingly worn or "experienced" face*
   rough, rugged-looking, craggy (features)

*having a tight or tense face*
   taut, drawn, hardened, hard (features)

*having a skull-like face*
   skull-faced, spectral, hollowed

Marigny type, Mediterranean, big-nosed, lumpy-jawed, a single stitched-in wrinkle over his eyebrows from just above which there springs up a great pompadour of wiry bronze hair.            WALKER PERCY, *The Moviegoer*

Directly next to me, on the first cross seat, is a very fine-looking girl. She is a strapping girl but by no means too big, done up head to toe in cellophane, the hood pushed back to show a helmet of glossy black hair. She is magnificent with her split tooth and her Prince Val bangs split on her forehead. Gray eyes and wide black brows, a good arm and a fine swell of calf above her cellophane boot. One of those solitary Amazons one sees on Fifty-seventh Street in New York or in Nieman Marcus in Dallas.
            WALKER PERCY, *The Moviegoer*

Walter is a sickly-looking fellow with a hollow temple but he is actually quite healthy. He has gray sharklike skin and lidded eyes and a lock of hair combed across his forehead in the MacArthur style.    WALKER PERCY, *The Moviegoer*

Under all that powder her face black as Harpo. She got a long pointed nose and big fleshy mouth. Lips look like black plum. Eyes big, glossy. Feverish. And mean. Like, sick as she is, if a snake cross her path, she kill it.
            ALICE WALKER, *The Color Purple*

He just look her up and down. She bout seven or eight months pregnant, bout to bust out her dress. Harpo so black

*having a fleshy face*
    puffy, bloated, jowly, heavy-jowled, meaty

*having a blotched or spotted face*
    having a maple face

*having a double chin*
    double-chinned, having dewlaps

*having a concave face*
    push-faced, dish-faced

*elfin*
    impish, pixieish

*pert*
    cute

*baby-faced*
    cherubic

*looking worried or depressed*
    grim, grim-faced, gloomy, saturnine, with a February face

*unsmiling*
    grave, solemn, long-faced

*beaming*
    sunny-faced

*radiant*
    glowing

he think she bright, but she ain't that bright. Clear medium brown skin, gleam on it like on good furniture. Hair notty but a lot of it, tied up on her head in a mass of plaits. She not quite as tall as Harpo but much bigger, and strong and ruddy looking, like her mama brought her up on pork.

ALICE WALKER, *The Color Purple*

He walked over to her as quietly as if she were asleep, feeling strange to be by himself, and stood on tiptoe beside her and looked down into her sunbonnet towards her ear. Her temple was deeply sunken as if a hammer had struck it and frail as a fledgling's belly. Her skin was crosshatched with the razor-fine slashes of innumerable square wrinkles and yet every slash was like smooth stone; her ear was just a fallen intricate flap with a small gold ring in it; her smell was faint yet very powerful, and she smelled like new mushrooms and old spices and sweat, like his fingernail when it was coming off.

JAMES AGEE, *A Death in the Family*

Andrew is just as thin as I am fat, and his clothes hang on him in the most comical way. He is very tall and shambling, wears a ragged beard and a broad Stetson hat, and suffers amazingly from hay fever in the autumn.

CHRISTOPHER MORLEY, *Parnassus on Wheels*

The other was a remarkable fellow. He was in his middle forties, slim, a bit stoop-shouldered. His eyes were black and deep-set. His eyebrows were bushy. He had long arms and wrists, and although he used his hands constantly in making conversation, they were relaxed and delicate in their movements.    JAMES MICHENER, *Tales of the South Pacific*

*extremely round-headed*
   trochocephalic

*extremely short- or broad-headed*
   brachycephalic

*extremely large-headed*
   macrocephalic

*extremely long-headed*
   dolichocephalic

*having a high or dome-like head with short hair*
   bullet-headed, domey

Their commander was a middle-aged corporal—red-eyed, scrawny, tough as dried beef, sick of war.

KURT VONNEGUT, JR., *Slaughterhouse Five*

But the sweet young girl was the daintiest thing these premises, within or without, could offer for contemplation: delicately chiseled features, of Grecian cast; her complexion the pure snow of a japonica that is receiving a faint reflected enrichment from some scarlet neighbor of the garden; great, soft blue eyes fringed with long curving lashes; an expression made up of the trustfulness of a child and the gentleness of a fawn; a beautiful head crowned with its own prodigal gold; a lithe and rounded figure, whose every attitude and movement was instinct with native grace.

MARK TWAIN, "The Loves of Alonzo and Rosannah"

Hurree Babu came out from behind the dovecot, washing his teeth with ostentatious ritual. Full-fleshed, heavy-haunched, bull-necked, and deep-voiced, he did not look like 'a fearful man'.    RUDYARD KIPLING, *Kim*

Tall, powerful, barefoot, graceful, soundless, Missouri Fever was like a supple black cat as she paraded serenely about the kitchen, the casual flow of her walk beautifully sensuous and haughty. She was slant-eyed, and darker than the charred stove; her crooked hair stood straight on end, as if she'd seen a ghost, and her lips were thick and purple. The length of her neck was something to ponder upon, for she was almost a freak, a human giraffe, and Joel recalled photos, which he'd scissored once from the pages of a *National Geographic,* of

# Hair, Coiffures, Mustaches, and Beards

hair
> tress, lock, strand, shock, hank, coil, tendril, curl, ringlet, swirl

hairy
> hirsute, unshaven, shaggy, crinose

having no hair
> hairless, bald, bald-headed, glabrous, depilous, a cueball

having little hair
> balding, thin, thin on top, sparse, wispy, scant, thinning

mid-forehead point formed by the hairline
> widow's peak

having or resembling a monk's circular fringe or shaven crown
> tonsured

having a full or bushy head of hair
> mop-headed, mop top, lion-headed, leonine, thick-haired, luxuriant

having short hair
> close-cropped, close-thatched, cropped, short-cropped

having very light or whitish hair (like spinning fiber)
> towheaded

having soft and lustrous hair
> silken-haired

having fine hair
> fine-haired, thin-haired

curious African ladies with countless silver chokers stretching their necks to improbable heights.

TRUMAN CAPOTE, Other Voices, Other Rooms

The skinny girl with fiery, chopped-off red hair swaggered inside, and stopped dead still, her hands cocked on her hips. Her face was flat, and rather impertinent; a network of big ugly freckles spanned her nose. Her eyes, squinty and bright green, moved swiftly from face to face, but showed none a sign of recognition. . . .

TRUMAN CAPOTE, Other Voices, Other Rooms

His face was like a black withered apple, and almost destroyed; his polished forehead shone as though a purple light gleamed under the skin; his sickle-curved posture made him look as though his back were broken: a sad little brokeback dwarf crippled with age.

TRUMAN CAPOTE, Other Voices, Other Rooms

Mrs. Haydon was a short, stout, hard built, German woman. She always hit the ground very firmly and compactly as she walked. Mrs. Haydon was all a compact and well hardened mass, even to her face, reddish and darkened from its early blonde, with its hearty, shiny cheeks, and doubled chin well covered over with the up roll from her short, square neck.

GERTRUDE STEIN, Three Lives

Mr. Barbecue-Smith belonged to the old school of journalists. He sported a leonine head with a greyish-black mane of

*having hair with turns or twists*
　crinkly
*having hair in disorder*
　unkempt, messy, mussed up, unruly, tangled, ratty, tousled,
　rumpled, snarled
*having wild and thickly coiled (snake-like) hair*
　Medusa-like

*long and loose*
　flowing
*loose or streaming in the wind*
　windblown, flyaway
*long but lacking body*
　lank, stringy
*stiff*
　bristly, brush-like
*rough*
　bristly, bristling, scraggy, scrubby
*with pointed tufts*
　spiky
*in thick strands*
　ropy
*downy*
　fuzzy (face or skin)

*having unkempt or untrimmed facial hair (short of a mustache or beard)*
　unshaven, stubbly, stubbled, scraggy, bristly
*having soft or delicate facial hair*
　downy
*needing a shave*
　with five-o'clock shadow

*formed into curls or ringlets*
　curled, crimped
*formed into small and tight curls*
　frizzed, frizzed out, frizzy

oddly unappetising hair brushed back from a broad but low forehead. And somehow he always seemed slightly, ever so slightly soiled.                     ALDOUS HUXLEY, *Crome Yellow*

Next to Mary a small gaunt man was sitting, rigid and erect in his chair. In appearance Mr. Scogan was like one of those extinct bird-lizards of the Tertiary. His nose was beaked, his dark eye had the shining quickness of a robin's. But there was nothing soft or gracious or feathery about him. The skin of his wrinkled brown face had a dry and scaly look; his hands were the hands of a crocodile. His movements were marked by the lizard's disconcertingly abrupt clockwork speed; his speech was thin, fluty, and dry.

ALDOUS HUXLEY, *Crome Yellow*

In the midst of this brown gloom Mr. Bodiham sat at his desk. He was the man in the Iron Mask. A grey metallic face with iron cheek-bones and a narrow iron brow; iron folds, hard and unchanging, ran perpendicularly down his cheeks; his nose was the iron beak of some thin, delicate bird of rapine. He had brown eyes, set in sockets rimmed with iron; round them the skin was dark, as though it had been charred. Dense wiry hair covered his skull; it had been black, it was turning grey. His ears were very small and fine. His jaws, his chin, his upper lip were dark, iron-dark, where he had shaved. His voice, when he spoke and especially when he raised it in preaching, was harsh, like the grating of iron hinges when a seldom-used door is opened.

ALDOUS HUXLEY, *Crome Yellow*

*ruffled and given more body by coming toward the scalp*
  teased, back-combed
*combed up toward the top of the head*
  upswept, swept back, raked back
*having certain strands bleached or colored*
  highlighted, streaked, frosted, tinted, lightened, darkened
*given aligned soft waves (by means of heated curling irons)*
  marceled
*dried (and usually given a fluffed shaping) with a blow dryer*
  blow-dried
*straightened chemically*
  processed, conked, relaxed
*cut in different lengths for a fuller look*
  layered
*cut all one length*
  having a blunt cut

*oiled*
  greased, slicked, slick, pomaded, brilliantined, plastered,
  pasted

*matted patches of hair*
  elflocks
*lock hanging at the front of the head*
  forelock
*groomed curl of hair displayed against the forehead or side of the face*
  spit curl
*curled lock of hair*
  ringlet
*tuft of hair growing awry or hanging over the forehead*
  cowlick
*dampened curl held with a hairpin or clip*
  pin curl
*twisted or intertwined length of hair*
  braid, plait

He was charmed by the pale face, the lissome figure, draped in pearl gray, with a coiled string of pearls at the throat.

THEODORE DREISER, *Sister Carrie*

Miserable food, ill-timed and greedily eaten, had played havoc with bone and muscle. They were all pale, flabby, sunken-eyed, hollow-chested, with eyes that glinted and shone and lips that were a sickly red by contrast. Their hair was but half attended to, their ears anemic in hue, and their shoes broken in leather and run down at heel and toe.

THEODORE DREISER, *Sister Carrie*

Captain Marpole's grizzled head emerged from the scuttle. A sea-dog: clear blue eyes of a translucent truth-worthiness: a merry, wrinkled, morocco-coloured face: a rumbling voice.        RICHARD HUGHES, *A High Wind in Jamaica*

*Emily,* with her huge palm-leaf hat, and colourless cotton frock tight over her minute impish body: her thin, almost expressionless face: her dark grey eyes contracted to escape the blaze yet shining as it were in spite of themselves: and her really beautiful lips, that looked almost as if they were sculptured.        RICHARD HUGHES, *A High Wind in Jamaica*

This was the first time I had seen Fletcher for nearly a year. He was a tall man who must once have been a handsome figure in the fine clothes he always wore and with his arrogant air and his finely chiseled face set off by his short-cropped black beard and brilliant eyes. Now a heaviness was

*tight braid usually worn down the back of the head*
  pigtail, rat's tail, rat tail

*cinched lock of hair hanging loosely down the back of the neck*
  ponytail

*braid(s) worn flat against the scalp*
  cornrow

*knot of hair worn at the back of the head*
  chignon, bun

*knot of folded-under hair at the back of the head*
  French knot, French twist

*knot of hair worn on the top of the head*
  topknot

*wave set in lotioned or wet hair with a finger*
  finger wave

*long and row-like braids as worn by Rastafarians*
  dreadlocks

*single long lock worn on a bare scalp*
  scalp lock

*attachable woman's hairpiece for creating a hanging length of hair down the back of the head*
  fall

*any attachable thick strand of hair for a woman's coiffure*
  switch

*front down-hanging hair cut evenly across*
  bangs

*woman's conical coil of hair worn at the back of the neck*
  Psyche knot

*roll of hair combed up from the forehead or temples*
  roach

*curl or lock of hair worn in front of the ear, earlock*
  payess (Yiddish)

*cylindrical roll of hair*
  puff

*curl that is tubular*
  sausage curl

setting in about his features and a fatty softness was beginning to show in his body.        JACK  SCHAEFER, *Shane*

She heard the feet cross the diningroom, then the swing
door opened and Luster entered, followed by a big man who
appeared to have been shaped of some substance whose par-
ticles would not or did not cohere to one another or to the
frame which supported it. His skin was dead looking and
hairless; dropsical too, he moved with a shambling gait like a
trained bear. His hair was pale and fine. It had been brushed
smoothly down upon his brow like that of children in da-
guerrotypes [*sic*]. His eyes were clear, of the pale sweet blue
of cornflowers, his thick mouth hung open, drooling a little.
        WILLIAM  FAULKNER,  *The Sound and the Fury*

He was tall, gaunt and ill-formed, with a snake-like neck,
terminating in a small, bony head. Under his close-clipped
hair this repellent head showed a number of thick ridges, as if
the skull joinings were overgrown by layers of superfluous
bone. With its small, rudimentary ears, this head had a posi-
tively malignant look.
        WILLA  CATHER,  *Death Comes for the Archbishop*

Not much taller than the Bishop in reality, he gave the
impression of being an enormous man. His broad high
shoulders were like a bull buffalo's, his big head was set
defiantly on a thick neck, and the full-cheeked, richly coloured, egg-shaped Spanish face—how vividly the Bishop
remembered that face! It was so unusual that he would be
glad to see it again; a high, narrow forehead, brilliant yellow

*curl that is spiral*
> corkscrew curl

*coiffure in which the hair is chemically curled or waved*
> permanent wave, permanent, perm, cold wave

*permanent wave that is looser and gives more body to the hair*
> body wave

*coiffure in which the (curly or frizzy) hair is chemically straightened and flattened or slightly waved*
> conk, process

*coiffure in which the hair is slicked back from either side to meet or overlap behind*
> ducktail, duck's ass, DA

*coiffure featuring spiky or irregularly chopped hair*
> punk

*short and brush-like haircut*
> crewcut, butch, burr-cut

*short and brush-like haircut with a flattened top*
> flattop

*having a short haircut that makes one's ears appear large*
> crop-eared

*coiffure with a brush-like strip down the center of an otherwise shaved head*
> Mohawk

*coiffure in which the hair is a naturally round and bushy mass*
> Afro

*coiffure in which the hair shape widens above the head to a flat top but is progressively shorter (or "faded") toward the ears*
> fade

*woman's coiffure in which the hair is cut in downward overlapping and uneven layers*
> shag

*woman's coiffure in which the brushed-up hair appears as a full and loose roll around the face*
> pompadour

eyes set deep in strong arches, and full, florid cheeks,—not blank areas of smooth flesh, as in Anglo-Saxon faces, but full of muscular activity, as quick to change with feeling as any of his features. His mouth was the very assertion of violent, uncurbed passions and tyrannical self-will; the full lips thrust out and taut, like the flesh of animals distended by fear or desire.    WILLA CATHER, *Death Comes for the Archbishop*

Someone advanced from the sea of faces, someone tall and gaunt, dressed in deep black, whose prominent cheek-bones and great, hollow eyes gave her a skull's face, parchment-white, set on a skeleton's frame.

DAPHNE DU MAURIER, *Rebecca*

He was a big, hefty fellow, good-looking in a rather flashy, sunburnt way. He had the hot, blue eyes usually associated with heavy drinking and loose living. His hair was reddish like his skin. In a few years he would run to fat, his neck bulging over the back of his collar. His mouth gave him away, it was too soft, too pink. I could smell the whisky in his breath from where I stood.

DAPHNE DU MAURIER, *Rebecca*

The eyes—and it was my destiny to know them well—were large and handsome, wide apart as the true artist's are wide, sheltering under a heavy brow and arched over by thick black eyebrows. The eyes themselves were of that baffling protean gray which is never twice the same; which runs through many shades and colorings like intershot silk in sunshine; which is gray, dark and light, and greenish gray, and

*woman's coiffure in which the hair is cut short and evenly all around the head*
> bob

*woman's coiffure in which the short cut is neither layered nor graduated*
> blunt cut

*woman's coiffure in which the hair is cut irregularly short toward the face and with the ears exposed*
> pixie, French cut

*woman's coiffure in which the hair is teased for a puffed-out look*
> bouffant

*woman's conical coiffure*
> beehive

*woman's coiffure with a rounded or cap-like top that is tapered at the back of the neck*
> mushroom

*woman's coiffure in which the usually shoulder-length hair is combed down and turned under or inward at the ends in a roll*
> pageboy

*woman's coiffure with bangs and the unlayered hair at chin length*
> Buster Brown, cap cut

*woman's coiffure in which the combed-down hair is curled outward*
> flip

*woman's coiffure that is short in which the hair arcs over the forehead and forms a triangle at the back*
> wedge, Dorothy Hamill

*woman's coiffure in which the short and uneven-length curls are given featherlike ends*
> feather cut

*woman's coiffure that is close-cropped in layers and short in the back*
> shingle

*woman's coiffure in which the hair is combed or swept up toward the top of the head and held by pins or combs*
> upsweep, updo

*woman's coiffure with a braid or braids "woven" close to the head and attached with pins*
> French braid

sometimes of the clear azure of the deep sea. They were eyes that masked the soul with a thousand guises, and that sometimes opened, at rare moments, and allowed it to rush up as though it were about to fare forth nakedly into the world on some wonderful adventure,—eyes that could brood with the hopeless sombreness of leaden skies; that could snap and crackle points of fire like those which sparkle from a whirling sword; that could grow chill as an arctic landscape, and yet again, that could warm and soften and be all a-dance with love-lights, intense and masculine, luring and compelling, which at the same time fascinate and dominate women till they surrender in a gladness of joy and of relief and sacrifice.                              JACK LONDON, *The Sea Wolf*

She shut her book and slowly looked up; her hat-brim partially shaded her face, yet I could see, as she raised it, that it was a strange one. It looked all brown and black: elf-locks bristled out from beneath a white band which passed under the chin, and came half over her cheeks, or rather jaws: her eye confronted me at once, with a bold and direct gaze.

                              CHARLOTTE BRONTË, *Jane Eyre*

Mrs. Reed might be at that time some six or seven-and-thirty; she was a woman of robust frame, square-shouldered and strong limbed, not tall, and, though stout, not obese; she had a somewhat large face, the under-jaw being much developed and very solid; her brow was low, her chin large and prominent, mouth and nose sufficiently regular; under her light eyebrows glimmered an eye devoid of ruth; her skin was dark and opaque, her hair nearly flaxen; . . .

                              CHARLOTTE BRONTË, *Jane Eyre*

*woman's coiffure in which the hair is combed back to form a long or vertical roll at the back of the head*
>French twist, French roll

*woman's coiffure (eighteenth century) with the hair worn in cylindrical rolls or puffs*
>pouf


*artificial covering of (another's or synthetic) hair*
>hairpiece, wig

*man's covering of hair over a bald spot*
>toupee, piece, rug

*seventeenth- and eighteenth-century man's wig often powdered and gathered at the back*
>periwig, peruke

*woman's fringe of hair or curls worn on the forehead*
>frisette (archaic)


*having a mustache*
>mustached, mustachioed (usually a long mustache)

*mustache that is slight and thin*
>pencil mustache

*narrow mustache under the middle of the nose*
>toothbrush mustache

*thickly shaggy or droopy mustache*
>walrus mustache

*thick mustache with long and curving ends*
>handlebar mustache, military mustache

*curving and dressed mustache*
>waxed mustache


*having a beard*
>bearded

*beard covering most of the lower face*
>full beard, beaver

*small chin beard or tuft*
>goatee

The lower part of his physiognomy was over-developed; his narrow and low forehead, unintelligently furrowed by horizontal wrinkles, surmounted wildly hirsute cheeks and a flat nose with wide, baboon-like nostrils.

JOSEPH CONRAD, *Victory*

Her hair was very elaborately done with two ringlets on the left side of her scraggy neck; her dress was of silk, and she had come on duty for the afternoon.

JOSEPH CONRAD, *Victory*

He was a muscular, short man with eyes that gleamed and blinked, a harsh voice, and a round, toneless, pock-marked face ornamented by a thin, dishevelled moustache sticking out quaintly under the tip of a rigid nose.

JOSEPH CONRAD, *Victory*

She was a small, plump, fair woman, with a bright, clear eye, and an extraordinary air of neatness and briskness.

HENRY JAMES, *Washington Square*

Her shape was not only exact but extremely delicate, and the nice proportion of her arms promised the truest symmetry in her limbs. Her hair, which was black, was so luxuriant that is reached her middle before she cut it to comply with the modern fashion, and it was not curled so gracefully in her neck that few would believe it to be her own.

HENRY FIELDING, *Tom Jones*

*beard that is long and rectangular*
    patrician, square-cut beard

*trim and pointed beard extending back to the ears*
    Vandyke, pickedevant

*beard shaped like a pointed or broad spade*
    spade beard

*pointed beard beginning at the lower lip*
    imperial

*beard following the line of the chin*
    galways

*whiskers extending below the ears*
    sideburns, burnsides, side-whiskers, sideboards

*side-whiskers that become broader at the lower jaw*
    muttonchops, muttonchop whiskers, dundrearies

## Colors of Hair

*white*
    hoary, silvery, platinum, snow white

*blond*
    blonde, blondish, straw-colored, flaxen-haired

*golden blond*
    goldilocks

*bleached blond*
    peroxide blond, bottled blond, drugstore blond

*pale grayish blond*
    ash blond

*black or brown*
    brunette, dark-haired, dark

*black*
    raven, jet, jet black, coal black, ebony

*brown*
    chestnut, wheaten, nut brown

His manners, she thought, were very dignified; the set of his iron-grey hair and his deep eye sockets made him resemble the portrait of Locke. He had the spare form and the pale complexion which became a student; as different as possible from the blooming Englishman of the red-whiskered type represented by Sir James Chettam.

GEORGE ELIOT, *Middlemarch*

The cousin was so close now, that, when he lifted his hat, Dorothea could see a pair of grey eyes rather near together, a delicate irregular nose with a little ripple in it, and hair falling backward; and there was a mouth and chin of a more prominent, threatening aspect than belonged to the type of the grandmother's miniature.

GEORGE ELIOT, *Middlemarch*

William Dampier . . . had written his famous account. . . . "Their eyelids are always half-closed to keep the flies out of their eyes . . . They had great bottle noses, pretty full lips, and wide mouths."

ALAN MOOREHEAD, *The Fatal Impact*

The girls were sisters. One wore a green frock, the other a tunic of mauve jersey with an orange sash around her bottom. Their cheeks were rouged, their hair shingled, and their nostrils were cavernous.

BRUCE CHATWIN, *On the Black Hill*

She was a short and very courageous woman with laugh wrinkles at the edge of her slaty eyes, and silver hair cut in a fringe.                              BRUCE CHATWIN, *On the Black Hill*

*drab brown*
    mouse-colored, mousy

*reddish brown*
    auburn

*red-haired*
    redheaded, a carrot top, ginger, gingery, titian

*reddish blond*
    strawberry blond

*gray or partly gray*
    grizzled, graying, hoary

*dyed reddish or orangish brown*
    hennaed

*dyed slightly bluish (to offset yellowed coloration)*
    having a blue rinse

She despised Nigel for lacing his plummy voice with working-class slang.    BRUCE CHATWIN, *On the Black Hill*

Chile was still in the chair when the new-wave barbers came back and began to comment, telling him they could perm what was left or give him a moderate spike, shave the sides, laser stripes were popular.

ELMORE LEONARD, *Get Shorty*

The child, who was diminutive for his years, had an aged expression of countenance: a pale complexion, and sharp little features. He was dressed in knickerbockers, with red stockings, which displayed his poor little spindle-shanks; he also wore a brilliant red cravat.

HENRY JAMES, *Daisy Miller*

He plucked a flower and stuck it in his buttonhole, and something a little doggish peeped out of the black buttony eyes, a hint of the seraglio.

GRAHAM GREENE, *Brighton Rock*

There was a deep humility in Hale; his pride was only in his profession: he disliked himself before the glass, the bony legs and the pigeon breast, and he dressed shabbily and carelessly as a sign—a sign that he didn't expect any woman to be interested.    GRAHAM GREENE, *Brighton Rock*

And Loerke was not a serious figure. In his brown velvet cap that made his head as round as a chestnut, with the brown

*having large eyes*
large-eyed, saucer-eyed, wide-eyed, fish-eyed

*having small eyes*
beady-eyed, piglike, ferret-like, ferrety

*having the eyes wide apart*
wide set, far set

*having the eyes close together*
close set

*having sunken eyes*
hollow-eyed, deep set

*having bulging or protruding eyes*
pop-eyed, banjo-eyed, prominent, protuberant, starting, exophthalmic, hyperthyroid, bug-eyed, proptosed, bulbous, goggle-eyed

*having narrow eyes*
slit-eyed

*having lively eyes*
bright-eyed, twinkle-eyed, flashing, luminous, beaming, glinting, glowing

*having expressionless eyes*
flat, cold, dull-eyed, lusterless, blank, fish-like, glassy

*blinking frequently*
blinky-eyed, blinky

velvet flaps loose and wild over his ears, and a wisp of elf-like, thin black hair blowing above his full, elf-like dark eyes, the shiny, transparent brown skin crinkling up into odd grimaces on his small-featured face, he looked an odd little boy-man, a bat.    D. H. LAWRENCE, *Women in Love*


Tashtego's long, lean, sable hair, his high cheek bones, and black rounding eyes—for an Indian, Oriental in their large-ness, but Antarctic in their glittering expression—all this sufficiently proclaimed him an inheritor of the unvitiated blood of those proud warrior hunters, who, in quest of the great New England moose, had scoured, bow in hand, the aboriginal forests of the main.

HERMAN MELVILLE, *Moby-Dick*


His face was pale as death, and far more ghastly; the broad forehead was contracted in his agony so that his eyebrows formed one grizzled line; his eyes were red and wild, and the foam hung white upon his quivering lip.

NATHANIEL HAWTHORNE,
"My Kinsman, Major Molineux"


He was a snub-nosed, flat-browed, common-faced boy enough, and as dirty a juvenile as one would wish to see, but he had about him all the airs and manners of a man. He was short of his age, with rather bow-legs, and little, sharp, ugly eyes.    CHARLES DICKENS, *Oliver Twist*


He placed himself at a corner of the doorway for her to pass him into the house, and doated [*sic*] on her cheek, her ear,

*having the eyes narrowed*
squinting

*having inwardly turned eyes*
cross-eyed, cockeyed, strabismic

*having outwardly turned eyes*
walleyed, cockeyed, strabismic

*squinting*
cockeyed, strabismic

*having restless or moving eyes*
shifting, shifty, darting, swivel-eyed

*having soft and dark eyes*
sloe-eyed

*having moist or wet eyes*
dewy-eyed, watery, aqueous, glistening

*having slanted eyes*
slanty-eyed, sloe-eyed

*having horizontally long or somewhat oval eyes*
almond-eyed

*having half-closed eyes*
heavy-lidded, sleepy-eyed, with drooping lids, slumberous, slumbrous

*having motionless eyes*
staring, transfixed, unblinking, glazed clear, limpid

*having reddened eyes*
red-eyed, bloodshot, cranberry, pink-veined

*having weary or strained eyes*
bleary-eyed

*having wrinkles around the eyes*
crinkly-eyed

*having fleshy folds under the eyes*
pouchy, pouched, baggy, bagged

and the softly dusky nape of her neck, where this way and that the little lighter-coloured irreclaimable curls running truant from the comb and the knot—curls, half-curls, root-curls, vine-ringlets, wedding-rings, fledgeling [*sic*] feathers, tufts of down, blown wisps—waved or fell, waxed over or up or involutedly, or strayed, loose and downward, in the form of small silken paws, hardly any of them much thicker than a crayon shading, cunninger than long round locks of gold to trick the heart.

GEORGE MEREDITH, *The Egoist*

Zilla was an active, strident, full-blown, high-bosomed blonde.                 SINCLAIR LEWIS, *Babbitt*

To the eye, the men were less similar: Littlefield, a hedge-scholar, tall and horse-faced; Chum Frink, a trifle of a man with soft and mouse-like hair, advertising his profession as poet by a silk cord on his eyeglasses; Vergil Gunch, broad, with coarse black hair *en brosse;* Eddie Swanson, a bald and bouncing young man who showed his taste for elegance by an evening waistcoat of figured black silk with glass buttons; Orville Jones, a steady-looking, stubby, not very memorable person, with a hemp-colored toothbrush mustache.

SINCLAIR LEWIS, *Babbitt*

In the flesh, Mrs. Opal Emerson Mudge fell somewhat short of a prophetic aspect. She was pony-built and plump, with the face of a haughty Pekingese, a button of a nose, and arms so short that, despite her most indignant endeavors, she could not clasp her hands in front of her as she sat on the platform waiting.                 SINCLAIR LEWIS, *Babbitt*

| | |
|---|---|
| sheep-like | sad, mournful, doleful |
| rolling | hard, steely, piercing, |
| darting |     penetrating, gimlet-eyed |
| anxious | soft |
| seductive, bedroom | wild |

## COLORS OF EYES

blue, cornflower blue, steely blue, china blue, sapphire blue, baby blue

brown, velvet brown

gray, gooseberry, slate gray, slaty

green, greenish, emerald

light or golden brown, hazel

violet

amber

## EYEBROWS

*contracted (as in a frown)*
    knitted

*thick*
    bushy, beetling, beetle-browed

*thinned to a line with tweezers*
    tweezed, plucked

*accented cosmetically*
    penciled

Dr Messinger, though quite young, was bearded, and Tony knew few young men with beards. He was also very small, very sunburned and prematurely bald; the ruddy brown of his face ended abruptly along the line of his forehead, which rose in a pale dome; he wore steel-rimmed spectacles and there was something about his blue serge suit which suggested that the wearer found it uncomfortable.

EVELYN WAUGH, *A Handful of Dust*

Col. Grangerford was very tall and very slim, and had a darkish-paly complexion, not a sign of red in it anywhere; he was clean-shaved every morning, all over his thin face, and he had the thinnest kind of lips, and the thinnest kind of nostrils, and a high nose, and heavy eyebrows, and the blackest kind of eyes, sunk so deep back that they seemed like they was looking out of caverns at you, as you may say. His forehead was high, and his hair was black and straight, and hung to his shoulders. His hands was long and thin. . . .

MARK TWAIN, *The Adventures of Huckleberry Finn*

Good heavens! it was Dorian Gray's own face that he was looking at! The horror, whatever it was, had not yet entirely spoiled that marvellous beauty. There was still some gold in the thinning hair and some scarlet on the sensual mouth. The sodden eyes had kept something of the loveliness of their blue, the noble curves had not yet completely passed away from chiselled nostrils and from plastic throat.

OSCAR WILDE, *The Picture of Dorian Gray*

Romeo was a stout elderly gentleman, with corked eyebrows, a husky tragedy voice, and a figure like a beer-barrel.

OSCAR WILDE, *The Picture of Dorian Gray*

*large*
    prominent

*having a pronounced downward bend from the bridge of the nose*
    hooked, hook-nosed, hawk-nosed, beak-nosed,
    parrot-nosed, having an arched nose

*having a slight or fine downward bend from the bridge of the nose*
    Roman, aquiline

*having a long nose*
    leptorrhine, blade-like

*having a nose curving out or upward*
    ski-jump nose

*having a wide nose*
    wide-nosed, broad-nosed, flat-nosed

*having a short and sometimes turned-up nose*
    snub-nosed, simous, blunt, stubby

*having a broad and sometimes turned-up nose*
    pug-nosed

*having a large and bulbous nose*
    cob-nosed

*having a somewhat flattened nose*
    button-nosed

*having a protuberant or swollen-looking (and sometimes red) nose*
    bottle-nosed

*having a crooked or injured nose*
    broken-nosed, irregular

Had orange blossoms been invented then (those touching emblems of female purity imported by us from France, where people's daughters are universally sold in marriage), Miss Maria, I say, would have assumed the spotless wreath, and stepped into the travelling carriage by the side of gouty, old, bald-headed, bottle-nosed Bullock Senior. . . .

WILLIAM THACKERAY, *Vanity Fair*

A withered face, with the shiny skin all drawn into wrinkles! The stretched skin under the jaw was like the skin of a plucked fowl. The cheek-bones stood up, and below them were deep hollows, almost like egg-cups. A short, scraggy white beard covered the lower part of the face. The hair was scanty, irregular, and quite white; a little white hair grew in the ears.   ARNOLD BENNETT, *The Old Wives Tale*

And the men of the regiment, with their starting eyes and sweating faces, running madly, or falling, as if thrown headlong, to queer, heaped-up corpses—all were comprehended.

STEPHEN CRANE, *The Red Badge of Courage*

His pallid bloated face expressed benevolent malice and, as he had advanced through his tidings of success, his small fatencircled eyes vanished out of sight and his weak wheezing voice out of hearing.

JAMES JOYCE, *A Portrait of the Artist as a Young Man*

The droning voice of the professor continued to wind itself slowly round and round the coils it spoke of, doubling, tre-

*having an inflamed nose (as from habitual drunkenness)*
  copper nosed

*turned up at the end*
  upturned, uptilted, retroussé

*wrinkled up*
  crinkled

bling, quadrupling its somnolent energy as the coil multi-
plied its ohms of resistance.

JAMES JOYCE, *A Portrait of the Artist as a Young Man*

She was a slender, small-breasted girl, with an erect carriage,
which she accentuated by throwing her body backward at
the shoulders like a young cadet. Her gray sun-strained eyes
looked back at me with polite reciprocal curiosity out of a
wan, charming, discontented face.

F. SCOTT FITZGERALD, *The Great Gatsby*

His sister, Catherine, was a slender, worldly girl of about
thirty, with a solid, sticky bob of red hair, and a complexion
powdered milky white. Her eyebrows had been plucked and
then drawn on again at a more rakish angle, but the efforts of
nature toward the restoration of the old alignment gave a
blurred air to her face.

F. SCOTT FITZGERALD, *The Great Gatsby*

In softness of features, body bulk, leanness of legs, apish
shape of ear and upper lip, Dr. Pavil Pnin looked very like
Timofey, as the latter was to look three or four decades later.
In the father, however, a fringe of straw-colored hair re-
lieved a waxlike calvity; he wore a black-rimmed pince-nez
on a black ribbon like the late Dr. Chekhov; he spoke in a
gentle stutter, very unlike his son's later voice.

VLADIMIR NABOKOV, *Pnin*

The good Doctor had perceptibly aged since last year but
was as sturdy and square-shaped as ever with his well-padded

*having large and projecting ears*
   big-eared, jug-eared

*having large and floppy ears*
   spaniel-eared

*having an injury-deformed or battered ear*
   cauliflower-eared

*small or delicately shapely ears*
   seashell ears

*having ears upright and somewhat pointed*
   prick-eared, having satyr-like ears

shoulders, square chin, square nostrils, leonine glabella, and rectangular brush of grizzled hair that had something topiary about it.                    VLADIMIR NABOKOV, *Pnin*


Her hair was as grey as her companions's, her face as bloodless and shrivelled, but amber-tinted, with swarthy shadows sharpening the nose and hollowing the temples.

EDITH WHARTON, *Ethan Frome*


She held the light at the same level, and it drew out with the same distinctness her slim young throat and the brown wrist no bigger than a child's. Then, striking upward, it threw a lustrous fleck on her lips, edged her eyes with velvet shade, and laid a milky whiteness above the black curve of her brows.                    EDITH WHARTON, *Ethan Frome*


Heathcliff did not glance my way, and I gazed up, and contemplated his features almost as confidently as if they had been turned to stone. His forehead, that I once thought so manly, and that I now think so diabolical, was shaded with a heavy cloud; his basilisk eyes were nearly quenched by sleeplessness—and weeping, perhaps for the lashes were wet then; his lips devoid of their ferocious sneer, and sealed in an expression of unspeakable sadness.

EMILY BRONTË, *Wuthering Heights*


. . . while the Haiti-born daughter of the French sugar planter and the woman whom Sutpen's first father-in-law had told him was a Spaniard (the slight dowdy woman with

*having a loose or slightly open mouth*
   slack-mouthed, drooping

*having an open mouth (as in surprise)*
   gaping, agape, cavernous

*well-shaped*
   shapely, full, sensual, ripe, generous

*small but prominent or shapely*
   beestung

*thick*
   blubber, lubber

*having a thin mouth or lips*
   thin-lipped, slash-mouthed

*having a crooked or twisted mouth*
   having a screw mouth

*having (or showing) contracted or squeezed lips*
   pursed, puckered

*having somewhat everted lips*
   pouty, truculent

*having a protruding upper lip*
   satchel mouth, shad mouth, gate mouth

*having a classically shapely upper lip*
   Cupid's bow

*having grayish or reddish brown lips*
   liver-lipped

*with much or bright lipstick*
   rouged

untidy gray-streaked raven hair coarse as a horse's tail, with parchment-colored skin and implacable pouched black eyes which alone showed no age because they showed no forgetting, whom Shreve and Quentin had likewise invented and which was likewise probably true enough). . . .

W I L L I A M   F A U L K N E R ,   *Absalom, Absalom!*

Parsons, Winston's fellow tenant at Victory Mansions, was in fact threading his way across the room—a tubby, middle-sized man with fair hair and a froglike face. At thirty-five he was already putting on rolls of fat at neck and waistline, but his movements were brisk and boyish. His whole appearance was that of a little boy grown large, so much so that although he was wearing the regulation overalls, it was almost impossible not to think of him as being dressed in the blue shorts, gray shirt, and red neckerchief of the Spies.

G E O R G E   O R W E L L ,   *Nineteen Eighty-four*

It was a lean Jewish face, with a great fuzzy aureole of white hair and a small goatee beard—a clever face, and yet somehow inherently dispicable, with a kind of senile silliness in the long thin nose near the end of which a pair of spectacles was perched. It resembled the face of a sheep, and the voice, too, had a sheeplike quality.

G E O R G E   O R W E L L ,   *Nineteen Eighty-four*

His body, which was nearly naked, presented a terrific emblem of death, drawn in intermingled colors of white and black. His closely shaved head, on which no other hair than the well known and chivalrous scalping tuft was preserved,

*having protruding upper teeth*
  bucktoothed, having an overbite

*having a space or spaces between teeth*
  gap-toothed, gat-toothed

*having a jutting tooth*
  snaggle-toothed

was without ornament of any kind, with the exception of a solitary eagle's plume, that crossed his crown and depended over the left shoulder.

JAMES FENIMORE COOPER, *The Last of the Mohicans*

His features, keen and regular, with an aquiline nose, and piercing black eyes; his high and wrinkled forehead, and long grey hair and beard, would have been considered as handsome, had they not been the marks of a physiognomy peculiar to a race which, during those dark ages, was alike detested by the credulous and prejudiced vulgar, and persecuted by the greedy and repacious nobility. . . .

SIR WALTER SCOTT, *Ivanhoe*

The hermit, as if wishing to answer to the confidence of his guest, threw back his cowl, and showed a round bullet head belonging to a man in the prime of life. His close-shaven crown, surrounded by a circle of stiff curled black hair, had something the [*sic*] appearance of a parish pinfold begirt by its high hedge. The features expressed nothing of monastic austerity or of ascetic privations; on the contrary, it was a bold bluff countenance, with broad black eyebrows, a well-turned forehead, and cheeks as round and vermilion as those of a trumpeter, from which descended a long and curly black beard.          SIR WALTER SCOTT, *Ivanhoe*

At thirteen or fourteen he was a mere bag of bones, with upper arms about as thick as the wrists of other boys of his age; his little chest was pigeon-breasted; he appeared to have no strength or stamina whatever. . . .

SAMUEL BUTLER, *The Way of All Flesh*

*having smooth skin*
> lustrous, unwrinkled, soft-skinned, shining, glowing, glabrous, flawless

*having healthily reddish skin*
> ruddy, rosy-cheeked, apple-cheeked, rubicund, rubescent

*having wrinkles*
> wrinkled, rugose

*having large pores*
> large-pored, grainy

*having aged skin*
> withered, shriveled, dried up, wizened, like parchment, puckered, cracked, shrunken

*having weathered skin*
> tough, leathery, leathern

*having freckles*
> freckled, lenticular

*having small spots or discolorations*
> mottled, blotchy, splotchy, splodgy (British)

*having warts*
> warty, verrucose

*having pockmarks*
> pockmarked, pocked, pitted

*pimply*
> papuliferous, eruptive

*having sores or lesions*
> ulcerated, broken

He was dressed all in decent black, with a white cravat round his neck. His face was as sharp as a hatchet, and the skin of it was as yellow and dry and withered as an autumn leaf. His eyes, of a steely light grey, had a very disconcerting trick, when they encountered your eyes, of looking as if they expected something more from you than you were aware of yourself. His walk was soft; his voice was melancholy; his long lanky fingers were hooked like claws.

WILKIE COLLINS, *The Moonstone*

A tall man stood in the doorway. He held a crushed Stetson hat under his arm while he combed his long, black, damp hair straight back. Like the others he wore blue jeans and a short denim jacket. . . . This was Slim, the jerkline skinner. His hatchet face was ageless. He might have been thirty-five or fifty.    JOHN STEINBECK, *Of Mice and Men*

A girl was standing there looking in. She had full, rouged lips and wide-spaced eyes, heavily made up. Her fingernails were red. Her hair hung in little rolled clusters, like sausages. She wore a cotton house dress and red mules, on the insteps of which were little bouquets of red ostrich feathers.

JOHN STEINBECK, *Of Mice and Men*

At twenty-seven Alice was tall and somewhat slight. Her head was large and overshadowed her body. Her shoulders were a little stooped and her hair and eyes brown.

SHERWOOD ANDERSON, *Winesburg, Ohio*

*oily*
> greasy

*pale*
> pallid, wan, chalky, pasty, blanched, etiolated, peaked, whey-faced

*dark*
> swart, swarthy, dark-complexioned

*white*
> alabaster, pearly, creamy, porcelain, milk white, translucent, light complexioned

*brown*
> cocoa, chocolate, coffee

*black*
> coal black, ebony

*grayish blue*
> livid

*yellowish*
> sallow, waxen, jaundiced, waxlike, parchment-colored, tallow-hued

*reddish*
> ruddy, raw, blowzy, flushed, suffused

*blushing*
> flushing, mantled

*sunburned*
> sunburnt, tan, bronzed, brown, coppery

*reddish brown*
> liverish

*bluish*
> cyanotic

*black and blue*
> livid

*spotted in coloring*
> mottled, blotched, liver-spotted

Elmer Cowley was extraordinarily tall and his arms were long and powerful. His hair, his eyebrows, and the downy beard that had begun to grow upon his chin were pale almost to whiteness. His teeth protruded from between his lips and his eyes were blue with the colorless blueness of the marbles called "aggies" that the boys of Winesburg carried in their pockets.

SHERWOOD ANDERSON, *Winesburg, Ohio*

. . . there stood the stereoscopic images, locked in one another's arms, of a gigantic negro and a golden-haired young brachycephalic Beta-Plus female.

ALDOUS HUXLEY, *Brave New World*

His face was profoundly wrinkled and black, like a mask of obsidian. The toothless mouth had fallen in. At the corners of the lips, and on each side of the chin, a few long bristles gleamed almost white against the dark skin. The long unbraided hair hung down in grey wisps round his face. His body was bent and emaciated to the bone, almost fleshless period.

ALDOUS HUXLEY, *Brave New World*

A hundredweight of ringed and brooched blubber, smelling to high heaven of female smells, rank as long-hung hair or blown beef, her bedroom strewn with soiled bloomers, crumby combinations, malodorous bust-bodices. She had swollen finger-joints, puffy palms, wrists girdled with fat, slug-white upper arms that, when naked, showed indecent as thighs. She was corned, bunioned, calloused [*sic*], varicose-veined.

ANTHONY BURGESS, *Inside Mr. Enderby*

*bent and knobby or somewhat deformed*
    gnarled, horny, knotted

*thick*
    square

*short (fingers)*
    stubby

*fat and ugly (fingers)*
    sausage fingers

*delicate*
    slender, fine

*long*
    tapered

*worn*
    coarse, rough, callused, chapped

Mrs. Opisso the daily woman had come in, dusky, hippy, bosomy, garlicky, moustached, leering brilliantly, a wartime Gibralterian evacuee in whose blood seethed Genoese, Portuguese Jewish, Saracen, Irish and Andalusian corpuscles. . . .

ANTHONY BURGESS,  *Inside Mr. Enderby*

She had all her front teeth, black hair, naughty eyes, earrings that jangled tinnily—clusters of minute coins—a snub nose and a comfortable round chin.

ANTHONY BURGESS,  *Inside Mr. Enderby*

He was a tight brisk little man, with the air of an arrant old bachelor. His nose was shaped like the bill of a parrot; his face slightly pitted with the smallpox, with a dry perpetual bloom on it, like a frost-bitten leaf in autumn. He had an eye of great quickness and vivacity, with a drollery and lurking waggery of expression that were irresistible.

WASHINGTON IRVING,  *The Sketch Book*

Little Britain has likewise its sages and great men. One of the most important of the former is a tall, dry old gentleman, of the name of Skryme, who keeps a small apothecary's shop. He has a cadaverous countenance, full of cavities and projections, with a brown circle around each eye, like a pair of horn spectacles.

WASHINGTON IRVING,  *The Sketch Book*

## Legs, Knees, and Feet

*having long legs*
　　leggy, long-limbed, dolichocnemic

*stick-legged*
　　spindly, spindle-shanked

*bowlegged*
　　bandy-legged

*knees touching*
　　knock-kneed

*having shapely legs*
　　well-turned (ankle)

*having large knees*
　　knobby

*muscular*
　　thick, sinewy

*short and thick*
　　stumpy, stubby, piano legs

*crooked*
　　gnarled, twisted

*withered*
　　atrophied

*having turned-in feet*
　　pigeon-toed

The father seemed to repress his feelings, but his fixed eye, contracted brow, and deeply-furrowed face showed the struggle that was passing within.

WASHINGTON IRVING, *The Sketch Book*

The cognomen of Crane was not inapplicable to his person. He was tall, but exceedingly lank, with narrow shoulders, long arms and legs, hands that dangled a mile out of his sleeves, feet that might have served for shovels, and his whole frame most loosely hung together. His head was small, and flat at top, with huge ears, large green glassy eyes, and a long snipe nose, so that it looked like a weathercock, perched upon his spindle neck, to tell which way the wind blew.

WASHINGTON IRVING, *The Sketch Book*

The latter, a young man of about forty, was of Gabriel's size and build, with very round shoulders. His face was fleshy and pallid, touched with colour only at the thick hanging lobes of his ears and at the wide wings of his nose. He had coarse features, a blunt nose, a convex and receding brow, tumid and protruded lips. His heavy-lidded eyes and the disorder of his scanty hair made him look sleepy.

JAMES JOYCE, *Dubliners*

Aunt Julia was an inch or so taller. Her hair, drawn low over the tops of her ears, was grey; and grey also, with darker shadows, was her large flaccid face. Though she was stout in build and stood erect her slow eyes and parted lips gave her the appearance of a woman who did not know where she was or where she was going. Aunt Kate was more vivacious.

*square-jawed*
  lantern–jawed
*straight-jawed*
  orthognathous
*having a crooked jaw*
  skew–jawed, agee–jawed
*firm-jawed*
  with the jaw set
*having a projecting lower jaw*
  wopple–jawed, jimber–jawed, prognathous, prognathic
*having a projecting upper jaw*
  jutting, opisthognathous
*having the lower jaw hanging down (often stupidly)*
  slack–jawed

Her face, healthier than her sister's, was all puckers and creases, like a shrivelled red apple, and her hair, braided in the same old-fashioned way, had not lost its ripe nut colour.

JAMES JOYCE, *Dubliners*

Lenehan's eyes noted approvingly her stout short muscular body. Frank rude health glowed in her face, on her fat red cheeks and in her unabashed blue eyes. Her features were blunt. She had broad nostrils, a straggling mouth which lay open in a contented leer, and two projecting front teeth.

JAMES JOYCE, *Dubliners*

With a fierce delight in his own realism he described the woman who had opened the door for him. She was dark, small, and fat, quite young, with black hair that seemed always on the point of coming down. She worn [*sic*] a slatternly blouse and no corsets. With her red cheeks, large sensual mouth, and shining, lewd eyes, she reminded you of the Bohemienne in the Louvre by Franz Hals.

W. SOMERSET MAUGHAM, *Of Human Bondage*

He was a small, shrivelled person, with bad teeth and a bilious air, an untidy grey beard, and savage eyes; his voice was high and his tone sarcastic.

W. SOMERSET MAUGHAM, *Of Human Bondage*

He was a man of somewhat less than average height, inclined to corpulence, with his hair, worn long, arranged over the scalp so as to conceal his baldness. He was clean-shaven. His

*walking*
   stepping, pacing, treading, ambulating, perambulating

*walking in an orderly way*
   marching, processing, filing

*walking slowly*
   shuffling, shambling

*walking slowly and heavily*
   lumbering, loping

*walking swiftly*
   rolling, barreling, swooping

*walking with quick and hurried steps*
   scuttling

*walking in a jerky or uncertain way*
   reeling, lurching, staggering, tottering, toddling, wobbling,
   unsteady, faltering

*walking quietly or with muffled sound*
   tiptoeing, padding

*walking in a lively way*
   bouncy, sprightly, skipping, tripping

*walking easily or confidently*
   light-footed, sure-footed, striding briskly, gliding,
   sauntering, ambling, strolling

*walking effeminately*
   mincing, flouncing, flitting

*walking haltingly*
   limping, hobbling, claudicant

features were regular, and it was possible to imagine that in his youth he had been good-looking.

W. SOMERSET MAUGHAM, *Of Human Bondage*

The baroness gave him a flashing, brilliant smile. She was a woman of more than forty, but in a hard and glittering manner extremely beautiful. She was a high coloured blonde with golden hair of a metallic lustre, lovely no doubt but not attractive, and Ashenden had from the first reflected that it was not the sort of hair you would like to find in your soup. She had fine features, blue eyes, a straight nose, and a pink and white skin, but her skin was stretched over her bones a trifle tightly; she was generously *décolletée* and her white and ample bosom had the quality of marble.

W. SOMERSET MAUGHAM, "Miss King"

The Hairless Mexican was a tall man, and though thinnish gave you the impression of being very powerful; he was smartly dressed in a blue serge suit, with a silk handkerchief neatly tucked in the breast pocket of his coat, and he wore a gold bracelet on his wrist. His features were good, but a little larger than life-size, and his eyes were brown and lustrous. He was quite hairless. His yellow skin had the smoothness of a woman's and he had no eyebrows nor eyelashes; he wore a pale brown wig, rather long, and the locks were arranged in artistic disorder. This and the unwrinkled sallow face, combined with his dandified dress, gave him an appearance that was at first glance a trifle horrifying. He was repulsive and ridiculous, but you could not take your eyes from him. There was a sinister fascination in his strangeness.

W. SOMERSET MAUGHAM, "The Hairless Mexican"

*walking in search of or with effort*
trekking, traipsing, tramping

*walking or moving about in search of pleasure*
gallivanting

*walking awkwardly or loudly*
clomping, stomping, galumphing

*walking arrogantly*
strutting, swaggering, promenading, parading, prancing

*walking loudly*
clomping, marching

*walking heavily or wearily*
plodding, tramping, trudging, slogging, dragging, straggling, drooping, slogging

*walking with purpose or without hesitation*
striding, marching, bearing down

*walking aimlessly*
rambling, wandering, roving, traipsing, gadding

*walking with duck-like short steps*
waddling

*walking furtively*
prowling, skulking

*walking warily or timidly*
pussyfooting, creeping

*walking or moving in a grand or stylish manner*
sweeping

*walking in a conspicuous or ostentatious way*
sashaying

He was wearing mirrored sunglasses, a soft cap with a buttoned visor, white rubber boots, and yellow rubber overalls slashed at the crotch. Of middle height, blond and fine-featured, he had sandy hair around his ears and a large curl in back, like a breaking wave.

JOHN MCPHEE, *The Control of Nature*

Back at the guest house Mrs. Starling introduced me to George Windus, who had sidewhiskers and baggy pants and a florid face.    PAUL THEROUX, *The Kingdom by the Sea*

She hobbled around, leaning on a gnarled stick, muttering to herself in a language I could not quite understand. Her small withered face was covered with a net of wrinkles, and her skin was reddish brown like that of an overbaked apple. Her withered body constantly trembled as though shaken by some inner wind, and the fingers of her bony hands with joints twisted by disease never stopped quivering as her head on its long scraggy neck nodded in every direction.

Her sight was poor. She peered at the light through tiny slits embedded under thick eyebrows. Her lids were like furrows in deeply plowed soil. Tears were always spilling from the corners of her eyes, coursing down her face in well-worn channels to join glutinous threads hanging from her nose and the bubbly saliva dripping from her lips. She looked like an old green-gray puffball, rotten through and waiting for a last gust of wind to blow out the black dry dust from inside.    JERZY KOSINSKI, *The Painted Bird*

She was a tall beanpole of a girl with a prognathous mouth and stick-out grinning teeth.

THOMAS WOLFE, *Look Homeward, Angel*

*clear*
> audible, firm, resolute, authoritative, carefully articulated, crisp, distinct

*high*
> high-pitched, soprano, shrill, girlish, treble

*squeaky*
> twittery

*low*
> deep, dark

*cold*
> hard, steely, dry

*warm*
> intimate

*soft*
> muted, subdued, whispery, low, breathy, modulated

*loud*
> strong, robust, ringing, stentorian, prodigious, booming, commanding

*loud and irritating*
> sharp, grating, harsh, piercing, brassy, screechy, ear-splitting

*pleasant or soothing*
> euphonious, melodious, sweet, dulcet, mellifluous, seductive, rich, lyrical, languid, sweet, silken, soft, honey-voiced

*bright*
> chirpy, chirrupy, bubbly

She was a powerful old lady, six feet tall, with the big bones of a man, and a heavy full-jawed face, sensuous and complacent, and excellently equipped with a champing mill of strong yellow horse-teeth. It was cake and pudding to see her at work on corn on the cob.

THOMAS WOLFE, *Look Homeward, Angel*

He had aqueous gray eyes, and a sallow bumpy skin. His head was shapely, the forehead high and bony. His hair was crisp, maple-brown. Below his perpetual scowl, his face was small, converging to a point: his extraordinarily sensitive mouth smiled briefly, flickeringly, inwardly—like a flash of light along a blade.

THOMAS WOLFE, *Look Homeward, Angel*

There was a boy named Otto Krause, a cheese-nosed, hair-faced, inch-browed German boy, lean and swift in the legs, hoarse-voiced and full of idiot laughter, who showed him the gardens of delight. There was a girl named Bessie Barnes, a black-haired, tall, bold-figured girl of thirteen years who acted as model.

THOMAS WOLFE, *Look Homeward, Angel*

Then, amid their laughter, the door opened, and several of the others came in—Eliza's mother, a plain worn Scotch-woman, and Jim, a ruddy porcine young fellow, his father's beardless twin, and Thaddeus, mild, ruddy, brown of hair and eye, bovine, and finally Greeley, the youngest, a boy with lapping idiot grins, full of strange squealing noises at which they laughed.

THOMAS WOLFE, *Look Homeward, Angel*

*slow-speaking and somewhat mannered (or with prolonged vowels)*
> drawling

*mournful*
> sepulchral, funereal

*artificial or pretentious*
> affected

*falsely or overly sweet*
> cloying, saccharine, ingratiating

*having pronounced S sounds*
> sibilant, hissing

*affectedly elegant, lisping*
> mincing

*stammering*
> stuttering, sputtering

*like a flute*
> fluted, fluty

*shrill and piping*
> reedy

*gruff*
> husky, throaty, scratchy, raspy, hoarse, gravel-voiced, wheezy, roupy, guttural

*deep*
> resonant, sonorous

*deep and refined in articulation*
> plummy

*hollow*
> tinny

*without intonation*
> monotonous, flat

*nasal*
> catarrhal, asthmatic

*whiny*
> whimpering, puling

A grass widow, forty-nine, with piled hair of dyed henna, corseted breasts and hips architecturally protuberant in a sharp diagonal, meaty mottle arms, and a gulched face of leaden flaccidity puttied up brightly with cosmetics, rented the upstairs of Wooden Street while Helen was absent.

THOMAS WOLFE, *Look Homeward, Angel*

He was a comely, handsome fellow, perfectly well made, with straight strong limbs, not too large, tall and well-shaped, and, as I reckon, about twenty-six years of age. He had a very good countenance, not a fierce and surly aspect, but seemed to have something very manly in his face, and yet he had all the sweetness and softness of an European in his countenance, too, especially when he smiled. His hair was long and black, not curled like wool; his forehead very high and large; and a great vivacity and sparkling sharpness in his eyes. The colour of his skin was not quite black, but very tawny; and yet not of an ugly yellow, nauseous tawny, as the Brazilians and Virginians, and other natives of America are; but of a bright kind of a dun olive colour that had in it something very agreeable, though not very easy to describe. His face was round and plump; his nose small, not flat like the Negroes;, a very good mouth, thin lips, and his fine teeth well set, and white as ivory.

DANIEL DEFOE, *Robinson Crusoe*

Marineau was a handsome tall man, somewhat in the Levantine style, with red lips a little too full, a tiny silky mustache, large limpid brown eyes, shiny black hair that might or might not have been marceled, and long, pale, nicotined fingers.     RAYMOND CHANDLER, "Try the Girl"

*rising and falling monotonously*
    singsong, jingly

*nervous*
    uncertain, quavering, quavery, edgy

He had a big, flat face, a big, high-bridge, fleshy nose that looked as hard as the prow of a cruiser. He had lidless eyes, drooping jowls, the shoulders of a blacksmith. If he had been cleaned up a little and dressed in a white nightgown, he would have looked like a very wicked Roman senator.

RAYMOND CHANDLER, "Mandarin's Jade"

The forehead was high, and very pale, and singularly placid; and the once jetty hair fell partially over it, and overshadowed the hollow temples with innumerable ringlets now of a vivid yellow, and jarring discordantly, in their fantastic character, with the reigning melancholy of the countenance. The eyes were lifeless, and lustreless, and seemingly pupilless, and I shrank involuntarily from their glassy stare to the contemplation of the thin and shrunken lips.

EDGAR ALLAN POE, *Berenice*

Tall, lean, loosely and feebly put together, he had an ugly, sickly, witty, charming face, furnished, but by no means decorated, with a straggling moustache and whisker. He looked clever and ill—a combination by no means felicitious; and he wore a brown velvet jacket. He carried his hands in his pockets, and there was something in the way he did it that showed the habit was inveterate. His gait had a shambling, wandering quality; he was not very firm on his legs.

HENRY JAMES, *Portrait of a Lady*

Carey Carr wore spectacles and he had a cleft chin. At forty-two he still looked very young, with round plump cheeks and a prissy mouth, yet to people who knew him this air of

*thin*
> slender

*thick*
> squat, bull-necked

*curved*
> curving

*long and graceful*
> swanlike

*short*
> no neck

*flabby*
> baggy

*scrawny*
> turkey

cherubic vacancy and bloodlessness, at first so apparent, quickly faded: one knew that his face could reflect decision and an abiding passion.

WILLIAM STYRON, *Lie Down in Darkness*

Mr. Squeer's appearance was not prepossessing. He had but one eye, and the popular prejudice runs in favour of two. The eye he had was unquestionably useful, but decidedly not ornamental, being of a greenish grey, and in shape resembling the fanlight of a street door. The blank side of his face was much wrinkled and puckered up, which gave him a very sinister appearance, especially when he smiled, at which times his expression bordered closely on the villainous. His hair was very flat and shiny, save at the ends, where it was brushed stiffly up from a low protruding forehead, which assorted well with his harsh voice and coarse manner. He was about two or three and fifty, and a trifle below the middle size; he wore a white neckerchief with long ends, and a suit of scholastic black, but his coat sleeves being a great deal too long, and his trousers a great deal too short, he appeared ill at ease in his clothes, and as if he were in a perpetual state of astonishment at finding himself so respectable.

CHARLES DICKENS, *Nicholas Nickleby*

Ransie was a narrow six feet of sallow brown skin and yellow hair. The imperturbability of the mountains hung upon him like a suit of armor. The woman was calicoed, angled, snuff-brushed, and weary with unknown desires. Through it all gleamed a faint protest of cheated youth unconscious of its loss.

O. HENRY, "The Whirligig of Life"

*healthy*
> hearty, hale, robust, vigorous, sound

*thoughtful*
> deliberative, meditative, ruminative, reflective, pensive

*unthinking*
> thoughtless, heedless, careless, disregardful

*direct*
> straightforward, candid, forthcoming, forthright, frank,
> open, outspoken, aboveboard, straight

*mature*
> grown-up, adult, mellowed, full grown, seasoned,
> full-blown, experienced

*immature*
> puerile, callow, green, sophomoric, juvenile, half-baked,
> inexperienced, adolescent, untutored, wet behind the ears

*lively*
> alive, animated, vibrant, vivacious, energetic, spirited, feisty,
> spry, perky, effervescent, bubbly, pert

*jaunty*
> airy, devil-may-care, happy-go-lucky, insouciant,
> pococurante, breezy, easygoing, casual, nonchalant, offhand,
> carefree

*confident*
> self-confident, assured, self-assured, self-possessed, poised,
> self-reliant

His mother's great chest was heaving painfully. Jimmie paused and looked down at her. Her face was inflamed and swollen from drinking. Her yellow brows shaded eyelids that had grown blue. Her tangled hair tossed in waves over her forehead. Her mouth was set in the same lines of vindictive hatred that it had, perhaps, borne during the fight. Her bare, red arms were thrown out above her head in an attitude of exhaustion, something, mayhap, like that of a sated villain.

STEPHEN CRANE, "Maggie: A Girl of the Streets"

He was tall, slim, rather swarthy, with large saucy eyes. The rest of us wore rough tweed and brogues. He had on a smooth chocolate-brown suit with loud white stripes, suede shoes, a large bow-tie and he drew off yellow, wash-leather gloves as he came into the room; part Gallic, part Yankee, part, perhaps, Jew; wholly exotic.

EVELYN WAUGH, *Brideshead Revisited*

Her black hair cascaded over one clavicle, and the gesture she made of shaking it back and the dimple on her pale cheek were revelations with an element of immediate recognition about them. Her pallor shone. Her blackness blazed. The pleated skirts she liked were becomingly short. Even her bare limbs were so free from suntan that one's gaze, stroking her white shins and forearms, could follow upon them the regular slants of fine dark hairs, the silks of her girlhood. The iridal dark-brown of her serious eyes had the enigmatic opacity of an Oriental hypnotist's look (in a magazine's back-page advertisement) and seemed to be placed higher than usual so that between its lower rim and

*friendly*
> sociable, gregarious, amicable, approachable, affable,
> companionable, chummy, congenial, convivial, neighborly

*charming*
> winning, winsome, engaging, endearing, gallant, debonair

*happy*
> cheerful, gay, merry, blithe

*innocent*
> simple, guileless, ingenuous, artless, angelic, naive

*contented*
> pleased, placid, at peace, serene, untroubled, unworried

*disappointed*
> crestfallen, disheartened, crushed, dejected

*stylish*
> sophisticated, debonair, polished, worldly, worldly-wise

*courteous*
> considerate, polite, courtly, well-mannered, gracious

*discourteous*
> impolite, uncourtly, ungracious, rude

*graceful or seductive*
> languorous

*eager to please*
> accommodating, well-disposed, willing, ingratiating,
> wheedling, smarmy, complaisant

*enthusiastic*
> eager, earnest, zealous, avid, fervid

*passionate*
> impassioned, ardent

*imposing*
> impressive, forbidding, intimidating

*regal*
> imperious, kingly, queenly, princely, autocratic, aristocratic,
> lordly

the moist lower lid a cradle crescent of white remained when she stared straight at you. Her long eyelashes seemed blackened, and in fact were. Her features were saved from elfin prettiness by the thickish shape of her parched lips. Her plain Irish nose was Van's in miniature. Her teeth were fairly white, but not very even.

VLADIMIR NABOKOV, *Ada*

He advanced, hand outstretched, in pale blue trousers and a dark blue shirt, an unexpected flash of Oxford and Cambridge, a red silk square. He was white-haired, though the eyebrows were still faintly gray; the bulbous nose, the misleadingly fastidious mouth, the pouched gray-blue eyes in a hale face. He moved almost briskly, as if aware that he had been remiss in some way; smaller and trimmer than David had visualized from the photographs.

JOHN FOWLES, *The Ebony Tower*

If the Mouse was odd, this creature was preposterous. She was even smaller, very thin, a slightly pinched face under a mop of frizzed-out hair that had been reddened with henna. Her concession to modesty had been to pull on a singlet, a man's or a boy's by the look of it, dyed black. It reached just, but only just, below her loins. The eyelids had also been blackened. She had the look of a rag doll, a neurotic golliwog, a figure from the wilder end of the King's Road.

JOHN FOWLES, *The Ebony Tower*

Wolkowicz smiled, his old sardonic grin that narrowed his slanted eyes and lit up his shrewd muzhik face.

CHARLES MCCARRY, *The Last Supper*

*arrogant*
> superior, haughty, snobbish, imperious, overbearing, patronizing, condescending, stuck-up, supercilious

*dictatorial*
> demanding, peremptory

*cocky*
> bumptious, nervy, cheeky, brash

*fresh*
> brazen, impudent, impertinent, saucy, pert

*forward*
> pushy, offensive, obnoxious, outrageous

*artificial*
> studied, stagy, mannered, affected, phony, pretentious

*irritable*
> edgy, touchy, testy, tetchy, fractious

*combative*
> scrappy, challenging, provocative, rambunctious, defiant, pugnacious, belligerent, bellicose, truculent

*angry*
> incensed, indignant, furious, wrathful, enraged, boiling, outraged

*conciliatory*
> placatory, placating, mollifying

*sorry*
> regretful, repentant, penitent, contrite, apologetic, remorseful

*disagreeable*
> morose, sullen, sulky, crabbed

*unsociable*
> unfriendly, unapproachable, standoffish, inamicable, cool, chilly, asocial, antisocial, inimical

*defensive*
> protective, self-protective

Everything about her person is honey-gold and warm in tone; the fair, crisply-trimmed hair which she wears rather long at the back, knotting it simply at the downy nape of her neck. This focuses the candid face of a minor muse with its smiling grey-green eyes. The calmly disposed hands have a deftness and shapeliness which one only notices when one sees them at work, holding a paint-brush perhaps or setting the broken leg of a sparrow in splints made from match-ends.                          LAWRENCE DURRELL, *Justine*

Physical features, as best I remember them. He was fair, a good average height and strongly built though not stout. Brown hair and moustache—very small this. Extremely well-kept hands. A good smile though when not smiling his face wore a somewhat quizzical almost impertinent air. His eyes were hazel and the best feature of him—they looked into other eyes, into other ideas, with a real candour, rather a terrifying sort of lucidity. He was somewhat untidy in dress but always spotlessly clean of person and abhorred dirty nails and collars. Yes, but his clothes were sometimes stained with spots of the red ink in which he wrote. There!
                          LAWRENCE DURRELL, *Balthazar*

His fatless, taut, weather-yellowed features, his deep eye sockets and long creased cheeks and dry gray hair were those of a man ending rather than beginning his forties. Jason was forty-two, like Carol. In his arms she looked young, and her broad hips suggested a relaxed and rounded fertility rather than middle-aged spread. Though Jason's eyelids were low-ered in their deep sockets, and seemed to shudder in the firelight, Carol's blue eyes were alertly round and her face as

*hostile*
> antagonistic, malevolent, ill-disposed, surly

*evil*
> wicked, sinister

*frightening*
> menacing, intimidating

*sneaky*
> furtive, sly, stealthy, surreptitious, secretive

*displeased*
> discontented, malcontent, disgruntled, out of sorts, dyspeptic

*sad*
> dejected, melancholic, downcast, grim-faced, chapfallen, hangdog, bowed, low, blue, crestfallen, dispirited, heavyhearted, depressed, despondent, glum, mopish, mopy, gloomy, disconsolate, inconsolable

*humble*
> self-effacing

*subservient*
> fawning, sycophantic, toadying, servile, obsequious, craven, slavish, cringing

*lacking energy*
> enervated, lifeless, effete, listless, leaden, sluggish

*without liveliness or flair*
> stolid, lumpish, plodding

*shy*
> timid, sheepish, mousy, diffident, uncertain, reticent, reluctant

*meek*
> docile, weak-kneed

*cautious*
> wary, chary, hesitant, guarded, suspicious, gingerly, circumspect, leery

pristine and blank as a china statuette's each time the slow
music turned her around so Ed could see her.

JOHN UPDIKE, *Couples*


But in no regard was he more peculiar than in his personal
appearance. He was singularly tall and thin. He stooped
much. His limbs were exceedingly long and emaciated. His
forehead was broad and low. His complexion was absolutely
bloodless. His mouth was large and flexible, and his teeth
were more wildly uneven, although sound, than I had ever
before seen teeth in a human head. The expression of his
smile, however, was by no means unpleasing, as might be
supposed; but it had no variation whatever. It was one of
profound melancholy—of a phaseless and unceasing gloom.
His eyes were abnormally large, and round like those of a
cat. The pupils, too, upon any accession of diminution of
light, underwent contraction or dilation, just such as is ob-
served in the feline tribe. In moments of excitement the orbs
grew bright to a degree almost inconceivable; seeming to
emit luminous rays, not of a reflected but of an intrinsic
lustre, as does a candle or the sun; yet their ordinary condition was so totally vapid, filmy, and dull, as to convey the
idea of the eyes of a long-interred corpse.

EDGAR ALLAN POE, "A Tale of the Ragged Mountains"


It was hard to know whom he was speaking to. His eyelids
looked swollen—leaden hoods set slantwise over the eyes,
eclipsing them but for a glitter. His entire body appeared to
have slumped away from its frame, from the restless rumi-
nating jowl to the undershirted beer belly and bent knees.
His shuffle seemed deliberately droll. His hands alone had

*slow*
> lethargic, phlegmatic, sluggish, snail-like, ponderous, laggard, poky, lumbering

*uneasy*
> restless, fidgety, fidgeting, fluttery, restive, nervous, unnerved, edgy, jittery, ill at ease

*disturbed*
> discomposed, discomfited, troubled, bothered, disconcerted

*quiet*
> reserved, subdued, retiring, unobtrusive, reclusive, withdrawn, conservative, self-contained, restrained

*imperturbable*
> unflappable, unfazed, airy

*impassive, cold*
> unfeeling, impervious, icy, affectless, impersonal, stone-like, unyielding

*inexpressive*
> unforthcoming, reserved, uncommunicative, unresponsive, withdrawn

*unyielding*
> unrelenting, uncompromising, implacable, unbending, unreachable, obstinate, stubborn, dogged, balky, contrary, mulish, recalcitrant, pervivacious, inflexible, obdurate

*unaware*
> unconscious, oblivious, unmindful, mindless, heedless

*lost*
> absent, remote, distant, faraway

*preoccupied*
> distracted, abstracted, absent-minded, distrait

*dazed*
> stunned, numb, benumbed

firm shape—hands battered and nicked and so long in touch with greased machinery that they had blackened flatnesses like worn parts. The right middle finger had been shorn off at the first knuckle.    JOHN UPDIKE, "The Gun Shop"

Madame Merle was a tall, fair, plump woman; everything in her person was round and replete, though without those accumulations which minister to indolence. Her features were thick, but there was a graceful harmony among them, and her complexion had a healthy clearness. She had a small grey eye, with a great deal of light in it—an eye incapable of dullness, and, according to some people, incapable of tears; and a wide, firm mouth, which, when she smiled, drew itself upward to the left side, in a manner that most people thought very odd, some very affected, and a few very grace- ful. Isabel inclined to range herself in the last category. Ma- dame Merle had thick, fair hair, which was arranged with picturesque simplicity, and a large white hand, of a perfect shape—a shape so perfect that its owner, preferring to leave it unadorned, wore no rings.

HENRY JAMES, *The Portrait of a Lady*

Charlie La Farge was just sixteen. He was of medium height, nice-looking, with the close-cropped hair that was the fash- ion among high-school boys that year.

WILLIAM STYRON, *Lie Down in Darkness*

It appeared, indeed, from the countenance of this proprie- tor, that he was of a frank, but hasty and choleric, temper. He was not above the middle stature, but broad-shouldered,

*puzzled*
> uncomprehending, bewildered, confounded, at sea, befuddled, perplexed

*speechless*
> tongue-tied, mortified, paralyzed, dazed, stunned, dumbfounded, insensible, overcome, overwhelmed

*businesslike*
> all business, officious, punctilious, conservative, bureaucratic, methodical, efficient

*acting in an automatic way*
> perfunctory, matter-of-fact, rote, prescribed, mechanical

*abrupt*
> brusque, unmannerly, rude, curt, bluff, unceremonious, peremptory, giving short shrift

*stiff*
> rigid, severe, strict, harsh

*girlish*
> maidenly, virginal

*manly*
> masculine, virile, manful

*womanly*
> feminine, ladylike

*effeminate*
> mincing, swishy, epicene

*mannish*
> unladylike, masculine, butch

*fatherly*
> paternal, patriarchal

*motherly*
> maternal, matriarchal

*like an uncle (offering affectionate guidance)*
> avuncular

long-armed, and powerfully made, like one accustomed to
endure the fatigue of war or of the chase; his face was broad,
with large blue eyes, open and frank features, fine teeth, and
a well-formed head, although expressive of that sort of good
humour which often lodges with a sudden and hasty temper.
Pride and jealousy there was in his eye, for his life had been
spent in asserting rights which were constantly liable to inva-
sion; and the prompt, fiery, and resolute disposition of the
man had been kept constantly upon the alert by the circum-
stances of his situation. His long yellow hair was equally
divided on the top of his head and upon his brow, and
combed down on each side to the length of his shoulders: it
had but little tendency to grey, although Cedric was ap-
proaching to his sixtieth year.

SIR WALTER SCOTT, *Ivanhoe*

He was a tall man of middle-age with two goggle eyes
whereof one was a fixture, a rubicund nose, a cadaverous
face, and a suit of clothes (if the term be allowable when they
suited him not at all) much the worse for wear, very much
too small, and placed upon such a short allowance of buttons
that it was quite marvellous how he contrived to keep them
on.    CHARLES DICKENS, *Nicholas Nickleby*

Therefore Ikey's corniform, be-spectacled nose and narrow,
knowledge-bowed figure was well known in the vicinity of
the Blue Light, and his advice and notice were much de-
sired.

O. HENRY, "The Love-Philtre of Ikey Schoenstein"

*lively*
> animated, bright-eyed

*alert*
> comprehending, sharp

*direct*
> pointed, fixed, glaring, penetrating, hard-eyed, challenging, piercing, unflinching, sharp-eyed, gimlet-eyed, unwavering, steadfast

*bold*
> brazen, unflinching, shameless, impudent, flinty, steely

*fierce*
> intense, fiery

*sidelong*
> askance

*squinting*
> squinched up

*glancing*
> fleeting, flitting

*furtive*
> sly, secretive

*disapproving*
> withering, hard, baleful, stern, glaring, frowning, dismissive, glowering, dirty, cold, displeased, critical, deprecatory

*resentful*
> reproachful, indignant, aggrieved, offended

One was a shaky and quick-eyed Swede, with a great shining cheap valise; one was a tall bronzed cowboy, who was on his way to a ranch near the Dakota line; one was a little silent man from the East, who didn't look it, and didn't announce it. Scully practically made them prisoners.

STEPHEN CRANE, "The Blue Hotel"

Her position before was sheltered from the light: now, I had a distinct view of her whole figure and countenance. She was slender, and apparently scarcely past girlhood: an admirable form, and the most exquisite little face that I have ever had the pleasure of beholding: small features, very fair; flaxen ringlets, or rather golden, hanging loose on her delicate neck; and eyes—had they been agreeable in expression, they would have been irresistible—fortunately for my susceptible heart, the only sentiment they evinced hovered between scorn and a kind of desperation, singularly unnatural to be detected there. EMILY BRONTË, *Wuthering Heights*

Considering all this, it was unexpected to meet a middle-aged man with a broken nose and a wide smile. He had a large face to match his broad body, and his head was half bald, crowned with a circle of strong curly hair. He had eyes you noticed. They were bright blue, and when he smiled, they were alive, and his broken nose gave him a humorous look. NORMAN MAILER, *The Deer Park*

The lieutenant walked in front of his men with an air of bitter distaste. He might have been chained to them unwillingly—perhaps the scar on his jaw was the relic of an escape.

*angry*
> furious, dark, savage, black, glowering, scowling

*threatening*
> menacing, fierce, ferocious

*expressionless*
> blank, vacant

*inscrutable*
> mysterious, sphinx-like

*bemused*
> distracted

*questioning*
> puzzled, mystified, nonplussed, quizzical

*surprised*
> astonished

*stunned*
> dazed, dumbfounded

*disbelieving*
> incredulous

*guilty*
> chastened

*shamefaced*
> sheepish

*guarded*
> wary, hesitant

*afraid*
> fearful, apprehensive, worried, concerned

*alarmed*
> distressed, panicked

*upset*
> disturbed, troubled, agitated, distraught, disquieted

*dismayed*
> aghast, horrified, horror stricken

His gaiters were polished, and his pistol-holster: his buttons were all sewn on. He had a sharp crooked nose jutting out of a lean dancer's face; his neatness gave an effect of inordinate ambition in the shabby city.

GRAHAM GREENE, *The Power and the Glory*

He was in his early forties, balding, with a pinky glabrous complexion and square rimless spectacles: the banker type of academic, circumspect and moral.

JULIAN BARNES, *Flaubert's Parrot*

You must picture Mr. Thomas Marvel as a person of copious, flexible visage, a nose of cylindrical protrusion, a liquorish, ample, fluctuating mouth, and a beard of bristling eccentricity. His figure inclined to embonpoint; his short limbs accentuated this inclination.

H. G. WELLS, *The Invisible Man*

One was rather short and very stoutly built, with a big bullet-shaped head, a bristly grey moustache, and small pale-blue eyes, a trifle bloodshot. The other was a slender young fellow, of middle height, dark in complexion, and bearing himself with grace and distinction.

ANTHONY HOPE, *The Prisoner of Zenda*

Sometimes, when a fierce wind blows out of the north, the faces of the scurrying citizens, drawn tight by the bluster of it, all seem to acquire a Lappish look, their eyes rather slanted, their cheekbones heightened, their skulls apparently

*pained*
   stricken, haunted, wounded
*sad*
   downcast, saturnine, brooding, long-faced, gloomy, glum
*injured*
   sulky, pouting, sullen

*watchful*
   appraising, measured

*inviting*
   beckoning, come-hither, enticing

*knowing*
   meaningful, pregnant, wise, charged

*confiding*
   reassuring, conspiratorial

*distant*
   faraway, far off, dreamy
*longing*
   wistful
*expectant*
   hopeful, imploring, pleading, beseeching

*odd*
   queer, strange, quizzical, enigmatic, fishy, weird

*despairing*
   despondent, hopeless

narrowed, until they too, tending as they often do anyway toward an ideal androgyny, seem like a species devised especially for the setting by fablers or geneticists.

J A N   M O R R I S ,   *Journeys*

Moore wore a splendid black silk robe with a gold lamé collar and belt. He sports a full mustache above an imperial, and his hair, sleeked down under pomade when he opens operations, invariably rises during the contest, as it gets water sloshed on it between rounds and the lacquer washes off, until it is standing up like the tope of a shaving brush.

A .   J .   L I E B L I N G ,   "Ahab and Nemesis"

On the wall were three heads, carved in relief and adorned with touches of red paint. One had a pronounced "imperial,"—a pointed tuft of beard.

T H O R   H E Y E R D A H L ,   *Easter Island: The Mystery Solved*

Ezra Stowbody was a troglodyte. He had come to Gopher Prairie in 1865. He was a distinguished bird of prey— swooping thin nose, turtle mouth, thick brows, port-wine cheeks, floss of white hair, contemptuous eyes.

S I N C L A I R   L E W I S ,   *Main Street*

He was taller than Gustav, a thin man with rough-cut dark-grey hair and beard and an aquiline nose. He turned by chance and faced us and I had a full view of his gaunt face. What surprised me was its fierceness. A severity that was almost savagery. I had never seen a face that expressed such

# Dress and General Appearance

*appropriate*
correct, suitable, apropos, seemly

*proper*
respectable, conservative, modest

*formal*
dressed up, elegant, dressy

*meticulous*
exquisite, impeccable

*fashionable*
smart, stylish, modish, chic, swell, à la mode

*smart*
snappy, modish, chic, toney, dashing, spiffy, snazzy, dapper,
natty, swanky, to the nines, becoming

*sporty*
rakish

*inappropriate*
incorrect, unsuitable, inapropos, unseemly, outlandish

*not fashionable*
frumpy, dowdy, frowsy, frowzy

*heterogeneous or of different colors*
motley

*informal*
casual, come as you are

*not neat or tidy*
unkempt, disheveled, rumpled, slovenly, sloppy

violent determination never to compromise, never to deviate. Never to smile. And what eyes! They were slightly exophthalmic, of the most startling cold blue. Beyond any
doubt, insane eyes.      JOHN FOWLES, *The Magus*


Dominating the scene by his height and force was Nathan:
broad-shouldered, powerful-looking, crowned with a shock
of hair swarthy as a Sioux's, he resembled a more attenuated
and frenetic John Garfield, with Garfield's handsome,
crookedly agreeable face—theoretically agreeable, I should
say, for now the face was murky with passion and rage, was
quite emphatically anything but agreeable, suffused as it was
with such an obvious eagerness for violence. He wore a light
sweater and slacks and appeared to be in his late twenties. He
held Sophie's arm tight in his grasp, and she flinched before
his onslaught like a rosebud quivering in a windstorm. Sophie I could barely see in the dismal light. I was able to
discern only her disheveled mane of straw-colored hair and,
behind Nathan's shoulder, about a third of her face. This
included a frightened eyebrow, a small mole, a hazel eye,
and a broad lovely swerve of Slavic cheekbone across which
a single tear rolled like a drop of quicksilver.
               WILLIAM STYRON, *Sophie's Choice*


The reddleman turned his head, and replied in sad and occu-
pied tones. He was young, and his face, if not exactly handsome, approached so near to handsome that nobody would
have contradicted an assertion that it really was so in its
natural colour. His eye, which glared so strangely through
his stain, was in itself attractive—keen as that of a bird of
prey, and blue as autumn mist. He had neither whisker nor

*overdressed*
> showy, flashy, flamboyant, dandyish, dandified, garish, foppish, frilly, extravagant, obvious

*cheap*
> gaudy, vulgar, tacky, common, tawdry

*immodest*
> sexy, provocative, revealing, daring, scantily clad

*worn*
> ragged, threadbare, shabby, tatterdemalion, seedy, ragtag, in tatters

*shabby but trying to appear dignified*
> shabby-genteel

moustache, which allowed the soft curves of the lower part of his face to be apparent. His lips were thin, and though, as it seemed, compressed by thought, there was a pleasant twitch at their corners now and then.

THOMAS HARDY, *The Return of the Native*

He had a pale, bony, high-crowned head, across which a thin wave of brown hair curled and was plastered to his skull. He had a long, pale, joyless face. His eyes jumped at me. His hand jumped towards a button on his desk.

RAYMOND CHANDLER, "The Man Who Liked Dogs"

She looked about twenty-six and as if she hadn't slept very well. She had a tired, pretty little face under fluffed-out brown hair, a rather narrow forehead with more height than is considered elegant, a small inquisitive nose, an upper lip a shade too long and a mouth more than a shade too wide. Her eyes could be very blue if they tried. She looked quiet, but not mousy-quiet. She looked smart, but not Hollywood-smart.

RAYMOND CHANDLER, "Mandarin's Jade"

Flat padded faces, flattish noses, and "double" upper eyelids—the epicanthic folds—appear to be adapted to protect the exposed and vulnerable face and eyes from cold.

ASHLEY MONTAGU, *Introduction to Physical Anthropology*

David Grambs, a graduate of Haverford College, has been a hunter and gatherer of words since his first job in publishing, with the pioneering *American Heritage Dictionary*. He has worked as a juvenile mystery fiction writer, encyclopedia editor, textbook writer, translator, magazine copy editor, and travel reporter, and is author of four other books pertaining to the English language. When not riffling through unabridged dictionaries, he likes to play very unclassical piano in all possible keys or to run at least three times around the reservoir in New York's Central Park.